Literacy and
the Politics of Writing

Albertine Gaur

intellect™
Bristol, U.K.
Portland OR, USA

Hardback Edition First Published in Great Britain in 2000 by
Intellect Books, PO Box 862, Bristol BS99 1DE, UK

First Published in USA in 2000 by
Intellect Books, ISBS, 5804 N.E. Hassalo St, Portland, Oregon 97213-3644, USA

Consulting Editor:	Masoud Yazdani
Cover Design:	Robin Beecroft
Copy Editor:	Wendi Momen

A catalogue record for this book is available from the British Library

ISBN 1-84150-011-9

Printed and bound in Great Britain by Cromwell Press, Wiltshire

Contents

Author Biography

Albertine Gaur received her doctorate from the University of Vienna, where she specialised in Ethnology and Philosophy. She studied Tamil and Hindi at the School of Oriental and African Studies, University of London, and spent five years in India, two of them teaching at a rural university in Rajasthan. After a short spell at the India Office Library and Records she joined the British Museum (later the British Library) as Assistant Keeper in charge of South Indian materials, going on to become Deputy Keeper and Head of the Department of Oriental Manuscripts and Printed Books until 1990. Since then she has served a four-year term in local government with the Royal Borough of Kingston-upon-Thames and is at present on the governing board of two local schools. She also acts as outside examiner for the University of Malaya, Kuala Lumpur. She is the author of many books, including the widely acclaimed A History of Writing *(British Library, 1984, 3rd revised edition, 1992), which has been translated into Japanese, Persian, Spanish, Italian and Korean. Another relevant publication is her* A History of Calligraphy *(British Library, 1994) and she is the co-author of* Signs, Symbols and Icons *(Intellect, 1997).*

Acknowledgements

Plates 8 (National Museum, Taiwan), 15 (Aleppo Museum, Syria), 16 (Idrib Museum, Syria), 23 (Museo National de Arqueologia e Ethnologia, Guatemala), 24 (Palenque Museum, Mexico), 25 (Museuo de Arqueologia e Ethnoligia, Guatemala), 29 and 33 (Damascus Museum, Syria), 34 (Villa Giulia National Museum, Italy), 35 (Vatican Museum), 40 and 42 (National Palace Museum, Taiwan), 46 (Bangkok National Museum, Thailand), 50 (National Library of Russia, Petersburg), 51 (National Historical Museum, Sofia), 58 (National Place Museum, Taiwan), 62 and 64 (Royal Library of Rabat, Morocco), 68 (Idrib Museum, Syria), 69 (National Palace Museum, Taiwan), 70 (Bangkok National Library, Thailand). Reproduced from the Morisawa Calendars Man and Writing, *produced by the Morisawa Company, Tokyo Branch, with kind permission of the President, Mr Yoshiaki Morisawa, and the Art Director in General, Mr Ikko Tanaka. The photographers were Mr Taishi Hirokawa and Mr Takashi Hatakeyama. I would also like to thank Prof. F. Yajima for his support and advice.*

Plate 43 has been reproduced by permission of the Syndics of Cambridge University. Plate 73 examples shown here are the work of the contemporary bookbinder Hilary Henning and are reproduced with her permission. Plates 3, 4, 11, 20, 21 and 87 have been photographed by the author. Plate 37 has been reproduced by permission of the Department of India and Oriental Collection, British Library. Plate 77 is reproduced by permission of Glasgow University Library.

The rest of the illustrations are reproduced from the author's A History of Writing *and* A History of Calligraphy, *both published by the British Library. Information about oral traditions in Judaism have been reproduced with the author's kind permission, from an unpublished article on* A Jewish Perspective of Oral Tradition *(1999) by Dr David A. Glatt-Gilad of Beersheba University.*

Introduction

This is neither a history of writing nor a handbook of existing scripts and writing systems. I have already tried to deal with these subjects in *A History of Writing* (1984), especially in the enlarged American/British edition of 1992.

The main questions I am trying to examine are: (1) What exactly is the primary purpose of writing? (2) How does the ability to put down information in permanent form relate to the concept of literacy? and (3) Does literacy depend on writing? In attempting an answer I have tried to look at the questions in a purely pragmatic manner, taking into account data that is at present available to us. New data, contradicting much of what we now take for granted may, after all, reach us at any time. One has only to consider how profoundly our understanding of human history has been changed during the last few centuries by the discovery and decipherment of hitherto unknown scripts, which served quite different, highly sophisticated, but now extinct civilisations.

Writing is (and has always been) a purely practical phenomenon insofar as it stores available, and for a particular society vital, information. As such, it is an essential part of the infrastructure of a given society. Literate are those able to access and/or contribute to this infrastructure. Many societies have, of course, functioned perfectly well with oral traditions alone and oral traditions have indeed never been wholly abandoned — to some extent they form an essential pre-condition for written literacy. But by being part of the infrastructure, writing is influenced less by linguistic, philosophical or philological considerations than by elements of power politics: how can what passes for writing at a given time aid a particular group to survive, develop and/or maintain a dominant position. Infrastructures deal not with abstract speculations but with purely practical problems. In fact, as far as written information storage is concerned, we had already left the age of linguistic philosophy when we started to rely on computers that are no longer based on language but on the interplay of just two numbers, 0 and 1.

If we look at past attempts to deal with the history of writing, we can see a dividing line between the efforts of those who addressed the question up until the mid-20th century and those who came afterwards. The 18th and the 19th centuries were largely dominated by scholars greatly influenced by biblical traditions, be they Jewish or Christian. Or, if they were of a non-religious disposition, by the values of the Enlightenment that put everything within human reach, promising, at least by implication, the possibility of a solution to all problems. In addition, most scholars were also familiar with Darwin's theory — it is difficult not to be influenced by prevailing theories, even if one only feels called upon to dispute them. They saw the origin of writing ('proper' writing) either as an act of divine inspiration or as the work of (often just one) human genius. By subscribing to such retrospective interpretation and, in addition, to a purely linear concept of historical (or evolutionary) development,

1

which moved towards one (Platonic) goal, they arrived, generally, at one overriding conclusion: the history (or evolution) of writing has moved from pictures to linear script forms, towards the representation of phonetic elements, reaching its eventual peak in the alphabet.

Towards the middle of the 20th century came the time of specialisation. It is true that the previous 'generalists' had often lacked deep insight into every possible subject. But as the view of the post-1950s specialists grew more and more narrow, they paid for their insight into one particular field (or sub-field) with an often almost complete disregard for all other subject areas. They began to look at writing, and what they imagined to have been the development of writing, only from their own narrow, specialised background and in consequence arrived at times at quite startlingly naive conclusions. (A similar trend made itself felt in the field of anthropology).

Harris (1995) regrets that so far no comprehensive theory of writing itself has been produced, a theory which does not prejudice the relation between writing and other forms of communication, while at the same time offering a coherent rational underlying the conduct of such an acquisition. If we look at this 'acquisition' (I would be happier with the term 'development') from a purely pragmatic point of view and concern ourselves less with the question of 'semiology' and the place of writing in 'a certain academic tradition', we may avoid phrasing questions in a manner that pre-judge the answer. Facts should, after all, not be manipulated to make a particular phenomenon fit into a particular 'academic tradition'.

Perhaps the time has come to admit that we simply do not know the whole story and that we may perhaps never do so. For example, not only the Egyptian script but the whole of Egyptian culture emerges into our consciousness in such a highly sophisticated form that we simply cannot continue to dismiss our ignorance of its early forms of development, or act as if such developments had never taken place. Early scripts on lost materials? But what materials? Leaves? This may hold true in the case of India where insects and a damp climate destroyed many early documents. But Egypt's climate was especially well-suited for the preservation of perishable materials — most surviving early Greek papyri have been found in Egypt, not on the European mainland. The uncomfortable fact is that we simply do not know how Egyptian writing and Egyptian culture developed. The same holds true for many other scripts. Can we pinpoint the exact origin of Chinese writing? Or that of the Indus Valley? Or Mesoamerica? There can be many (as yet unknown) reasons for our inability: natural cataclysms, the loss of oral traditions, meteoric impacts (which are now moving from the area of science fiction towards a rather uncomfortable reality), epidemics, climate changes (we are only just realising quite how devastating these can be). It might therefore be advisable to admit that much of what so far has been taken as proof simply rests on speculation and that we might be well advised to examine the whole question of writing from a quite different angle: an angle that looks at writing not as an intellectual achievement which by itself furthered civilisation, but as an essential part of the political infrastructure of a given society. And infrastructures do not create new societies, they simply serve them.

1. What is writing?

Few subjects have acquired such a variable collection of prejudices and confusing terminologies as has the subject of writing. A good many studies start with the words 'writing was the greatest invention ever made by mankind' — but was it an invention? 'Since the time of Aristotle it has been assumed that writing is a graphic device for transcribing speech' — but why credit a Greek philosopher, living over two millennia ago, with an insight into the needs of a past civilisation he did not know and a future he could never visualise? 'Writing is visible speech' (DeFrancis, 1989) — in some cases, perhaps, but why has this assumption been made by English-speaking scholars when the Roman alphabet is demonstratively ill-suited for representing their own mother tongue? One has only to remember that there are at least five different ways of pronouncing the vowel sign '*a*' by looking at such words as 'drought', 'love', draft', 'shut' or asking oneself why the '*g*' in 'George' should stand for a different sound than the '*g*' in 'grey'.

The material and political advantages brought about by the Industrial Revolution, Western colonial and economic expansion, produced a grossly Euro-centric outlook which eventually felt justified to call the alphabet 'the key to the history of mankind' (Diringer, 1968). Biblical traditions, as well as the promises of the Enlightenment, conspired in insisting that writing as such was invented only once by just one — divinely or otherwise — inspired human being. Post-colonial guilt censors us for calling the Chinese system of writing basically pictographic, since only the alphabet made Plato, and with it Western scientific thinking, possible (Olson, 1985; McLuhan, 1985; Goody, 1987; Ong, 1982) — in other words, to be our equals the Chinese have to be 'just like us'.

With writing itself having 'dwindled to microchip dimensions' (Harris, 1986), we should perhaps stop talking about the history of writing altogether since the term 'history' is too closely linked with a predominately linear, and as such wholly Western concept of evolution that moves towards one final, and by implication achievable, goal. In the same way, terms which have over the past centuries established themselves in this context like 'literacy', 'invention', 'text' , 'oral traditions', etc. may bear re-examination.

We should at least try to look at them, not as universal abstracts but as complex phenomena, which at different times, under different situations, fulfilled some basic but finally variable needs.

What then exactly is writing? How did it come about?

Why did some forms of writing successfully adapt themselves to various uses, even to languages for which they were singularly ill-suited, whereas others restricted themselves to one particular level, one particular period, one particular civilisation?

Should we perhaps not so much ask 'what is writing?', rather 'what is the *purpose* of writing?'

Plate 1. *Scribes and written accounts have always been an important part of the infrastructure, especially in times of war. The Assyrian armies had their 'war correspondents', skilled scribes, who kept detailed records of all events. Their work legitimized conquests and proclaimed the prowess of the war leaders. Among the many details seen at the palace relief of Tiglathpileser III, king of Assyria (745-727 BC), are two scribes registering the spoils from the city of Babylon. One is writing on a clay tablet, the other on a (leather?) scroll.*

The purpose of writing

Writing (preferably in the alphabet) is not a magic wand which, by its very existence, 'transforms the savage mind' (Goody, 1977). The sole purpose of writing is to store information essential to the survival and development of a particular society (see Plate 1). The amount of information and the way a particular society stores it depend largely on its needs. It is not the form of writing (be it pictographic or phonetic) that is decisive but the prevailing needs of a particular social group. In other words, what information is stored, and in what manner, depends largely on the needs of a particular society. Sometimes the essential information required may simply have been the ability to record numbers, either for commercial purposes (Mesopotamia) or astronomical/dynastic (Mesoamerica) ones; sometimes the core of a particular community may rest on religion or magic. It is in the end irrelevant what form of writing existed and how it appears to us today, as long it fulfilled the purpose for which it was designed.

Writing is, as such, an essential form of the infrastructure and infrastructures evolve differently in different places, in answer to different communal needs and problems. We could say, if we wanted to retain the concept of history, that there is not one history of writing but different histories, reflecting different forms of information storage, answering different needs. At the same time, the phenomenon of writing as such does not automatically go from cave painting to the alphabet (Weule, 1915; Sethe, 1939), nor are cave paintings inferior to the alphabet since they quite obviously effectively supported the needs of the cave dwellers.

Without writing there would be no history — but what about oral history? Oral recordings, the reciting of (sometimes mythologised) historical facts, existed long before the words were committed to writing: the Vedic literature of ancient India, the

Hebrew Bible, the Koran, Homer, the New Testament, the stories told by Celtic bards, folk poems, family histories — the story teller pre-dates the scribe in nearly all civilisations.

The main, and original, purpose of writing is not the recording of sounds but the ability to record facts and ideas. It is only because of the fact that ideas ('the king's brother must be killed') have to be expressed in what we now call a sentence that words ('king', 'brother', 'killed') come into the equation: in order to express or represent these words, first perhaps in the mind, then verbally, and eventually (making it an order) in writing, there arises a need for sounds. Saying that the main purpose of writing is the expression of language is to start at the end, not at the beginning of the actual phenomenon — turn the effect into the cause. Political power is embedded in the idea. It is not the group of phonemes in the word 'killed' that kill the king's brother.

Invention or evolution?

Theories about the origin of writing fall basically into two different, and one is often tempted to say, opposing camps: biblical or Darwinian — invention or evolution. But on closer examination the difference is perhaps more one of style than of substance. Both theories employ a basically linear way of reasoning which invariably leads towards one final goal: 'proper writing' — the alphabet, here often identified with all scripts representing sound elements be they syllabic, alphabetic or consonantal. The decisive step from thought writing (picture) to sound (phonetic) writing, the *Urerfindung* (Schmitt 1940/1980) is supposed to have been made only once, by just one human being, in one particular place. It will not surprises us to learn that this place is supposed to have been Mesopotamia, the place which creationist identify loosely with the biblical Eden.

Harris censures Gelb for doubting that writing was ever invented (Gelb, 1963), on the ground that if inventions were in reality simple improvements on what had preceded them, then the human race would never have invented anything at all. In a way both Harris and Gelb are right: it is highly doubtful that anything has ever been invented in the sense of creating something totally new out of practically nothing — an ability even biblical thinkers attribute only to a divine authority. But Gelb's 'improvements of what has preceded them' steer in fact closely towards the Darwinian theory of evolution, in the sense that different developments may in themselves be finite but, taken as a whole, move towards a definite, if not predestined goal — in this case (again), the alphabet. Harris in the above mentioned work continues his criticism of Gelb's theory that 'writing was established when a certain systematic correlation was established between graphic marks and words' . Though leaving out the somewhat embarrassing concept of Schmitt's *Urerfindung*, it nevertheless looks suspiciously like a correlation between historical and evolutionary thinking. We are again coming closely to the concept of 'pre-writing', 'forerunners of writing' and 'proper writing'. Though the route is different, the alphabet becomes once more some form of Platonic idea towards which all forms of 'proper' writing must by necessity progress. It thus seems that in the final instance Darwinians, the rational thinkers of the Enlightenment, as well as Creationists are closer to each other than it may at first appear. All subscribe ultimately to a linear concept of history, a movement towards a final goal which humans (by their own efforts or by divine inspiration) must finally reach, if their efforts can be deemed successful. This goal, needless to say, is again the alphabet.

Before going any further we should perhaps here briefly reflect on the causes and the true nature of invention. Inventions hardly ever happen spontaneously or, more importantly, out of context. They happen whenever a particular need coincides with the means available to satisfy this need. Printing did not start with Gutenberg. Block printing, and indeed printing from moveable type, had already been used in China for many centuries — though, strangely, early Western travellers tell us nothing about it. All the ingredients necessary for printing were known in 15th-century Europe: the oil press and the technique of cutting type as practised by goldsmiths — indeed Gutenberg (c. 1400-68) himself spent the earlier part of his life working as a goldsmith. The critical element for the explosion of printing in Europe was the availability of cheap paper (the first Bibles printed on parchment each needed the skins of some 300 sheep). This coincided with the growing secularisation and the consequent spread of education, the rise of wealthy book collectors in the newly rich towns and, eventually, the needs of the Church to provide proselytising texts for overseas territories. In China, where paper had been in use since at least the 2nd century AD, printing was stimulated by the expanding administrative needs following the unification of the country and the spread of Buddhism; indeed the first surviving printed book, complete and dated, is not the Gutenberg Bible but a Chinese translation of the *Diamond Sutra* dated 868 AD (now in the British Library). The elements congenial to printing go, however, much further back. There is the Phaistos disc found in Crete and dated c. 1700 BC, a clay disc into which (as yet undeciphered) picture signs have been impressed with individual fonts. Even earlier are the roll seals of ancient Mesopotamia which combine elements of a block printed text with pictorial illustration. In fact, inventions function rather like a kaleidoscope: at every turn new patterns emerge but the basic components from which these patterns are made remain the same.

Writing is therefore in most cases less an invention than the result of specific needs, at a specific time. Indeed, as we shall see later, truly invented scripts (scripts with a historically documented and named inventor) have nearly always been derivative and, when not supported by a strong establishment (e.g. Cyrillic for writing the Bible in Slavonic languages), they were often short lived (e.g. the scripts invented during the 19th century as a form of self-respect movements by indigenous people in America and Africa). Scripts, writing systems and other forms of non-oral communications do evolve and they do have a history, but not in the form of one linear movement towards one final goal. The goal differs greatly within different civilisations, just as the needs differ. We have as such not one history of writing but various histories of different forms of writing which came into existence or were invented or evolved (it is really rather tiresome to place the importance of the term above the purpose and the validity of a particular phenomenon), moving towards their own (not one universal), purpose-determined goal.

Plate 2. The Lukasa ('long hand' or 'claw') is a secret mnemonic device used by the Luba people of Zaire (Congo). It provides the mbudye *with means to pass on mythological knowledge and moral lessons to new members to the powerful, secret Luba society. The front of the board shows anthropomorphic carvings in high relief, the back depicts a turtle, an often-used* mbudye *symbol.*

Equally tenuous is the connection between language and writing. Speculation, for example, about how well (or how badly) the alphabet represents the English language is more or less spurious for the simply reason that the alphabet was never meant to write English in the first place. The present alphabet goes back some three thousand years via Etruscan and Roman forms of writing to a Greek alphabet which was, in turn, simply an adaptation of the Phoenician consonant script, to a time when the English language did not even exist.

Neither the appearance nor the success of a particular writing system is necessarily connected with the ability to represent a particular language. More decisive is in many cases the desire to promote political motivated aims (see Plate 2). Those aims can be secular or religious or both, religion being more often than not the continuation of politics by other means. Equally decisive are the vested interests of a particular group, or that of a particular (in most cases ruling) minority. A script originally designed for one particular language can be voluntarily adopted, or forced upon, an entirely different language, even one for which it seems totally unsuited. The cuneiform script, designed for the agglutinative Sumerian language which boasts a large number of syllabic (root) words, was taken over by the Akkadians (Babylonian/Assyrian) for their Semitic, consonant-orientated language. In Korea and Japan the equally ill-suited Chinese form of writing survived, in one or the other way, even after the creation of more appropriate, locally-created script forms.

Transmitting stored information

How much and in which manner information is stored depends largely on the amount and the type of information a particular society needs in order to function. The purpose of information storage is of course the wish to make it available for transmission, either to selected members of a particular group or to all those who have learned how to gain access to this information — in other words, to all those who have learned how to decode (read), though not necessarily also write, a particular script. It is, for various reasons, hardly ever the whole group.

Information can be transmitted in different ways: orally, in writing or by a combination of both, the latter being still more in use than is perhaps realised. But information can also be transmitted by gestures, expressions or body language (Barakat, 1975; Kendon, 1988; Mallery, 1972). Indeed we should at least ask ourselves, whether, far from writing simply reflecting language, the ability to record information in permanent form (a picture on a cave wall, marks on a stick) affected, perhaps even encouraged, the development or at least the codification of certain linguistic (spoken) terms.

Oral transmission needs personal and, depending on the nature and complexity of the information, often prolonged contact between two or more individuals who have to be physically present at the same time, in the same place. Orality has ownership (Ong, 1982), in the sense that one particular person possesses the information and is in a position to chose to whom he/she will pass it on. This person can also chose how much of the information stored in his/her memory should be passed on to whom and at what point — it thus also implies choice. In addition, enough time has to be spent to satisfy, at least superficially, the one who transmits the information that the one receiving it has effectively stored it in his/her memory, that he/she will be able to retain and eventually transmit it correctly. There is an inherent ability for censorship on the part of the one who passes on the information. But at the same time, the person receiving the information can wilfully, or through simple ignorance, corrupt and alter it. Ownership was perhaps one of the reasons why civilisation with a codified hierarchical (caste) structure, such as ancient India, preferred, even insisted, on orality. The group 'owning' the information had vested interest in its appropriate storage and transmission.

In the case of writing, information is stored mechanically, on an independent object, and can be retrieved and used at any time. When it comes to inscriptions, storage is restricted to one particular place, though the information loses much of its exclusiveness by being made public. Books, being moveable objects, can be consulted practically anywhere. Information begins to travel, affecting a much wider circle of people, covering much wider areas. A frequently held fallacy is the equation between writing, texts and literacy. We are supposed to be literate if we can read a (written) text. But texts do not depend on writing. Ancient Indian literature was based on oral traditions; Vedic texts were transmitted orally, as were the first scholarly examinations of phonology. In medieval Japan, scholarly achievements were jealously guarded and passed orally from teacher to pupil to prevent them from becoming publicly accessible. Oral transmissions prevailed among the Arabs, a highly literate people. It was indeed only after a large number of Huffaz (traditional story tellers) had been killed in the battles following the Prophet's death (663 AD) that the verses of the Koran were put into writing. Even in Judaism, an exceedingly script conscious religion, '. . . the concept of oral tradition in the making of the Jewish Scriptures (the Hebrew Bible) and its exegesis (the various Rabbinic Midrashic works, Mishna and Talmud, codes of law, and responsa literature) must be viewed in two broad planes: (1) The role of oral transmission of the sagas, legends, laws, poems, prophetic sayings, etc. which ultimately crystallised into the written form of the Bible, and (2) the role of oral interpretation which accompanied the above collections, primarily the laws, in order to render them both understandable and practical for the religious life of the community . . .' (Glatt-Gilad, 1999). Oral traditions not only continued, they still play a vital part in the interpretation and the understanding of the written texts.

Writing does, however, have its own, very definite advantages. There are limits to the amount of data human memory can retain. There is, in theory, no limit to the amount of information that can be stored in written form, especially if we consider the latest possibilities of storage — modern information technology. In addition, freed from the onerous task of having to remember and assimilate, completely and preferably permanently, a larger amount of orally transmitted information, information in written form provides a basis for new ideas, new speculation, additional information — data can create new data. But this ability has inherent dangers: it encourage heresy and has as such often been looked upon with mistrust by those who feared independence of thought, new ideas, new visions. Learning by heart does not encourage critical thinking but it is less easily controlled than written data. It is true, one can burn, and has burned, people as well as books but there is no reliable way to look into the minds of people the way one can look at a written or printed document.

The two most stable components

Looking at writing as a whole, from cave paintings to contemporary information technology, the two most stable components have always been the picture and the number. Both stand at the very onset of information storage and both appear and reappear, like some persistent *leitmotif* throughout the various forms of writing, until, eventually, they have once more regained a dominant position in our modern communication system.

Plate 3. Contemporary picture signs along the road can supply a multitude of information, each serving a different purpose.

Plate 3 (a) Simple, straightforward information, letting the traveller know what is available in this neighbourhood: a town hall, a marina, schools, parks, a museum, a tourist information centre, a church and a university. The three fishes in the top hand left corner are the logo of the town: Kingston upon Thames.

Plate 3 (c)

Plate 3 (b)

Both traffic signs (3b and 3c) issue a warning. The one on the left is clearly useful to the motorist; it states, 'there is no bridge in front of you and if you continue to drive on, your car will fall into the water.' The one above also gives a warning but its usefulness is highly doubtful since apart from turning back (not always possible on a narrow mountain road), there is little one can do about stones falling from a mountain.

Pictures such as those found in the Dordogne area or in northern Spain are already a dominant feature of the early (though not the earliest) Cro-Magnon period. They show mainly animals and, slightly later and less realistically, also human beings. Pictures retain their importance in nearly all tribal communications and also in secret forms of writing like those used by the Naxi people of south-western China or the various Hobo and gypsy signs. Pictures play a decisive part in Egyptian hieroglyphic writing, in the earliest Cretan scripts, on Mesopotamian seals, and those coming from the cities of the Indus Valley. They stand at the basis of Chinese writing and that of Mesoamerica. They can, under certain circumstances, acquire a secondary meaning, by being used as phonetic components, or determinatives, but this need not necessarily distract from their pictorial importance. Even within the framework of purely phonetic scripts (consonantal, syllabic or alphabetic), pictures, in the form of illustrations, remain an important and often essential part of the actual text. In many cases illustrations are meant to assist the reader, who is not yet fully literate, to understand the text. Pictures play a leading role in all forms of notations: for dance, music, the education of pre-school or special educational needs children. They also communicate in the form of contemporary strip cartoons where they tell whole stories, similar to the way some Southeast Asian manuscripts relate the previous lives of the Buddha. In some early Western chiroxylographic books, like the *Biblia Pauperum,* tentatively dated about 1420 and now in Heidelberg, illustrations were first produced by block print and the text was later added by hand. Such books seem generically related to earlier single printed sheets meant to provide cheap tracts for the semi-literate to whom the picture was more 'readable' than the text.

In the last decades pictures have again become important means of communication, affecting wide areas of our daily life. With the growing power of vast multinational concerns, goods are produced which, eventually, have to be sold in widely different geographical areas, to people belonging to different language groups. Pictures are effectively used as traffic signs (see Plate 3) and in all situations where, because of the international character of our life, language is more a hindrance than an asset and thus counter productive. Pictures, or 'windows' as they are referred to, are the key which allows us entrance into our computer systems, systems which, incidentally, work basically on the use of numbers, 0 and 1.

Returning to the Cro-Magnon period, simple notches cut into stone, bone or wood seem to precede pictures and is it not unjustified to consider them representations of numbers, perhaps even part of some numerical system. In fact, even more than pictures, numbers form a permanent and stable component of all forms of written information storage. They also provide added possibilities for political manipulation. Numbers can be used in different ways. They can serve the purpose of counting and accounting, showing ownership of possessions belonging to a particular group, a person or the state. They can assist the legitimate transfer of property (trade) and document the existence of debts. The practical use of numbers played an important part in Mesopotamia where clay tokens are documented from c. 8000 BC onwards (Schmandt-Besserat, 1996). Harris (1986) sees in the difference between iterative counting and slot listing (i.e. instead of drawing a picture for each sheep, you draw the picture of one sheep and add strokes indicating how many sheep there are) the beginning of what eventually became the cuneiform script. A typical example of a highly successful counting, or perhaps better, accounting system, which provided an infrastructure designed to exercise strict political control over people and their possessions were the *quipus,* used by the Incas of Peru. Tallies are a world-wide phenomena, they can be used for the recording of debts as well as that of important events. In England they provided a receipt for payments into the Royal Treasury until the early part of the 19th century.

Numbers can, however, also be used for measuring time, lunar phases, dynastic histories and dynastic legitimacy based on astronomical calculations. Marshak (1972), inspired by finding a bone with scratch marks in Ishango, a Mesolithic site at the head waters of the Nile in Central Africa, which he dated from about 6500 BC, considered these marks an early form of notation relating to lunar phases and periods. Building on this theory he claimed that 'already back as far as 30,000 BC Ice Age hunters of Western Europe [from Russia to the Atlantic, the Pyrenean foothills along the coast of Spain and Italy] seem to have used a system of notation that was already evolved, complex and sophisticated, and would seem to have been [in existence] thousand of years at this point'. The earliest evidence of a numerical recording device comes from a cave in the Lebembo Mountain in southern Africa, which shows 29 clearly visible marks made on the fibula of a baboon; it has been dated as far back as 35,000 BC (Joseph, 1991). Scholars working with such object have generally seen in the irregularity of the markings proof that those notches were not mere decorations but had very definite meanings.

Does counting in fact pre-date what we call writing? Were we in fact numerate before we could become literate? Did the number come before the picture? Historical evidence (however sparsely available) seems to point in this direction. If we accept (at least as a viable working hypothesis) that the need for permanent recording arising from the need for an infrastructure able to exercise control over a particular community, numbers recording time, measurements, people, animals, property, etc. represent a priority. The picture, in the form of name glyphs, place glyphs, etc. tends to look more like a qualifying addition.

There is, of course, also the practice of gesture counting which is widely used in Africa. Or the Oghams, considered by some to have originated from a finger alphabet used by Druids, that was eventually written down under the influence of the Roman alphabet. Indeed, it has been suggested that Roman numerals (interestingly based on the principle of subtraction i.e. CMXCVL = 995 reads in fact as 1000 minus 100 plus 100 minus 10 plus 50 minus 5) show traces of original finger counting: I for one finger, V for the whole hand with five fingers and X for two hands but together at the wrist pointing into opposite directions. This reliance on subtraction can incidentally also be observed among the Yoruba people of south western Nigeria. Their system of numeration is essentially based on 20. But whereas up to 14 this is expressed by using addition (14 = 10+4), afterwards numbers are expressed by deduction (e.g. 15 = 20-5), 45 = (20x3) - 10 - 5, or 108 = (20x6) - 10 - 2; and so on (Joseph, 1991). This exceedingly complex system was, moreover, not based on written records but on the use of heaps of cowry shells.

Numbers relating to a more abstract reality (lunar phases as opposed to the number of animals sold) become important whenever astronomical speculations are used to underscore the needs of society. In Mesoamerica, both the Mayas and the Aztecs enacted their ritual life around a cognition of time, which was looked upon as circular (unlike our own totally linear concept). It was the knowledge of dates and numbers that enabled them to record dynastic histories and astronomical events, thus creating some form of abstract stability in an otherwise insecure universe.

At the centre of the concept of the abstract use of numbers and numerical systems stands the cognition of zero. For us it is connected with what we call 'Arabic' numerals (0 - 9) which reached us from India, where their use was developed in the 1st century of the Christian era. A decimal system for whole numbers seems to have been known to the Indian astrologer Aryabhatta I. (b. 476 AD). This system reached Mesopotamia around 670 AD where the Nestorian bishop Severus Sebokht praised it as being superior to that used by the Greeks. Within a hundred years after the Prophet's death, Muslim influence extended over northern Africa, much of Spain and eastwards towards India. As a result of this expansion, Muslims began to acquire foreign learning and, by the time of the Caliph al-Mansur (d. 775), Indian and Persian astronomical texts were translated into Arabic and much of this new learning was in turn brought to Muslim Spain.

Zero is an active number, in fact probably the most active number-concept when it comes to higher mathematics and astronomical calculations. Why did it develop in India? In a way it could only have arisen against the implications of a Hindu/Buddhist background. In Panini's grammar (c. 500 BC) zero is characterised as *adrashana* (invisible) and there have been speculations as to whether the discovery of the mathematical zero might have been influenced by that of the linguistic zero, which pre-dates it. Similarly, there is the Buddhist notion of *sunyata* (emptiness). Both are by their very nature related to a scientific process of abstraction and generalisation. In both cases, by systematising the concept of zero, other general properties can be discovered, understood and formulated in a general manner — so much for the claim that only Plato and the alphabet made abstract thinking possible. We should here also remind ourselves that in India the concept of meaning was based mainly on the grammatical traditions of Paninian linguistics. Sanskrit terms for meaning relate mainly to words, sentences or other elements of language (Bhattacharya, 1962), not to metaphysics; there is no Sanskrit equivalent for terms such as 'the meaning of life', etc. Concepts like *adrashan* or *sunyata* (void) could in turn only arise within Hindu/Buddhist traditions; they would not fit into theistic religions where the void of non-existence is filled by a definite, always present deity. Thus the highly theistic Arabs accepted zero as a mathematical concept and brought it, in this form, to the West.

The concept of zero was, however, also known to the Mayas of Mesoamerica where it was represented by a stylised shell. Surprisingly, considering that zero reached us from India via the Arab world, this fact, if mentioned, has mostly been stated without much speculation about its origin and the reasons for its development and existence. But numbers played an important part in Maya information storage. The Mayas, and in all likelihood the Olmecs who preceded them, based their whole life around complex calendrical calculations which made an astoundingly sophisticated use of numbers. With just three signs, a shell for zero, a dot for one and a bar for five they were able to manipulate numbers up to millennia of years. They achieved this by using a system of place value that increased in multiples of 20 by placing signs vertically above each other. What provoked the Mayas or preceding culture to recognise the importance of zero? Their obsession with cycles and time? Zero, as far as we can perceive it, stood less for emptiness or void than for a definite beginning and a definite end. Or did it stand for the abstract (non-measurable?) space between both?

Bibliography

Barakat, R. A. *Cistercian Sign Language, a Study of Non-verbal Communication*. Kalamazoo: Cistercian Publications, 1975.

Barthel, G. *Konnte Adam schreiben: Weltgeschichte der Schrift*. Koeln: Du Mont Schauberg, 1972.

Bhattacharya, B. *A Study in Language and Meaning: a Critical Examination of some Aspects of Indian Semantics*. Calcutta, 1962.

Brown, M. P. *Writing and Script: History and Techniques*. London: British Library, 1998.

Cohen, M. *La grande invention de l'ecriture et son evolution*. Paris: Imprimerie Nationale, 1958.

Coulmas, F. *The Writing Systems of the World*. Oxford: Blackwell, 1989.

Coulmas, F. and Ehrlich, K. (ed.) *Writing in Focus*. Berlin: Mouton. 1983.

Danzel, T. W. *Die Anfaenge der Schrift*. Hamburg/Leipzig, Museum fuer Voelkerkunde, 1912.

DeFrancis, J. *Visible Speech — the Diverse Oneness of Writing Systems*. Honolulu: University of Hawaii. 1989.

Diringer, D. *The Alphabet - the Key to the History of Mankind*. 3rd edn., London: Hutchinson, 1968.

Gaur, A. *A History of Writing*. 3rd enlarged edn., London/New York: British Library, 1992.

Gelb, I. J. *A Study of Writing: The Foundations of Grammatology*. 2nd edn., Chicago: University of Chicago Press, 1963.

Goody, J. *The Domestication of the Savage Mind*, Cambridge: University Press, 1977.

Goody, J. *The Logic of Writing and the Organisation of Society*. Cambridge: University Press, 1987.

Harris, R. *The Origin of Writing*. London: Duckworth, 1986.

Jackson, D. *The Story of Writing*. 2nd edn., London: Barrie and Jenkins Ltd., 1987.

Jensen, H. *Signs, Symbols and Scripts: an Account of Man's Effort to Write*. London: George Allen and Unwin, 1970.

Joseph, G. G. *The Crest of the Peacock. Non-European Roots of Mathematics*. New York: I. B. Tauris and Co. Ltd., 1991.

Kendon, A. *Sign Language of Aboriginal Australia: Cultural Semiotics and Communication Perspectives*. Cambridge: University Press, 1988.

Mallery, G. *Sign Languages among North American Indians, Compared with that among other People*. The Hague: Moulton, 1972.

Marshak, A. *The Roots of Civilization. The Cognitive Beginnings of Man's first Art, Symbol and Notation*. New York: John Wiley and Sons, 1972.

McLuhan, M. *The Global Village. Transformation in Life and Media in the 21st century*. Oxford, 1985.

Olson, D. R. (ed.), *Literacy, Language and Learning, The Nature and Consequences of Reading and Writing*. Cambridge: University Press, 1988.

Ong, W. *Orality and Literacy, the Technologizing of the World*. London: Methuen, 1982.

Petterson, J. S. *Critique of Evolutionary Accounts of Writing*. Upsala: University of Upsala, 1991.

Robinson, A. *The Story of Writing*. London: Thames and Hudson, 1995.

Sampson, G. *Writing Systems*. London: Hutchinson, 1985.

Schmandt-Besserat, D. *How Writing came about*. Austin: University of Texas Press, 1996.

Schmitt, A. *Entstehung und Entwicklung von Schriften*. Herausgegeben von Claus Haebler. Vienna: Boehler Verlag, 1980.

Senner, W. M. (ed.). *The Origins of Writing*, London: University of Nebraska, 1989.

Sethe, K. H. *Vom Bild zum Buchstaben: Die Entstehungsgeschichte der Schrift*. Leipzig: Mit einem Beitrag von Siegfried Schott, 1939.

Weule, J. K. *Vom Kerbstock zum Alphabet: Urformen der Schrift*. Stuttgart: Frankh'sche Verlag Handlung, 1915.

2. Non-linguistic forms of writing

All forms of written information storage fall basically into one of two distinctly different groups: thought writing or sound writing. Thought writing communicates ideas and concepts directly — the terms do not really matter since they have in any case been imposed retrospectively. Thought writing can by-pass verbal expressions: it is not only independent of a particular language but, very often, of language as such. The reason for storing information in the first place is, of course, the desire to make it available for further communication. What is still less readily accepted is the fact that all forms of information storage and communication are of equal value, since within the cycle of necessity that brought about their existence, they effectively fulfil the same purpose: providing a commonly acceptable infrastructure around which the political and socio-economic life of the community can function.

Discussing the various forms and practices of thought (or non-linguistic forms) of writing, we shall see that though they represent various categories, they also show a good deal of interrelation. Tallies, property marks, memory aids, as well as pictorial narratives frequently overlap. In fact, it often seems that by using those terms we are simply trying to bring some order (our idea of order) into elements capable of representing different concepts under different circumstances. We may therefore do well to remember that nearly all those terms are retrospective inventions designed to explain situations about which we can, at best, speculate.

The power of pictures and signs

How far back does the ability to create, recognise and ultimately communicate by means of pictures and signs go? Does it presuppose a certain type of cognitive thinking and the ability of language? But then is cognitive thinking and the ability to communicate through sounds exclusively human? We now credit the Neanderthal with a recognition of death and the concept of an afterlife (Leroi-Gourhan, 1965) but is the recognition of death automatically connected with the idea of an afterlife? The almost ceremonial way in which elephants touch the bones of dead members of their species whenever they happen to come across them may at least create some doubt in our minds. In the same way, is the recognition of signs and the ability to communicate through them a human prerogative? Animals, we are told, do not have the ability to recognise pictures but they can recognise gestures and sounds. Our most direct relatives, such as chimpanzees and gorillas, live in social groups which by their very nature create a need for communication: gestures, postures, facial expressions, also sounds like contact calls, warnings, etc. (Terrace, 1979). But such communications need not be 'honest'. Richard Dawkins tells us that in some cases they can be purposely misleading so as to manipulate the listener in ways beneficial to the caller.

The earliest so far available evidence of the use of graphic signs and pictures, either incised (petroglyphs) or painted (petrograms), goes back to at least about 35,000 BC, a period which seems to have coincided with the use of colour (ochre, manganese) and jewellery. Some recent discoveries point towards the possibility that a form of abstract cognition may well have existed much earlier, in fact as far back as 60,000 years ago. With such a long time span and so little remaining evidence, speculations about purpose and meaning of prehistoric objects, incisions in stone or bone and — later — remarkably naturalistic pictures of animals on cave walls, must always remain tentative. Considering how difficult it is for most people to think themselves into another, contemporary, culture, any attempt to bridge a period of at least 35,000 years must be fraught with difficulty from the start. There have been arguments whether the much discussed, and much admired, wall paintings in the caves of central France and northern Spain were meant to represent religion or art. But art for art's sake is an exceedingly modern concept. Even early Christian icons do not, as a rule, bear the artist's signature. The same applies to wall paintings in Egyptian tombs and to the Indian carvers who, to this day, fashion the wooden chariots in which the divine images are pulled through the streets of the village in the course of annual festivals. For the pre-modern mind, the icon of the Virgin Mary, the figure of an Egyptian goddess or that of the god Vishnu in his chariot were not meant to represent anything as individualistic as art. The only thing we can more or less take for granted is that all these various forms were meant to store and convey information and were as such strictly functional tools of communication within the context of their particular communities. It is in fact much more likely that art as we understand it was simply a by-product of the need for information storage (writing). Were those paintings/engravings meant to serve religion and/or magic? Again we do not really know. They were, however, almost certainly less a form of self-expression than a means of communication. We cannot be sure what was communicated to whom — to the craftsmen himself, to a select group, to the whole community or to something outside and perhaps more powerful on which, in the opinion of the group, survival as such depended?

A system of communication was no doubt essential for the organisation of life in large (one is tempted to say urban-like) cave settlements like those found in Les Eyzies in the Dordogne region of France. But the ability to communicate was already necessary at a much earlier stage. The making of tools is thought to go back some two million years. The ability to make increasingly more sophisticated flints warranted some form of communication, an ability to hand down knowledge, if not orally, then at least by example. We are thus fairly safe to assume the existence of social organisations safeguarding the physical survival of groups. We may be justified to assume, with a certain amount of confidence, the existence of language or, better, some form of sound communication. But we have no means of knowing what form of sounds were used. We must be equally cautious if we say that those early surviving incised or painted signs, symbols and pictures represented a definite form of linguistic thought in support of linguistic utterance. It is perfectly possible that the stimulus worked the other way round — or indeed both ways. As soon as such definite forms of visual documentation were established, they became instrumental in assisting the development of definite linguistic expressions by making permanent statements about a particular concept or

Plate 4. Engraving of a mammoth as found in the Cro-Magnon caves of central France. Notches, probably older than the representation of the animal, run vertically through its body.

object. In other words, whosoever engraved or painted the picture of a mammoth or buffalo on a cave wall (see Plate 4) will (certainly at least in his own mind) have defined it by a specific term. Communicating the picture, it seems reasonable to assume, he also communicated the term.

Once emblematic symbols appeared they were predominately geometrical or abstract: circles, wheels, loops, triangles, spirals, zigzag lines, dots. Some archetypal images are quite clearly sexual in content: representations of a vulva, a phallus or female breasts. An intriguing feature is the recurring image of a hand stencilled with ochre on a wall. A signature, a commemoration of a person or an event? In India the Sati, leaving her dead husband's home to immolate herself on his funeral pyre, used to press her henna-coloured hands on the wall of the house. This image was then worshipped as a ritual commemoration of her sacrifice. Rajput ladies, in order to avoid the humiliation of capture, did the same before the enemies stormed the burning fort. Incidentally, the imprint of a stencilled hand is also a recurring motif in the visual vocabulary of Australian Aborigines.

Figurative representations, to begin with of single animals and, more rarely, abstract representations of human beings, seem to appear later, in fact not before around 30,000 BC. From an even later period are the large frescos like those found in Altamira,

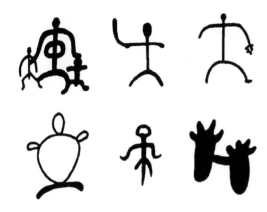

Plate 5. Hawaiian petroglyphs, mostly scratched into the ground formed by lava flows. They pre-date the arrival of the Europeans and supply information about Hawaiian history, deities, local heroes, kings, occurrences, annals of the arrival of immigrants, stylised pictures of animals, people, tools and so on.

Lascaux and other parts of the world, as well as narrative pictures: hunter surrounding animals, dancers (?) in front of animals, some seemingly wearing animal masks, or scenes of warfare. Animals are often surprisingly realistic whereas humans appear more stylised — indeed, in many cases they are shown in the form of abstract symbols such as squares, triangles, a succession of dots or straight lines (Leroi-Gourhan, 1965). Such paintings continue until about 9000 BC and can be found within a large geographical area stretching from the Ural to the Atlantic (Aubarbier, 1997), France and Spain, apparently reaching an apex between 18,000 to 10,000 BC. Should we assume a coherent prehistoric culture — a coherent state of civilisation which developed naturally on the basis of similar conditions? Or simply a coherent state of cognitive thinking? We do not know the social organisation of those civilisations but we can assume that such paintings were not wilful and individualistic but were meant to store information and commemorated data essential to the whole community.

An interesting point of those early signs, symbols and pictures is that they do not fit neatly into our linear concept of history. They appear, in no observable chronological order, in widely different parts of the world: Europe, Africa, America, Asia, Australia, the Polynesian Islands.

Scottish petroglyphs, the so-called 'cup and ring' sculptures dating from c. 2000 to 1500 BC are, for example, mainly found in the Argyll area on flat rock surfaces near the sea (Morris, 1977). Various suggestions about their purpose and meaning have been put forward: places of sacrifice, notices for new immigrants coming from the sea, burial sites, astronomical data relating to the winter sun rise, information about copper and gold deposits in the area, and so on.

In the last few decades ethnographic research into Hawaiian history has drawn attention to special forms of petroglyphs (see Plate 5) engraved on the lava or stone floors (McBride, 1997). Like in Scotland, they are mainly to be found in certain regions but they cover a much larger area. Distinct regional styles have encouraged speculation about their functional importance. A profusion of sail-shaped petroglyphs in Ka'upulehu has, for example, led to speculation about the possibility that at one time a school of navigation existed in this area. Special patterns of petroglyphs can be observed along boundaries, trails and sacred sites. Linear motifs seem the oldest; they have sometimes been overwritten by triangles or other forms. This apparent lack of care for earlier engravings can also be observed in the Dordogne caves — whether this indicates that a particular image was of only temporary importance, or that a particular place was especially suited for such activities, we simply cannot tell. It is however a fact that throughout history new religions have preferred to occupy previous sites of worship to benefit from existing communal memories and conventions and, at the same time, erase the power of previous traditions. Hawaiian petroglyphs, locally called *kaha ki'i* (*kaha*: to scratch/draw/mark; and *ki'i*: picture/image) are made either by pecking (a term also used for pictures scratched in sand), bruising (gentle scraping of the lava floor to change its colour) or abrading. According to local traditions, they were made by priests and had meaning to the initiated. Many signs are identical to the tattoo motifs seen by early visitor to the island. There are also indications that people had marks, or recognisable signs, which could be used like a signature (property marks?). No definite dating is possible since sea levels can change dramatically. Most petroglyphs appear to have been made about 1570 AD or earlier. In the north of the island, where sea levels have risen less, these are dated as early as 640 BC.

Narrative pictures

Can pictures ever be truly narrative? Or are they predominately descriptive? Or is there a simple but essential overlap? How then can pictures be used? What can they tell us? The power of the picture lies partly in the fact that it is able to make a definite, unequivocal statement. Seeing a picture of a buffalo tells us how a buffalo looks, what his main characteristics are. By making a definite statement — providing a snapshot — a picture also acts as a tool for further reference. Meeting a buffalo, after having seen its picture, enables the hunter to recognise it and recognise it instantly, a fact on which the success of the hunt as well as his own safety may depend. In a linguistic description much is left to the imagination of the listener and the descriptive skills of the story teller; neither can ever be sure that description and imagination have successfully overlapped.

   Whereas one picture describes a singular reality, an interrelated number of pictures can represent a narrative or, at least, a particular event within a narrative: a group of animals surrounded by armed figures may speak of a hunt, two opposing groups of armed men may describe a conflict. Two groups with foot prints leading in the opposite direction can record a parting of the ways. Such narrative pictures appear in the cave paintings of the Cro-Magnon period, at a much later date among the Bushmen of Africa, the Aborigines of Australia and, in an especially pronounced fashion, among the North American Indians (Mallery, 1893). They are also an important element of Maya writing. Since it is difficult to represent non-visual, abstract concepts by pictures, symbolic representations have to be added. Such narrative pictures are perfectly comprehensible, they can without too much difficulty be 'read', just as long as they communicate information between persons, or groups, who are able to draw on a pool of shared experience. Kipling in his *Just So Stories* gives a good account of the importance of this common pool of expectation and experience in the story about 'how the first letter was written'. A little girl, who lives with her family in a cave, one day accompanies her father on a fishing expedition. While they are away, the father breaks his spear and, trying to be helpful, the little girls draws a picture of the incident on a piece of bark. She then persuades a friendly stranger from another tribe, who does not speak the same language, but just happens to pass by, to take the picture to her mother. She hopes that the mother, once she has understood the father's predicament, will send another spear, so that the fishing expedition can continue. But the mother totally mis-`reads' the picture the girl has drawn, and, thinking that her husband had been hurt by the stranger, calls upon her women friends for help. Only after the stranger has been manhandled by the whole group is the misunderstanding eventually cleared up (we are never quite sure how) and the situation moves towards a satisfactory conclusion.

Objects

Apart from pictures, (abstract) signs and (recognisable) symbols, simple objects too can communicate data. Among the American Abnaki Indians a branch stuck in the ground at a certain angle shows the route taken, another one set up at an angle and close to the ground means that the person has not gone far, whereas a second stick further away says 'I have gone a long way'. Similarly, the number of days a person will probably be absent can be indicated by sticks stuck upright into the ground (Mallery, 1893). During the migration of the African Ewe tribe, the leaders scattered grass on side tracks which had to be avoided (Jensen, 1970). Many of these ancient forms of warning and informative data are still with us: walking though the forest or up a mountain we find coloured marks on trees to tell us in which direction we ought to go; travellers in the Himalayas pile stones on top of each other at a perilous pass; and in the Jewish cemetery in Prague stones are brought to the grave of the Rabbi whom Cabalistic tradition credits with the creation of the Golem (Scholem, 1972). Pictures, signs, symbols and, under certain conditions, objects can have lasting archetypal meaning by standing outside, not only of a particular language, but of linguistic thinking as such. Objects store and communicate information not only by their very existence, they can also be used as a medium for information storage. Painted pottery and weaving patterns are a pertinent example. We may, in fact, be well advised to look closer into the part such designs have played in the development of certain writing systems.

Pottery decorations are a worldwide phenomenon. Vessels from Anatolian villages, dating from c. 6000 BC, can be decorated with human figures, faces, Maltese crosses, hands making (what we assume) the gesture against the evil eye, and so forth. From pre-dynastic Egypt many examples of decorated pottery have survived which show well executed pictures of birds, animals, symbols of deities or other, often abstract, designs. In many cases they are already distinguished by a marked tendency towards codified abstraction, which was to become a characteristic of the hieroglyphic script. Pottery fragments from the Indus Valley repeatedly show an already well codified representation of a fish, a sign which prominently re-appears in the later Indus script. The Moche, a pre-Inca people, used marked beans for counting, perhaps in a way not altogether different from that employed by the *quipu* masters of Peru. Images of runners holding pouches filled with such beans feature prominently on some Moche pottery vessels.

Textiles are another medium that can be used for storing information. Traditional Arran or Jersey fisherman's pullovers are knitted in patterns characteristic of particular families, thus enabling identification in the case of drowning. The traditional jackets worn in Nepal by male members of the Rai tribe have a special type of embroidery at the back to show to which tribe a man belongs (Dunsmore, 1993). An interesting, though never fully verified claim, was made by the German scholar Gustav Barthel (1972) in the course of an international Congress of Americanists held in Lima. Barthel claimed that in addition to *quipus,* the Incas of Peru possessed a well developed form of iconographic writing consisting of geometrical designs, called *tocapus*, which appear on wooden cups and also on some woven material. Each individual sign is supposed to represent a definite character. Barthel claims to have identified 400 and deciphered at least 50 of them. However, nothing further has since been heard of this discovery.

Sally Sampson, a British artist who studied textiles at the Royal College of Art in 1979, introduced us, by means of exhibitions (Pitt River Museum, Oxford, 1995; Orleans House Gallery, Twickenham, 1998) to the somewhat mysterious Kitty Lake. The latter claims to have come across a particular type of weaving practised on the Rishmoo islands of Japan. There islanders are supposed to use weaving to record sayings and stories. Their roughly woven cloths incorporate fragments of bamboo and shells and Rishmoo children are at the age of seven given a piece of weaving, which is eventually joined to the pieces of other family members and passed on to further generations. The longest recorded piece is supposed to be made up of 24 parts and tells a poetic parable: 'Don't gaze at the stars too much while fishing / You shoot up into the starry heavens / And become part of eternity / Slightly too early.'

Tallies

The term tally has been applied to a wide variety of information storage. Tallies can act as memory aids, recalling the existence of objects, numbers or events (animals hunted, enemies killed, men or horse required at a particular camp, the days of a journey, the duration of a person's absence from home) or the number and (depending on the type of individual marks) the quality of goods sold. Once a society has advanced to the concept of ownership, the main purpose of the tally has mostly been the recording of debts. A marked stick spilt lengthwise gives the creditor and the debtor an incorruptible account of the amount of money or goods involved.

Harris (1986) has suggested that one notch could stand for one human finger but this would imply a decimal mode of counting, which is by no means universal. Indian school children, for example, still do their mental arithmetic based on multiples of twelve, using the thumb of each hand to count the three parts of each of the remaining four fingers of each hand. Another interpretation suggests that sometimes the series of notches incised on a piece of wood were made by different tools and over different periods, and that they may have been lunar notations constituting a calendar (Robinson, 1995).

Tallies have been used at all times and in almost all parts of the world. Some scholars have even suggested that the tally was instrumental in the development of the Chinese script. The earliest forms of Chinese writing materials — narrow slips of wood or bamboo and the mirror image of many Chinese characters — probably encouraged this speculation. According to this theory, the original notches on tallies were eventually supplemented by incised or painted ornaments and symbols. Once the Chinese script had been established, characters were used first in addition to and eventually in place of such ornamentation. Interesting, but purely anecdotal, is the story (Jensen, 1970) about the Swedish explorer Sven Hedin who, at the beginning of the 19th century, discovered in eastern Turkistan a wooden tablet that bore audit officials' check marks and signatures; the board had been spilt vertically, thus providing each party with documented proof of the original contract.

Physically, tallies can take a variety of forms. They need not be incised pieces of wood — notches can be cut into poles, the walls of houses or doors. Or pieces of wood can be attached to a string, such as the *kupe* once used in the Torres Strait Islands. Tallies as a means of enumeration, or for keeping archival records, can also take the form of knotted cords and have as such been used in ancient China, Tibet, Japan, Siberia, Africa, (pre-conquest) California and the Polynesian Islands. In Hawaii they played an important role in the gathering of taxes (rather like the tallies which recorded payments into the British treasury). In the Solomon Islands strings with knots and loops are still used for the exchange of news. The most sophisticated use of knotted cords is the *quipu* of pre-Conquest Peru.

Plate 6. Contemporary photograph of a Canadian totem pole.

Archival records

Archival records and genealogies fulfil a truly universal need. They establish the position of the individual, in his own estimation, in relation to the group he belongs to and in relation to the way this particular group relates to society as a whole. Much of what has been said above already touches this category.

The Maori of New Zealand used saw-shaped wooden boards called *he rakau whakapap* (*rakau* – wood, *wahapaku* – genealogy) for the recording of genealogy records. Young men were taught to recite the name of each ancestor with reference to each notch; the extinction of a male line was shown by a large gap. Though nowadays few people

Plate 7. Churingas *are among the sacred possessions of Australian Aborigines. They are kept well hidden from women and uninitiated youths. Their patterns belong to a form of sacred (non-figurative) geometry which can only be interpreted by someone who knows the meaning of a, probably orally, handed-down tradition.*

can 'read' these boards with fluency, some boards are still in the possession of certain Maori families.

A different rationale lies behind the concept of totems and the totem poles which play a significant part in the life of North American Indians (see Plate 6). They record not only the names and existence of ancestors but also the relationship of the individual to the ancestral totem, together with legends and important events in the history of the clan. Clan, individual, ancestors and totem become complementary aspects of the same identity. Heraldic devices fulfil similar needs, inasmuch as they establish a person's connection with a particular (usually prestigious) family or lineage.

Another form of establishing connections with one's ancestors and the place of one's origin is the mythological map which extends over a broad spectrum of culture and time. One of the oldest Hawaiian legends, for example, tells that when Aukelenuiaiku had to leave his homeland, his grandmother drew a map in the sand to show him faraway places beyond the sea, which he would eventually find on his journey (McBride, 1997). The Australian Aborigines have mythological maps called *churingas* (stone plaque or wooden tablets engraved with abstract line designs). They relate to a man's distant ancestors, who had the characteristics of both animals and men and who, during 'dream time' moved about the as yet undifferentiated country, shaping the environment and setting precedents which still govern human conduct (Burt, 1977). *Churingas* (see Plate 7) also provide proof of ownership by documenting the all-

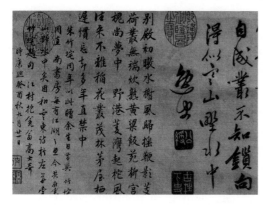

Plate 8. Chinese painters and calligraphers put their seal impression into the margin of their work. Sometimes a work would pass through the hands of several owners, who in turn might add their own seal-signatures, thus providing us with an invaluable proof of provenance.

important water holes and the ways by which they can be reached — to move through somebody else's land needs the owner's permission.

Archival information records not only the history of a person but also the events of past years. The wintercounts of the Dakota Indians (Mallery, 1893), for example, give a chronological account of the most recent history of the tribe and act as annals for the community. They can span a period of up to a century and consist of a series of pictures on buffalo skin, arranged in a circle, often from the centre outward. Each picture records the year's most important event: e.g. 30 Dakotas were killed by Crow Indians, an epidemic of whooping cough swept the village, a white man built a log cabin made of dry wood, many people drowned in a flood, an eclipse of the sun, and so on.

Property marks

At a first glance it may seem that much of the above falls into the category of property marks but there is one important difference. Whereas tallies, simple archival records, mythological maps and totem poles establish the relation of the individual with the group, property marks document the relation of a person with a particular piece of property. Property occurs only at a certain level of economic life: it depends on the ability to produce surplus available for exchange (trade). Property marks are thus not an end in themselves; they operate within a chain of owners and a particular economic climate. In some cases property can become, eventually, if not more important than the owner, then at least of equal value.

Property marks act as a simple form of signature, they establish ownership and with it authorise transactions. Simple forms of property marks have been used in all ages and by nearly all people. Nomadic herdsmen and settled cattle-breeders use them for the branding of their livestock. Societies whose economies depended on slave labour used in a similar way. Branding and tattooing can also signify a voluntary (or forced) identification with a particular religious or secular group. In the same category fall the house and clan marks, which can under certain circumstances also be used as signatures by people unable to read and write (Ebbinghouse, 1961). The pottery marks of ancient Egypt have their modern equivalent in ceramic marks and hallmarks identifying precious metals. There are furthermore the marks of masons found in the ancient Aegean regions, Palestine, Anatolia and medieval Europe.

The ultimate form of property mark is the seal. Seals played an important part in ancient Mesopotamia, in Crete and in the Indus Valley; in fact the only documentation

25

of the as yet undeciphered Indus script has reached us by way of seals. In China, painters and calligraphers authorise their works by 'signing' them with their personal seal; as the picture or calligraphy changes hands, each new owner adds his own seal impression, thus providing us with an accurate and often invaluable account of a work's provenance (see Plate 8).

Memory aids

Memory aids or mnemonic devices (from Mnemosyne, the personification of memory in Greek mythology) hold a transitional position between orality and writing. They depend on some method of coding but to make them effective a skilled interpreter, conversant with this coding, and/or a background of shared experience, is necessary. This pool of shared experience is the most important element in all forms of non-linguistic information storage. Without it the meaning of the message can not be 'read'. Even then there is sometimes a need for additional, orally given instructions. The message sticks of the Australian Aborigines were incised with marks in the presence of the messenger who had each sign explained to him. Message sticks were an essential part of the Aborigines' infrastructure, linking the widely scattered members of society. Carrying such a stick bestowed its own importance and could ensure safe conduct through hostile territories. Just as the *pustahas* — the personal note books of the Batak medicine men of Sumatra — protected the carrier who alone, after many years of apprenticeship, was in a position to interpret the notes taken .

Plate 9. Communities who either by birth or from choice stand outside conventional society need their own secret infrastructure which enables them to function and, at the same time, protect members of their group. In this category fall the gypsy and hobo signs. They supply secret information beneficial to the survival of all group members.

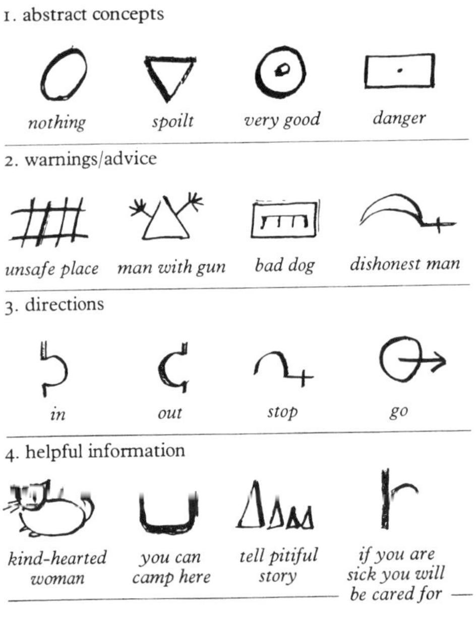

1. abstract concepts

| nothing | spoilt | very good | danger |

2. warnings/advice

| unsafe place | man with gun | bad dog | dishonest man |

3. directions

| in | out | stop | go |

4. helpful information

| kind-hearted woman | you can camp here | tell pitiful story | if you are sick you will be cared for — |

Like other forms of information storage, memory aids support the political infrastructure. The wampum belts of the North American Iroquois combined the use of patterns and colours to convey messages; they were also used in rituals, as currency and even for personal decoration. Wampum belts (Mallery, 1893) were first woven on a kind of loom and then decorated with beads. They played an important role in tribal politics, holding, more often than not, the balance between war or peace. Most belts showed designs in one colour on a differently coloured background. Dark colours signified danger, hostility and death. White stood for happiness, red for death. More elaborate belts interwoven with coloured symbols could serve as a declaration of war (a black belt with the sign of a tomahawk in red) or as a peace treaty (two dark hands on a white background) and so on.

Memory aids also support rituals. The knowledge necessary to perform the Midewiwin, or Medicine Dance, of the central Alonquin people of North America and the memory of the dances and songs performed at the meeting of the Mide society are inscribed on song-boards, or birch bark scrolls, which only the officiating medicine man can read correctly. Memory aids can play an essential role in the secret political life of certain communities. The *Lukasa* was created and used by the once powerful secret society of the Luba people of Congo (Reefe in *African Art*, vol. 10). This kind of coded information avoids 'spelling out' the full story by addressing only the initiate. Into the same category fall the so-called *Gaunerzeichen* (Streicher, 1928) and the hobo signs secretly drawn on walls or fences of targeted property (see Plate 9). They inform members of the community about how to obtain help from good-hearted individuals, point towards an opportunity to commit a theft, warn that a certain house is an 'unsafe place', keeps a 'bad dog' or, the opposite, that there is a 'kind-hearted woman' about who might fall for a 'pitiful story'.

Moreover, memory aids are by no means a thing of the past. We still use them in our own daily lives. We tie a knot in a handkerchief to remind us of a task which must not be forgotten. Devout persons use rosaries where the size and position of each bead help to recall (in correct order) certain prayers. Children draw lines on a calendar to mark the days left before the start of holidays, prisoners mark the passing of their imprisonment in a similar way. We still use often quite complex and self-invented forms of memory aids for remembering telephone or car registration numbers, important dates and so on. Finally, looking at it without conventional bias, all forms of writing (phonetic and non-phonetic) are basically a form of memory aid to be understood only by those sharing a common reading culture. After all, having been taught how to read Arabic does not enable one to read Chinese or any other script.

Modern picture writing

Much has already been written about the contemporary use of pictures and symbols which play an increasingly more complex and more dominant part in our daily life. They arise out of the way multinational and multilingual needs dominate large areas of our post-industrial society. In some ways we have already moved past the comforting promises of the much prophesied 'global village' into the harsh uncertainties of a 'punctuated equilibrium'. Ethnic, cultural and political realities are consistently overruled by the demands of a global economy and with it the need for a global, and by implication, non-linguist communications system. But the usefulness of such a non-verbal (picture dominated) system is restricted to well-defined, not necessarily interrelated fields of activities. In such a specific and restricted area we operate like our tribal ancestors within a pool of shared experience and expectations. Here language and specific writing systems would, especially in situations of acute danger, be more a hindrance than a useful tool for communications (see Plate 10).

Plate 10. *Narrative pictures have played an important part from Neotholitic and tribal cave paintings to the very present. Especially in situations of extreme danger, it is important to make sure that language does not interfere with survival. Today's air travel is totally international and travellers can belong to any linguistic or cultural background. In consequence, the safest way is to return to a series of pictures to show what to do in an emergency.*

One criticism that has repeatedly been made about any attempt to look upon prehistoric or tribal pictures as proper writing is that they were not a system of graphic symbols that could be used to convey all and any thoughts (DeFrancis, 1989). But this is exactly what they did. They conveyed all thoughts essential within the orbit of their own culture, just as modern picture signs represent all thoughts essential within a particular sphere of our own, greatly fractured, contemporary civilisation.

Finally, modern pictures and signs are not hieroglyphs — as they are sometimes, quite wrongly, called by some students of the subject. Hieroglyph is a very special (Greek) term denoting a particular style of Egyptian writing. Moreover, hieroglyph means 'sacred writing' and however important commerce and safety may be in our own, property- and market-orientated society, traffic signs and corporation logos are hardly sacred.

Bibliography

Aubarbier, J-L. and Binet, *Die Wege der Vorgeschichte im Perignon*. Sarlat: Editions Quest-France, 1997.

Bahn, P. G. and Verut, J. *Journey through the Ice Age*. London: Weidenfeld and Nicolson, 1988.

Barthel, G. *Konnte Adam schreiben: Weltgeschichte der Schrift*. Koeln: Du Mont Schauberg, 1972.

Burt, B. *Aborigines*. London: British Museum, 1977.

Danzel, T. W. *Die Anfaenge der Schrift*. Hamburg/Leipzig: Museum fuer Voelkerkunde, 1912.

Dunsmore, S. *Nepalese Textiles*. London: British Museum, 1993.

Ebbinghouse, K. *Die Hausmarken auf Hiddensee*. Berlin: Insistut fuer deutsche Volkskunde, 1961.

Frobenius, L. and Fox, D. C. *Prehistoric Rock Pictures in Europe and Africa*, New York: Museum of Modern Art, 1937.

Grand, P. M. *Prehistoric Art. Palaeolithic Painting and Sculpture*. New York: 1967.

Harris, R. *The Origin of Writing*. London: Duckworth, 1986.

Harris, R. *Sings, Language and Communication, Integrational and Segregative Approach*. London: Routledge, 1996.

Jensen, H. *Signs, Symbols and Scripts: an Account of Man's Effort to Write*. London: George Allen and Unwin, 1970.

Lehner, E. *American Symbols: a picture History*. New York: Dover Publications, 1966.

Leroi-Gourhan, A. *Hand und Wort: die Evolution von Technik, Sprache und Kunst*. Paris: Editions Albins Michel Press, 1969.

Mallery, G. *Picture-Writing of the American Indians. Introduction to the Study of Sign Language among the North American Indians, an illustration of the Gesture speech of Mankind*. Washington, 10th Report of the Bureau of Ethnology, 1893.

Non-linguistic forms of writing

Marshack, A. *The Roots of Civilisation. The Cognitive Beginnings of Man's first Art, Symbol and Notation.* New York: John Wiley and Sons, 1972.

McBride, L. R. *Petroglyphs of Hawaii.* Hawaii: Petroglyphs Press, 1997.

Morris, R. W. B. *The prehistoric Rock Art of Argyll.* Pool: Dophin Press, 1977.

Reefe, T. Q. *Lukasa: a Luba memory device.* African Art. vol. 10.

Robinson, A. *The Story of Writing.* London: Thames and Hudson, 1995.

Scholem, G. G. *Major Trends in Jewish Mysticism.* 6th edn., New York: Schocken Books, 1972.

Seobeck, T. Q. *How Animals Communicate.* Bloomingdale, 1985.

Smith, M. E. *Picture writing from ancient southern Mexico, Mixtec Place Signs and Maps.* Oklahoma: University Press, 1973.

Streicher , H. *Die graphischen Gaunerzinken.* Vienna: Kriminologische Abhandlung, 1928.

Stokes, W. M. and Stokes, W. L. *Messages on Stone. Selection of Native Western Rock Art.* Utah: Starstone Publications, 1980.

Terrace, H. M. *The Chimpanzee who had Sign Language.* New York: Knopf, 1979.

3. The introduction of language elements

Given the political and economic domination the West enjoyed during the last few centuries, it was perhaps inevitable that 'proper' writing became associated with the alphabet and the ability to represent language. But there still remained a certain unease about how to evaluate and account for those systems (be they called ideographic, pictographic or logographic) which existed, not necessarily always before, but also outside or parallel with 'proper' writing. Nor could those forms of information storage be dismissed as entirely irrelevant since they so obviously played an important role in the infrastructure of their own communities. To solve the problem, scholars began to look upon them simply as a (perhaps necessary) step in the development and the history of phonological scripts which, eventually, reached their apex in the alphabet. Somewhere, somehow — so the argument usually goes — there must have existed a 'missing link' that breached the gap between thought writing and sound writing. This missing link has, on the whole, been tracked down to the so-called 'mixed' forms of writing, like those used in Mesopotamia, Egypt or Mesoamerica. The deciding factor has generally been identified as the rebus, even if opinions about its exact position and role differed. Thus, we are told, pictograms and signs may convey messages by visual means but they move towards 'proper' writing only with the introduction of the rebus principle (Cohen, 1958). However, not everybody agrees entirely with this simple explanation. Does the rebus really provide the bridge from logographic representation (Gelb, 1963) to 'proper' writing? Or was the rebus never the beginning of phonography but merely the dead end of logography and did it therefore less promote the development of scripts than the transmission of information (Harris, 1996)? However, if we consider information storage the sole purpose of writing, the latter becomes less of a problem.

The riddle of the rebus

What then exactly is this so-called rebus principle? What were the needs that created it? The argument (often repeated) goes as follows: since a purely pictographic system not only demands an inordinate number of signs, it is also ill suited to express elements of grammar and syntax or more complex forms of meaning. The picture of a leg can stand for 'leg' or, by implication, for 'to go', but difficulties arise when one wants to express sentiments such as 'I very nearly went yesterday'. The rebus increased the possibilities of information storage and communication by allowing the same symbol to stand for the idea it represents as well as for the sound (originally) associated with the word used for this idea. The picture of the sun disk can become re-usable and represent words, or parts of a word, such as sun-day, sunny, son and so on. Both the Egyptians and the Sumerian/Akkadians made use of this principle and, we are told, thus initiated the important transitional step towards 'proper' writing, i.e. a purely phonetic writing. But those scripts, together with Chinese, did in fact go a step further in re-using symbols: a symbol could also act as a determinative (Egypt, Mesopotamia) or as a radical (China) to clarify meaning. The resemblance of the shape of such representational symbols (two leg for 'to go' in Egyptian, two legs for 'man' in Chinese, etc.) has sometimes been taken as proof of one script having developed from another (or all scripts from just one common ancestor), but it is more likely the result of the consistency in the shape of objects in the visible word itself. In other words, the same coloured pieces of glass form themselves into different pictures at the turn of a kaleidoscope. The question of course remains: who, or better, what turns the kaleidoscope? But then, how does one tell the dancer from the dance?

There can be no doubt that the representation of sounds and the re-useability of symbols increased the possibility to express forms of grammar and syntax (orthography is at this point irrelevant, as is any exact form of pronunciation) while at the same time limiting the number of signs necessary to cover all necessities. But the ability to express linguistic elements goes much further back than Egypt, Mesopotamia or Mesoamerica. Linguistic elements already appeared in simple forms of information storage: in objects, pictures and signs. In fact, we do not know how early such ideas made their first, tentative appearance. Nobody can tell what the animal pictures or notches seen in Palaeolithic caves 'told' the 'reader', how fixed and codified their verbal value was, or even, whether there was just one single verbal value which communicated itself, either directly or though an appointed interpreter. How far did written information storage, the creation of definite images, influence the development of language?

As with so many other elements connected with the concept of writing, we have to accept that there is much we simply do not know and may perhaps never know for certain. It seems that somehow the rebus arose out of a natural connection between orality and writing, between oral and written information's storage, oral and written literacy.

The emergence of the rebus in objects, proverbs and ritualistic memory aids

Does the rebus exist merely in an auxiliary capacity or as a principle in its own right? What is certain is the fact that the use of rebus transfer goes much further back than the appearance of the so-called mixed scripts. Under certain circumstances it can, in embryo, provide a link between language elements and objects or pictures of objects and events.

We know that information stored in objects may communicate a certain amount of linguistic expression. Can we call this a rebus? Or can we at least say that this form of communication moves towards such a direction? Nearer the actual rebus concept are examples which have definite linguistic, and as we shall see, syntactic significance. In other words, the rebus, as an enabling faculty, can inherently deal with exceedingly simple forms of information storage. Well known, and often quoted, are the so-called Yoruba love letters from Nigeria where six cowrie shells sent to a member of the opposite sex means 'I am attracted to you' because the Yoruba word *efa* means both 'six' and 'attracted'. If the recipient shares the sentiment, he or she might send a string

Plate 11. Pictorial representations of proverbs include elements of language insofar as they stand for a definite, verbal message. A ball of wool with a needle and a blanket made up of narrow woven strips represent a proverb used by the Ewe people of Togo (Africa): 'big things can come from little ones' or 'little causes, big effects'.

of eight cowrie shells to say 'I agree, I feel the same' because the Yoruba word *ejo* means 'eight' as well as 'attracted'. In a similar way, the so-called *aroko* of the Jebu people living in the hinterland of Lagos consist of a reed cord, two red knots, four cowrie shells and a piece of fruit-peel (Jensen, 1970). This is a letter a very sick person might send to a friend and it reads: 'The illness is getting worse, our only hope rests with God'. In both, as in many other cases, the rebus has its point of gravity more in orality than in writing as such.

Proverbs state cultural truism meant to re-enforce the listener's convictions by referring to lessons from parallel events in an attempt to convert him or her to one's own view. In general, proverbs fall into relative disuse once the literacy level increases in a particular society because proverbs basically rely on oral, face-to-face communications. With the aid of certain mnemonic devices, they can, however, be made visible, thus addressing a wider audience (see Plate 11). A knowledge of traditional proverbs was an essential element of everyday life in Ashante society (McLeod, 1981), vital to those who wanted to advance their social position. Proverbs were used to clinch debates and also for deciding arguments — they represented therefore an essential part of Ashante rhetoric. Their visual representation may have been prone to a variation of meanings but they provided a starting point for a mental or spoken chain of thoughts and sayings. The image of a bird turning his beak

Plate 12. Language elements can appear in seemingly simple memory aids. Much of the knowledge necessary to perform the Midewiwin (Medicine Dance) of the central Alonquin people, together with the memory of the dances and the songs performed at the meetings of the Mide society, is inscribed on song-boards or birch bark scrolls.

backwards could stand for 'a person should not hesitate to turn back on past mistakes'. A crocodile grasping a mud fish in its mouth could mean 'if the mud fish gets anything it will eventually go to the crocodile' but also 'only a bad crocodile eats the creature that shares the same hole in the river bed'. Such proverbs could be made visible on everyday objects — on a pipe, the walls of houses — making them an ever present factor in Ashante society.

Plate 13. A text written in pictures by the Cuna Indians of Panama. Such texts were used by singers during a special ritual. They describe the quest of the fugitive soul of a sick man. The lines are read in a boustrophedon manner. Unlike the representation of proverbs, the verbal meaning of the text must be correct to ensure the effectiveness of the ritual chant.

In this context linguistic elements can stand for words and/or a whole sentence. In the cases of ritualistic mnemonic devises, where precision of meaning is essential, they can represent the order in which sentences or songs have to read/sung so as to ensure the validity of the performance. They are thus less open to general interpretation and to acquiring meaning; they often need the aid of a trained interpreter well versed in the requirements of relevant rituals (see Plate 12). For example, the usual picture writing of the native North American Indians is usually referred to a *kekewin*. There exists however a second form of picture writing called *kekinowin*. The later is known only to the priests who use it to memorise the correct order and the exact wording of magic spells and incantations. Here the picture represents not just an idea but a definite sentence or word, and in each case only one possible spoken form will correspond to it. Those pictures are in fact read exactly like a text (see Plate 13).

Sign languages

In primary sign language various morphological and syntactic processes are employed that are different to those used in spoken language. But the element of language as such need not by necessity be absent. Signs function almost like logograms written into the air.

We shall here leave aside sign languages designed for the use of deaf or other special needs people and concentrate on those that developed in connection with specific tasks by people capable of using language and in many cases also writing. These type of sign languages span historically and geographically, as well as subject wise, a relatively large area. They can serve a double purpose: setting the signer apart from the rest of the community, enabling him or her to communicate, often secretly on his or her own terms. Specialised signs have to be learned and they must also, like pictures and symbols, relate to a common pool of shared experience. Consequently, they are in many cases able to break the political hold the community habitually asserts over all its members. By doing so, they become an infrastructure within an infrastructure and act as instruments of special empowerment.

Sign languages cover specialised fields and serve special sections of the community (Kendon, 1988). There are the sign languages used by Bushmen hunters in the Kalahari desert and those of the Aborigines of Australia. Here, abstaining from the use of language is essential for the success of the hunt. But we need not go so far afield. A SAS patrol will use sign language in exactly the same way to secure the success of an operation (McNab, 1995). A special occasion can also create the need for abstaining from language so as to shield an event from non-initiates. Apart from hunting signs, Australian Aborigines use special signs in connection with initiation ceremonies and mourning rituals. Into a somewhat different category fall the signs employed by the Plain Indians of North America which are used between groups who do not speak the same language. The great linguist and traveller Richard Burton, while Consul in West Africa (1961-3), claims to have created a special sign language to communicate with tribes whose language he did not understand. He tells us that he had devised some 200 different signs, adding that they were enough to enable any traveller to make his way through the same area.

Signs can also support taboos. Armenian married women in some remote areas were not permitted to speak in the presence of a wide range of affiliated relations and consequently took refuge in signing. Monks bound by a rule of silence (Barakat, 1975) are sometimes allowed to use a limited number of signs to communicate essential information to each other; in such cases signing can also be supported by short written notes.

A wide field is covered by sign languages attached to special professions. One extremely sophisticated and complex system is the one used to instruct Indian Bharat Natyam dancers, which even has rules for formation into comparable morphemes. In industrialised countries special sign languages have been developed for crane operation, aircraft marshalling, stock exchange transactions, bidding at auctions, broadcasting studies and between workers in especially noisy factories.

The failure of purely phonetic scripts

In 1886 the International Phonetic Association (IPA) was founded in Paris, based on the ideas of the Danish phonetician Otto Jespersen. Its aim was to devise a totally artificial and therefore, it was thought, internationally acceptable alphabet for all languages. This international phonetic alphabet (IPA), as it came to be known, would provide the academic community with a notional standard for the representation of all languages. Thus, at one time, students attempting to learn Hindi were, instead of being taught the Devanagari characters which provide an exact representation of the language, expected to struggle with a number of more or less meaningless signs before being allowed to learn Devanagari. Jespersen's idea was taken up not only by parts of the academic community but with even more enthusiasm and, as it turned out, often quite disastrous results, by language teachers who thought it would help to improve children's pronunciation. IPA, they argued, was so accurate that it could represent even the accent of the original speaker. Since hardly two people speak exactly alike, one wonders how this could have helped children towards literacy. In any case, any possible advantages gained by it were offset by the sheer lack of readability. Far from boosting children's confidence, it often destroyed their confidence in spelling and orthography altogether. In some cases it adversely affected their ability to read to such an extent as to turn perfectly capable students into artificial dyslexics.

What IPA did prove was the fact that scripts and writing systems have to develop naturally as a result of a communal need. Just as Esperanto never became an international success, the sheer artificiality of IPA made it from the beginning hardly more than an ultimately barren intellectual exercise. It also showed that artificial inventions do not advance causes or societies but lead towards a non-productive and, in the final instance, meaningless exercise.

An interesting fact is the sometimes overlooked difference between a phonetic script and the transcription or transliteration of an already existing writing system. Both use phonetic script signs and/or notations which aim to refer to the primary sounds of a language in an unambiguous way, with one symbol ideally being restricted to just one sound, though diacritics are often necessary to make a clearer distinction. For example, to transliterate Vietnamese as many as four diacritics must sometimes be attached to one letter of the alphabet. In many ways, the notion of 'visible speech' could perhaps more fittingly be applied to such transliteration systems than to phonetic scripts as such. It is not without interest to note that the Toronto Group's favourite concept had been taken up almost a century earlier by the elocution teacher A. M. Bell (1819-1905) who (another interesting feature) first lectured in Edinburgh before emigrating to Canada. In 1879 he gave a public demonstration of his new scheme for recording speech in writing, which he eventually brought out in a book entitled *Visible Speech, the Science of the Universal Alphabet* (1867). In all fairness to Bell, his system was never meant to provide a new way of writing or even spelling but was solely meant to assist children in learning how to read. In this way Bell hoped it would 'provide a sound bridge from language to language'. His symbols were iconic and meant to signify the vocal organs involved in pronouncing sounds. This in itself was nothing new: the Sanskrit grammarians and King Sejong of Korea had made similar attempts, though, it must be said, with more success. Bell never gained the support of the British government for his venture but the practice of using such a system for transcribing speech proved a useful tool for anthropologists trying to take down hitherto unrecorded languages (Powell, 1877). From the middle of the 20th century onwards the transcription or transliteration of, especially, Asian languages (Wellisch, 1978) has acquired a certain degree of political implication. To quote just one example, there was the long refusal of the American Library of Congress to use Pinyin for the transliteration of Chinese since, in the eyes of some orthodox (American) scholars, this was perceived as a Communist-friendly move. In the same way, some Asian librarians saw in the insistence of their Western colleagues to transliterate their scripts for the purpose of Western students a form of belated intellectual imperialism. This was perhaps less whimsical than those outside this subject area might think: many Asian scripts (certainly in the case of India) were frequently much better suited to express and represent a particular language. There was also the controversy surrounding authors' names which produced endless discussion amongst various interest groups. However, with the ability of modern computers to reproduce any script, in any form, running in any direction, this argument has lost much of its force and brought about a better accommodation between scripts and national sentiments.

Apart from using (artificially created) phonetic scripts as an aid to learning new scripts or transliterate languages not yet fully codified, there have been a number of local attempts to find phonetic forms of writing to increase literacy. The south western group of Thai languages, for example, covers an area where 90 different languages are spoken by a population of four millions. To further nation-wide literacy, a completely phonetic script had at one time been adopted. Its spread and success was however greatly hampered by a lack of qualified teachers and adequate teaching materials, as well as funding. Though in 1984 the government claimed to have erased illiteracy altogether, a later study, commissioned in 1987, showed that literacy, nationwide, was just about 31%. Considering the difficulties inherent in such a project, one should not look at this figure (if it was indeed a correct reflection of the then existing situation) necessarily as an all-out failure.

The elusive phoneme

It was to some extent the hunt for that elusive concept, the 'phoneme' which convinced the creators as well as the supporters of IPA that a purely phonetic script would, more than even the alphabet, provide a universal panacea for the lack of literacy and all related ills. Now one of the most used (though seldom fully understood) terms in modern linguistics (in most recent times unfortunately introduced into primary school education), it has had many different forms of usage since its first appearance in the early 19th century. Before the term itself was coined, the nearest technical term was 'letter' (Abercrombie, 1965) — something rather different and far less elusive.

What then exactly is a phoneme? It is generally considered to be the smallest possible unit in the sound system of any language. But unlike a letter in an alphabet, it has no existence independent of a particular language; it is not a real but an imaginary sound underlying spoken language. A phoneme in one language is not a phoneme in another; we cannot really pronounce *c* or *t*, except if connected within a word. For example, if we take the word *cat*, *c* and *t* achieve sound qualities only through the interpolated *a*. If we tried to pronounce *c* and *t* on their own, we would end up with something like *ce* and *ti* — syllables. Not only does each language have its own phonemic system, even within one and the same language different local dialects, or simply personal ways of speaking, have different phonemic values. Phonemes must be carefully distinguished from physical sounds which do not in themselves constitute a limited system but which can be said to be 'realisations' of the contrary(?) phonemes. Or as Schmitt (1980) put it: a phoneme cannot be produced as a sound. It is simply an abstract concept (*Gedankengroesse*) which can be made real only visually (as a letter) but not acoustically. The study of phonemes, we are told by other authorities, is part of phonology; the study of sound, on the other hand, falls under the subject of phonetics.

This may look like a somewhat amusing example of scholarly sophistry but it becomes less amusing when used for teaching primary school children. At present the

The introduction of language elements

National Literacy Strategy, based on educational reforms first introduced in 1988 and since then continuously modified, insists that children in primary schools should be able to understand the phonemic components of their own language so as to improve their spelling and help them to become fully literate. Something the planners seem to have overlooked is that, sadly, English is not a phonemic language. It is, to go back to Schmitt, a letter script (*Buchstabenschrift*) and not a sound script (*Lautschrift*). The same letter has a large variety of sound possibilities. Many English words (if not most) have to be read logographic, like Chinese. Indeed, scholars working on dyslexia have found that the brain waves of people reading English are very similar to those produced by people reading Chinese and that persons suffering from dyslexia in English do not suffer necessarily from dyslexia in Chinese or Japanese (two, from the point of alphabet-writing communities, much more 'difficult' scripts). In German, for example, a child who has learned how to pronounce the letters of the alphabet could, in most cases, read a German word even if he or she did not know its actual meaning. One is not quite sure how this same child would be able to read a word like, for example, 'hunt', since as a letter of the alphabet *u* would, in the English alphabet, be pronounced as *you*, *h* as *edge* and *t* as *te*. This apart from the fact that learning to spell through phonemic understanding would demand perfect speech on the part of the teacher and a perfect ear for sounds on the part of the child.

Bibliography

Abercrombie, D. *What is a letter? Studies in Phonetics and Linguistics.* London: Oxford University Press, 1965

Barakat, R. A. *A Cistercian Sign Language: a Study of Non-Verbal Communication.* Michigan: Cistercian Publications, 1975.

Bell, A. M. *Visible Speech, the Science of Universal Alphabets, or self-interpreting psychological Letters, for the writing of all Languages in our Alphabet.* London: N. Tuebner and Co.,1867.

Chao, Y. R. *Language and Symbolic Systems.* London: Cambridge University Press, 1968

Christaller, J. G. *A Collection of three thousand and six hundred Ishi Proverb in Use among the Negros of the Gold Coast speaking the Ashante or Fante Language. Together with their Variations and alphabetically arranged.* Basle, Evangelical Mission, 1879.

Chromsky, N. *Reflections on Language.* New York: Pantheon, 1975.

Cohen, M. *La grande invention de l'ecriture et son evolution.* Paris: Imprimerie Nationale, 1958.

Gelb, I. J. *A Study of Writing: The Foundations of Grammatology.* 2nd edn., Chicago, University of Chicago Press, 1963.

Glaser, M. and Pausch. M. *Between Orality and Writing,* Amsterdam: Rodopi, 1994.

Harris, R. *The Origin of Writing.* London: Duckworth, 1986.

Harris, R. *Signs, Language and Communication, Integrational and Segregative Approach.* London: Routledge, 1996.

Jensen, H. *Signs, Symbols and Scripts; an Account of Man's Effort to Write.* London: George Allen and Unwin, 1970.

Jones, D. *The Phoneme: its Nature and Use.* 2nd edn., Cambridge: Heffner.

Lepsius, C. R. *Standard Alphabet for reducing Unwritten Languages and foreign Graphic Systems to a Uniform Orthography in European Letters,* 2nd edn. Amsterdam: John Benjamins, 1981.

Kendon, A. *Sign Language of Aboriginal Australia, cultural, semiotic and communicative Perspectives.* Cambridge: University Press, 1988.

McLeod, M. D. *The Asante.* London: British Museum, 1981.

McNab, A. *Immediate Action,* London: Corgi Books, 1995.

Powell, J. N. *Contributions to North American Ethnology.* 3 vols., 1877.

Schmitt, A. *Untersuchungen zur Geschichte der Schrift, Entstehung und Entwicklung der Schriften.* Herausgegeben C. Haebler. Koeln: Boehler, 1980.

Terrace, H. M. Nim, *The Chimpanzee who had Sign Language.* New York: Knopf, 1979.

Wang, W. S-Y. *The Emergence of Language, Development and Evolution.* San Francisco, W. H. Fullman, 1991.

Wellisch, H. H. *The Conversion of Scripts, its Nature, History and Utilization.* New York: John Wiley and Sons, 1978.

4. Extinct scripts: the infrastructure of palace and temple

These much-discussed forms of writing have generally been quoted as examples of the so-called 'mixed' scripts, which are thought to have constituted the decisive link between 'forerunners' of writing and 'proper' writing. Though visually vastly different, they exhibit certain common features: the use of logographic pictures, phonetic elements usually based on the rebus principle and determinatives for the clarification of meaning. Another common element is a profound, if varied, reliance on numbers related to the counting and/or accounting of objects, property and events or for the measurement of time and/or the legitimacy of dynastic traditions. These scripts operated during different periods, in widely different geographical areas. None of them is still in use, some have never been properly, or indeed at all, deciphered. Unconvincing attempts have in the past repeatedly tried to link them to one common origin, or as Schmitt (1940) would have it, see in them the results of a *Urerfindung* — an original invention made just once, in just one place, which then served as a template for further developments. While this demands what more or less amounts to an act of faith, all those scripts did have something else in common — they successfully served the infrastructure of their respective societies, societies which rested broadly on a balance between the powers of the palace and temple, the temple being more often than not closely interlinked with the market.

What then do we know about them? We know, for example, the beginning, history and internal structure of the Mesopotamian cuneiform script; we also know the exact time when it ceased to be used. We know all about the internal construction, variations and the demise of the Egyptian script and the elements that caused this demise; but we know next to nothing about its beginning and early stages of development. We know something about the internal construction and nearly everything about the sudden and brutal end of scripts used in Mesoamerica. We can speculate about the motivations inherent in their origin, decipher parts of the whole system and, up to a point, understand the importance attached to numbers and the manner in which they were used to support the fabric of society. We also know (though it is for some reason seldom given due attention) that the Mayas had a knowledge of zero, something which none of the other scripts had developed in the same way.

As far as the ancient Mediterranean scripts are concerned, we can speculate about them but only two, Linear B and the Cypriote script, have so far been deciphered, mainly because we know the language they served. We know nothing about the origin, or even the end (or the reason for this end), of the Indus Valley script — we are unable to read it. We are also ignorant about the people who used this script and the type of language they spoke.

Plate 14. Clay tokens as used in Mesopotamia from c. 8000 BC onward.

The most stable components of early writing systems seem to have been pictures and numbers — in some civilisation the knowledge of numbers and their manipulation played a more important part than in others. This was almost certainly the case in Mesopotamia, where trade dominated the life of the people. Trade in turn depends on the amount (numbers) and the identification of goods. In the ancient civilisations of Mesoamerica numbers too were important but their primary purpose related to the manipulation and interpretation of calendrical elements connected with religion, politics and dynastic histories. An essential element of Mesoamerica's infrastructure revolved around dynastic genealogies, stories of migrations, wars and sacrifices. In Peru, on the other hand, where the main form of writing was the *quipu,* numbers were all-important for archival record-keeping, taxation and with it the success of a highly centralised political control.

Mesopotamia

It is now generally agreed that writing in the Middle East started solely in support of business transactions (Walker, 1989). Once we accept this as the basis for further discussions, it is of only secondary importance whether the inspiration for subsequent developments was based on property marks, seals, pictures — or whether the first impetus came in the form of clay tokens (see Plate 14). Clay tokens, incorporating some form of primitive accounting system (Schmandt-Besserat, 1992, 1996) are thought to have accompanied goods in transit. Numbers are inherent in the concept of ownership, just as proof of ownership forms the basis of property and all trading relations. But though tokens and numbers can play an important role, this role is strictly limited to a certain stage of socio-economic development. Tokens prove facts but the necessary infrastructure to protect, administer and creatively use those facts needs more complex methods of information storage. The suggestion has been made that writing arose from a slotting system that combined numbers and pictures, with a different picture representing each commodity (Harris, 1986). This may well have been the case in Mesopotamia but it becomes again an act of faith as soon as we try to move it into the realm of an overall explanation for the origin of writing as such.

Let us now briefly examine both theories: the token/slotting and the property mark/picture one and ask ourselves whether they are in fact complementary rather than contradictory. Considering known historical facts, they seem to follow different historical and socio/economic periods. The earliest tokens — at this point, only small objects made of clay — go back to the Neolithic period of c. 8000 BC. They are thought to have evolved in support of a simple form of agriculture and animal husbandry and served the purpose of keeping track of surplus goods produced by farmers. Later, with the growth of organised labour, the move from subsistence farming to specialisation and the development of increasingly larger urban settlements, they also related to goods manufactured in specialised workshops. As the variety of goods increased, clay tokens took on different shapes or were incised with patterns indicative of the commodities they represented. As society, especially in the cities, became more stratified, an increase in bureaucracy introduced a demand for archival storage. One method was to enclose tokens in a sealed clay envelope (*bullae*). Eventually the shape of the tokens inside the envelop was impressed on the envelop. A sealed *bullae,* Schmandt-Besserat argues, might accompany goods; in the case of dispute, it could be broken open to check the accuracy of the information. Such a system was in fact a form of pictorial writing in embryo, which eventually led to writing tablets and pictography. It was thus not the picture but a primitive accounting system which introduced writing to Mesopotamia. Though this theory is by no means universally accepted, it is interesting to note that simple clay tokens have also been found in Syria, Iraq, Iran, Turkey and Israel, and indeed (a fact which has so far received little attention), probably also in the remains of the Indus cities.

After about 3000 BC the use of tokens seems to have trailed off (Robinson, 1995). By the middle of the 4th century BC, with political control mostly in the hands of small city-states or short-lived empires, a form of economy had developed that depended increasingly on not just cooperation but centrally organised labour for the purpose of irrigation (left to itself most of the land is infertile for up to eight months of the year). The administrative control of the resulting surplus, the growing power of the various city-states, on which the new wealth depended, increased the importance of trade (see Plate 15). Trade in turn depends on contracts and laws, not just on information (tokens and *bullae*), and on the ability to defend (armies) not only trade but also increasingly more densely populated areas (cities/states). In this new and highly centralised economy the officials of the palace and the temple (the twin institutions around which life revolved) needed a more reliable and sophisticated form of information storage than human memory, tokens, *bullae* or simple property marks made by seals.

The people generally credited with the invention of what eventually became known as the cuneiform script were the Sumerians, who by the middle of the 4th millennium BC had established a prominent position in Mesopotamia. Neither their actual place of origin nor their ethnic/linguistic affinities have so far been established beyond doubt. The earliest known Sumerian tablets have for long been considered those coming from Uruk, dated about 3300 BC. Recent excavations in north eastern Syria do however indicate that a walled city already existed at Tell Brac around 3800 BC. By around 3500 BC the people of Tell Brac were certainly numerate. Excavators have also found early pictographic dockets showing animal representations accompanied by numbers — and pottery vessels with marks indicative of ownership.

Though we have generally come to associate Mesopotamian writing with the cuneiform (see Plate 16) script (Lat. *cuneus*, wedge, i.e. wedge-shaped impressions made with a blunt edged stylus on wet clay), the original Sumerian script was clearly

Plate 15. A system of weights is essential for trading. This particular weight is shaped in the form of a duck and inscribed with three Sumerian cuneiform characters. It was found in Ugarit and dates from c. 1300 BC.

pictographic. How far these original pictures depended on tokens, additional impressions made on clay envelopes or on clay tablets themselves is debatable. Much more far-fetched is the idea that the ability to replace tokens by two-dimensional signs would have made the rebus redundant. Even if the earliest written signs were only signs of signs, this (apart form leaving at least 1500 Sumerian signs unaccounted for) would still leave us with a purely logographic script, with no adequate explanation about its further developments.

Originally, the Sumerian script was in all likelihood predominately logographic (one sign/sign group for each term or concept without the addition of grammatical elements). However, this script acquired quite early on phonetic elements (phonograms) and determinatives (sense-signs placed before or after a character to determine categories of objects). The Sumerian language itself is agglutinative (the basic idea of a word being expressed by an unchanging syllable, or polysyllable, which may be modified by a series of prefixes or post-fixes). Phonograms stood for syllables which could be used either directly or like a rebus. In other words, the drawing of a particular object could stand for (the Sumerian word of the) object it depicted, or for its homonyms [to translate this into English. the drawing of a sun disc could stand for *sun* or *son*]. It could also be used to represent other homonymous syllables [i.e. the drawing of a bird's bill could stand for *bill,* the name *Bill,* it could also be used in such words a *buil*-ding, a-*bil*-ity and so on].

Plate 16. A Sumerian-Eblite lexicon, often referred to as the oldest dictionary in the world. It was discovered as part of the Royal Archives during excavations at Ebla (North Syria) in 1975; c. 2400-2000 BC.

Despite its complexity this was still a relatively simple script, though it never quite freed itself from the fact that its origins were based on practical bookkeeping and not on the expression of abstract ideas. But further problems arose when, after c. 2800 BC, the Semitic Akkadians (Babylonians/Assyrians) began to establish themselves in Mesopotamia. Culturally less advanced than the people they came to dominate, they took over certain features of Sumerian life, among them the Sumerian script. Since this script was particularly ill-suited to accommodate the structure of a Semitic language (where the root meaning of words depends on groups of consonants), a number of compromises became necessary. In the event, the Akkadians continued to use the Sumerian logograms but substituted the Semitic equivalent of the Sumerian word for it [transferring this situation again to German and English: the drawing of a bird's bill could now also be read as *Schnabel*]. In addition, they made use of the original (Sumerian) phonetic value of the (written) syllable [to return to our German-English example: the drawing of a bird's bill could also be read as *Bil*-dung, *bil*-lig, *Bil*-d, and so on] and an increased use of determinatives to overcome mounting problems of ambiguity. The number of cuneiform signs had by then been reduced to 600 (from the original 2000) but the number of possible values and variations was considerably higher.

This was by all accounts a complex and cumbersome way of writing. It was also, because of the writing material (clay bricks) and the writing implements (reed stylus), visually difficult to comprehend. Yet it successfully lasted well over three millennia. In addition, it was also chosen for the representation of a number of different languages until it eventually gave way to the more 'user friendly' Aramaic.

Ancient Mediterranean forms of writing

Of the five ancient Mediterranean scripts, three from Crete and two from the island of Cyprus, only two have so far been deciphered: Cretan Linear B and one of the Cypriote scripts. Both are syllabic and both were used for writing a contemporary form of the Greek language. The earlier Cypriote-Minoan, with about 85 symbols and dating from 1500 BC onwards, has remained undeciphered. The later Cypriote script, from about the 11th to the 3rd century BC and featuring some 50 to 60 signs, appears in bilingual inscriptions of classical Greek with a line in Cypriote underneath. It was deciphered in 1871.

From about 2300 BC onwards Crete's prosperity began to depend on trade supported by a powerful fleet, with the palaces of Knossos and, to a lesser extent, that of Phaistos providing administrative centres of gravity. Homer had already talked of Crete as 'a rich and lovely land, washed by the sea on every side; in it are many people and 90 cities. There one language mingles with another . . . Among the cities is Knossos, a great city.' The person who two and a half millennia later introduced us to the remains of Knossos, the archaeologist Sir Arthur Evans (1851-1941), not only excavated the site but used much of his own means to reconstruct parts of the palace of Knossos, an endeavour often ridiculed by purists. He was also responsible for introducing us to three hitherto unknown forms of Cretan writing, the earliest found on seal stones, the later two inscribed on clay tablets.

Early Cretan stone inscriptions, either on seal stones or marking property, are short and generally ascribed to a period between c. 1900 and 1600 BC. They consist of recognisable pictures, some perhaps based on ancient cult symbols. With only 140 different signs, they have so far resisted attempts to decipher them.

It seems that from around 1800 BC onwards linear forms of writing, mostly scratched into clay tablets, began to appear. The earlier form, eventually called Linear A, was mainly written on clay tablets, the text being divided by lines into square fields, with four to five lines in each field. Examples come from palaces in the south of the island; only few have been found in Knossos. The number of signs has been reduced to 75 (85 according to some scholars), with some pictorial signs still clearly visible. Evans laboured conscientiously on their decipherment but was greatly hampered by his ignorance of the (still unknown) Minoan language in which they were probably written. It has been suggested, though in no way proven, that Linear A was mainly used for personal documents and religious texts.

The last form of writing, Linear B, seems to bear some relation to Linear A but there are also many signs that do not match. This script is mostly written on clay tablets and documented from between 1450 BC to c. 1200 BC. This was the time when Knossos came under Mycenean influence and Cretan scribes seem to have adapted their syllabic script to the linguistic expression of the new ruling class, Minoan Greek (Green, 1981). This script was eventually deciphered by Michael Ventris in 1953, who recognised it as a (not very efficient) means for writing the (Indo-Aryan) Greek language.

Linear B seems to have served a large palace economy. There are lists of land holdings, craftsmen to whom allocations have been made, systems of weights, inventories, as well as day to day accounts (see Plate 17). Individual tablets were dried in the sun and kept in baskets for about a year before they could be re-used. Apart from phonetic expressions (mostly open syllables), there were also signs (ideograms?) representing commodities, goods, animals or humans, which usually appear before the (decimal) numerals. A form of slotting system similar to the one used in Mesopotamia? Maybe, maybe not. There are also special signs for names and places and — already quite an advanced concept — word divisions.

Peru

If in Mesopotamia writing developed out of an accounting system designed to assist trade, in Peru numbers seem to have been the main form of writing. Numbers, supporting a complex system of account keeping, enabled the ruling Inca elite to enforce a strictly centralised administrative control, thus providing it with an effective tool for the collection of taxes. Trade was of little importance, since nothing comparable to our concept of personal property seems to have been in existence. What trade did exist was basically run on a barter system.

We are, of course, severely handicapped in our speculations by the fact that nearly all information about the Inca Empire comes from hostile, and highly biased, sources. We know how the political infrastructure of the empire functioned at the time of Pizarro's arrival in 1531 AD. But the Spaniards did not come as colonisers or traders; they came purely for the sake of conquest and plunder, intentions thinly veiled by claims of religious motivation. Thus, at the very moment when we meet Inca civilisation for the first time, we already become witnesses to its destruction.

The Inca Empire that Pizarro encountered had reached its peak barely a century earlier. As in Mesoamerica, many of its finest achievements (weaving, building with

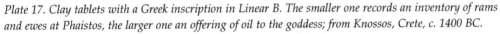

Plate 17. Clay tablets with a Greek inscription in Linear B. The smaller one records an inventory of rams and ewes at Phaistos, the larger one an offering of oil to the goddess; from Knossos, Crete, c. 1400 BC.

interlocking stones, fine metal work, etc.) were a legacy of earlier civilisation. The Incas had, however, unlike the Mayas or Aztecs, more clearly defined expansionist aims. Those were amply supported by a strong army (with officers from the Inca's own household), a centralised system of administration and a foolproof way of taxation — all of it supported by an awesome bureaucracy (about 1331 officials per 10,000 heads of population). This enabled them to assimilate new territories and ensure a centrally planned increase in overall productivity. Such centralisation of political power depends on the exact storage and the easy accessibility of information. It is generally thought that the Incas did not have any form of writing. They did — but their writing was based, more strongly than anywhere else, on the practical use of numbers. In addition, their infrastructure was supported by a network of roads, some 3250 miles long, running from north to south, with post houses every five miles, runners who could relay despatches at a rate of 150 miles per day and — most important of all — the means of information storage the runners carried: the *quipu*.

Quipus are knotted cords, some up to five kilograms in weight. Means by which data can be conveyed include the type and number of knots (from one to nine), the position of each knot (decimal place value), the colour and ply of each string and the position of the string along the main cord. Gracilaso de la Vega (b. 1539 AD), the son of a Spaniard and a niece of the last Inca ruler, tells that '. . . according to their position, the knots signify units, ten, hundreds, thousands, ten thousands and, exceptionally, hundred thousands, and they are all [as] well aligned on their different cords as the figures that an accountant sets down, column by column in his ledger' (Joseph, 1991). On their own, quipus could not be used for computation; they served basically as the storage of information. Computation was made with the assistance of an abacus-like board (see Plate 18) by specially appointed officials, the *quipu* masters (*quipucamayoc*). Quipus and the *quipu* masters enabled the Inca and the central administrators (the Inca's family) to know exactly how many inhabitants lived in the empire, what duties they fulfilled and what they possessed down to the last pair of sandals in each household.

Did *quipus* supply more than statistical information? Did they act as a form of slotting system? It has been suggested that verbal messages may have been sent with the runners who carried the *quipus* — which raises the question whether in some way they also acted as a form of memory aid. Did under certain circumstances *quipus* also contain some form of memory aid related to ritual and historical events? Opinions are divided. Quipus have been found in Inca graves which, at one point, encouraged speculation that their purpose may not have been purely statistical but that, under certain circumstances, they also contained magical combinations of numbers (Danzel, 1912). Since any strictly controlled administration depends on laws, and the enforcement of laws, it is possible that *quipus* were also used to record laws (Bankes, 1977), together with other information relevant to administration. Did they include the ability to count time? According to Poma de Ayala, the Inca week lasted ten days, with a month consisting of three weeks; sometimes an extra two days had to be added. Generally, the Incas seem to have been able to measure short periods, like the time of days by the position of the sun but were less successful when it came to

CO̅TADOR·MAIOR·ITE3ORERO
TAVANTIN·SVIOO·VIPOC
CVRACA·CON ⊕ DOR·CHAVA

con tador y tesouro   con tador

Plate 18. The infrastructure of the Inca Empire depended on the quipu, *used together with an abacus-like board by the local* quipu-masters. *Both are here depicted in a drawing made by Poma de Ayala, c. 1613. Guaman Pedro Cieza de Leon, writing immediately after the Spanish conquest, gives an account of the effectiveness of the system: 'in the capital of each province there were accountants whom they called* quipu camayocs, *and by these knots they kept the account of the tribute paid by the natives of that district in silver, gold, clothing, flocks, down to wood and other insignificant things, and by these* quipus *by the end of each year, or ten or twenty years, they gave a report to one whose duty it was to check the account so exactly that not even a pair of sandals was missing . . . the wars, cruelties, pillages and tyranny of the Spaniards had been such that if these Indians had not been accustomed to order and providence, they would all have perished . . . and after the Spaniards had passed through, the chieftains came together with the keepers of the* quipus, *and if one had expended more than the others, those who had given less made up the difference, so that all were on equal footing.'*

measuring long periods. Time, for the purpose of administration, is, after all, only important in the short term.

The Incas were probably not the originators of this system. Sending runners to convey recorded messages was already practised by the Moche (600 BC—200 AD), whose lives and customs can partially be reconstructed from scenes painted on their pottery. A certain category of Moche pottery is decorated with pictures showing runners, sometimes with animal, bird or insect (or even bean-shaped) heads, wearing military dress, carrying small pouches filled with marked beans (see Plate 19). Beans decorated with special designs such as parallel lines, dots, a combination of dots or lines, some comb-like shapes and other, not yet identified images, may have constituted a system of information storage that was perhaps even more complex than numbering. Like the Incas, the Moche also used such beans in connection with counting boards. There have even been suggestions that they constituted a form of writing comparable to that used by the Mayas of Mesoamerica (Bankes, 1977), though this is perhaps too adventurous an interpretation. Marked beans did however almost certainly constitute a well-understood system of information storage. Like *quipus*, they have also been found in Moche graves — which opens possibilities for further speculation.

This leaves us with another interesting question. How far did pictures (the second most stable component in the area of information storage) play a part in the country we now know as Peru? Incidentally, the name Peru itself is based, rather like Bishop Landa's Maya 'alphabet', on a basic misunderstanding. Garcilaso de la Vega relates how, in about 1515, a Spanish ship sailing close to the coast captured a local fisherman and asked him what the land was called. He is supposed to have replied *Beru* (possibly his own name) and that he was in *pelu* (a river). It was from the combinations of these two words that the Spaniards eventually arrived at the word Peru, a name which neither the Incas nor their predecessors ever used (Bankes, 1977).

When at the beginning of the 20th century Peruvian and American archaeologists began to interest themselves in local culture, they discovered cave paintings dating from c. 8000 to 6000 BC which show llama-like animals, horned and deer-like beasts, hunters using clubs and slings — paintings in every way comparable to those found in the Cro-Magnon caves of France and Spain. Whatever the exact type of animals

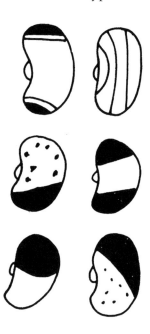

Plate 19. The Moche, a pre-Inca people used marked beans for the storage and communication of information. This system was no doubt an important element of their infrastructure. Moche pottery shows runners speedily carrying pouches filled with such beans. Marked beans have also been found in Moche graves, which may indicate that they provided more than just numerical information.

and weapons, these paintings made a definite statement; they stored, like their Western counterparts, information essential to the life of the community.

How far then did images painted on pottery vessels and certain designs on textiles contain a form of information storage we have so far been unable to comprehend? Barthel's claim that motifs on woven fabrics and also on some drinking vessels represented (logographic?) characters has neither been repeated nor verified. This, however, does not necessarily mean the end of the story.

Egypt

One of mysteries surrounding the Egyptian script is the fact that we come across it at a moment when it was already, structurally and visually, fully developed. We cannot, at present, say with any certainty where this form of writing came from and how (or even why) it developed.

Still relatively popular is the idea that Egyptian writing derived, or was at least influenced, by Mesopotamian examples. Even some quite recent works express doubt about the possibility that the Egyptians could have stumbled on the phonetic principle independently. But why not? A composition of pictures, sound elements and determinatives can be found in other forms of writing, such as, for example, those of Mesoamerica, which could hardly have been influenced by Sumeria. But then the idea that writing as such developed first in Mesopotamia and was from there introduced to Egypt has always rested on somewhat flimsy grounds. After all, around the time when pre-cuneiform Sumerian writing consisted of crude pictures scratched into clay, Egypt could already boast a fully developed and visually more or less perfect script painted on wood, written on papyrus or incised in stone (see Plate 20). Stone inscriptions demand great mastery of a particular script, a well laid out exemplar from which the stone mason can work, a carefully thought out arrangement of space, the placement of characters and so on. The argument that writing on perishable materials usually pre-dates stone inscriptions does not, as far as Egypt is concerned, provide any convincing explanation. Egypt's dry climate was especially well suited for the preservation of delicate materials. There exists, however, an additional element, which so far has perhaps not always been given enough consideration. Whatever we have found, or may still find, is but a fraction of what must have been the sum total of Egypt's material culture. Almost from the moment a royal tomb was completed, grave robbers went to work. Egypt may not have suffered the waves of foreign invasion which destroyed much documentation in other parts of the ancient world but it has always been well-versed in recycling its own resources. Stones could be use for new buildings, wooden status and mummies for burning. Gold, silver and precious stone could be re-used (though perhaps not in quite as crude a manner as the one practised by the Spaniards in the Americas, who melted priceless treasures into bullion to ensure an even distribution of loot). 'Abd al-Latif, a doctor from Baghdad who stayed in Egypt between 1193 and 1207, reported how Egyptian peasants were robbing graves to obtain mummy wrappings made of linen to use either as clothing or to sell to paper factories. Much damage has also been done by the forerunners of Western archaeologists, many of them

'specialists' like 'Abd al-Latif's peasants who looked for particular objects, discarding what they considered worthless. Even early archaeologists, who worked with (what they considered) to be the best intentions, often did more damage than good.

It has long been accepted that just before the beginning of the 1st Dynasty and the unification of Lower and Upper Egypt in c. 3100 BC, the (what came to be known as) hieroglyphic script appeared, suddenly and without clear examples of any earlier developments. Some recently discovered inscriptions do, however, suggest that an idea of Egyptian writing might well have existed earlier than has so far been thought. During the excavation of cemeteries near the site of the town of Abydos in Upper Egypt, in the vicinity of the tombs of the First Dynasty kings, Guenter Dreyer, the Head of the German Archaeological Institute, discovered, in an earlier royal tomb, together with vessels bearing ink smudges, some wooden tablets inscribed with the earliest as yet documented (proto?)-hieroglyphic signs. During his excavations Dreyer also found wooden tablets, some no bigger than postage stamps, showing recognisable pictures and symbols. As in the case of other early First Dynasty inscriptions, some of these signs refer to place names or quantities of commodities; others seem to have served to assist in the collection of taxes, allowing rulers to keep financial control of their subjects. Whether those early signs already included phonetic values is as yet impossible to tell.

But we are probably justified in saying that writing in Egypt seems to have developed out of the already familiar need for an infrastructure capable of providing political and economic stability and control. With this goes the desirability of recording the names of important places. The suggestion has at one point been made that Egyptian writing was an essential instrument for dating regal years (Fischer 1977). This presents some possibilities, especially when considering the position of the Pharaoh who became (certainly after his death) identified with divinity. Suggestions of a divine form of kingship, pointing towards Africa? Of equal importance, it has further been suggested, might have been the ability to calculate lunar phases, since they were closely interlinked with the annual inundations of the Nile on which both the prosperity of the country and the welfare of its rulers depended. But whatever the importance of numbers (mostly for internal account keeping — unlike the inhabitants of Mesopotamia, the Egyptians were not primarily traders), the picture, the second most stable component in the development of writing, played early on a strong and not to be overlooked role in Egyptian information storage.

Did pottery decorations figure prominently in the equation? Some pre-Dynastic vessels show well-executed pictures of birds, animals, symbols of deities. There are also abstract designs which already exhibit the characteristic ability of later Egyptian artists and scribes for observing nature and a strong tendency towards codified abstractions. Undoubtedly, a large number of Egyptian hieroglyphs were predominately pictorial or 'iconic' in character, insofar as they did not just represent logograms or other purely scriptorial elements. They could, it is true, be 'read' like any other script signs but in many cases they also had an additional, inherent significance (Horapollo, 1840; Arkell, 1975). The Ankh sign, for example, had not only hieroglyphic (scriptorial) value, it was also a symbol for eternal life (see Plate 21). Indeed, after the Egyptian script had long been forgotten, it was this particular quality of direct communication which kept the memory of Egyptian culture alive until the time when the scriptorial value of the script was eventually deciphered.

Apart from knowing next to nothing about the origin and the development of the Egyptian hieroglyphic script, we are also largely ignorant about the history of pre-Dynastic Egypt. The answer to many such questions probably lies not in Mesopotamia but much further south, inside Africa, Nubia or in some once fertile parts of the Sahara. Carbon dating of barley and einkorn found near Aswan in Upper Egypt show that a form of agriculture existed there as earlier as 16,000 BC. During the UNESCO-led operations to salvage the ancient monuments of Nubia, a large concentration of agricultural implements, dating from about 13,000 BC, was discovered (Joseph, 1991). The historian Diodorus (*Bibliotheca Historica*), who spent three years in Egypt during the middle of the 1st century BC, wrote that the Egyptians '. . . are colonists sent out by the Ethiopians ['Ethiopian' was the term then used for 'African'] . . . and a large part of the customs of the Egyptians . . . are Ethiopian, the colonists still preserving their ancient manners . . .'

The idea that Egyptian culture could have its origin in Africa has indeed occasionally been mentioned (Davidson, 1987), though only tentatively and without too much lasting effect. It had simply been unacceptable for political as well as religious reasons, though some of the wall paintings and funeral masks might have provided motives for reflection. But then, as Iversen (1961) pointed out, the Western world's preconceived notions about Egypt began with the Greek classical writers and 'none of the Greek writers had any first hand knowledge [of ancient Egypt and] of hieroglyphics'. Up to the middle of the 20th century, the idea that one of the world's greatest ancient civilisations could have originated in black Africa was not only unacceptable but totally beyond most people's comprehension. There were, in

Plate 21. Many Egyptian hieroglyphs, especially those acting also as determinatives, had inherent meaning which could be understood even if divorced from their linguistic content. The hieroglyph for 'scribe' (left) shows the instruments used for writing: a reed pen-case, a bag and a pallet for mixing ink. The symbol for Ankh (right) stood for eternal life and was placed on the body of the dead Pharaoh to ensure him a safe journey into the other world. It is shown in many illustrated texts and wall paintings. It could also (and still does so among certain members of our own society) act as an amulet. In Coptic Christianity it reappeared as the looped cross, together with many other Egypt-inspired motives, such as the Osiris-Christ or Isis-Mary concepts.

addition, the Bible-backed Hebrew/Christian traditions, which for two millennia had dominated Western thinking, which clung to the monogenesis of all things worthwhile, simply because all things had begun as a result of divine intervention, preferably in the biblical garden of Eden. Hence the, at times, almost fanatical insistence that writing could have been invented only once, in only one place.

Surviving Egyptian documents cover a wide subject area. There are legal documents, bills, letters but there is also a noticeable corpus of literature, much of it connected with the dead, Pyramidic texts and text relating to magic. In addition, we have collections of proverbs and examples of scientific literature dealing with questions of mathematics, medicine, chemistry and astronomical data relating to calendrical calculations. Though the number of people able to read and write was no doubt small and class related, Egyptian culture as such was highly literate.

We should here perhaps remind ourselves that the term hieroglyph (Greek *hieroglyphica grammata* — sacred carved letter), as indeed the terms for the other two variations of the Egyptian script, namely hieratic (*hieratikos* — priest) and demotic (*demotikos* — popular), have been coined relatively late, in fact only after Greek rulers

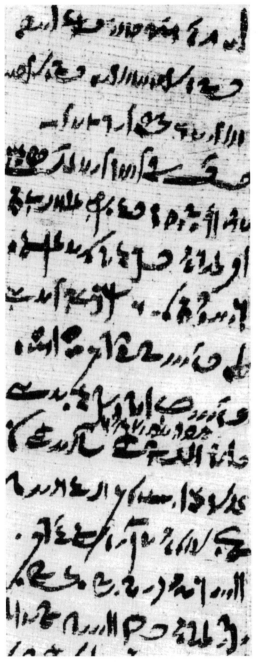

Plate 22. Hieroglyphs, and to some extent the hieratic script, were mostly written in vertical columns but in the course of the 12th dynasty (c. 1999-1786 BC) scribes began to write in horizontal lines, which allowed for more speed and a more cursive hand. By the 8th century BC demotic became the new alternative. Speed was now an important factor. Too elaborate hieroglyphs were sometimes replaced by an oblique stroke or (more rarely) by new signs; groups of hieroglyphs could sometimes be amalgamated into one single sign and abbreviations came into use. This demotic document, written in 270 BC, looks totally different from a hieroglyphic text but as far as the internal structure of the script is concerned, and apart from the above mentioned, mostly minor alterations, no real difference exists between the two forms of writing.

appeared in Egypt in the wake of Alexander's conquests. These terms therefore tell us more about how the Greeks perceived the Egyptian form of writing than what the Egyptians themselves thought about it (who seem to have used the same verb for 'to write' and 'to paint').

By the time the Greek terms came into common existence (c. 200 BC), hieratic served mainly for religious compositions, though in earlier times it had also been used for literary texts, business documents and private letters, while demotic was reserved exclusively for secular purpose (see Plate 22). In fact, the term *demotikus* (popular, for the people) is rather misleading; being a cursive form of the hieroglyphic/hieratic script, it is a good deal more difficult to read. It certainly did not spread literacy to a wider section of society and thus in no way endangered the position of Egyptian scribes.

The structure of the hieroglyphic script is well known and has repeatedly been discussed by various writers (Davies, 1987, etc.). Briefly, it consists of logograms which can represent nouns (picture of a leg for 'leg') or actions (two legs for 'to go'). The ancient Egyptian language belongs to the Hamitic group, where the root meaning of a word (as in Semitic) is represented by consonants. In fact, we do not really know the exact pronunciations of the language but have to rely for clues on Coptic, a modern form of ancient Egyptian. Consonant signs can represent one consonant, two consonants or, more rarely, three. In addition, there are the determinatives which indicate to what sphere of meaning a word belonged (for example: the sign of man added to sun disc can only mean 'son' and so on).

Another interesting feature of the Egyptian script is the fact that it already contained 24 single consonant signs. But those were never used to form a purely phonetic (and as we, probably wrongly, would say, simpler) basis for writing the Egyptian language. We do not really know why this never happened, though several suggestions have been put forward. Was it to protect the position of a powerful scribal class or because there was simply no conceivable need for such a step — inventions being largely based on the combination of needs and the ability to satisfy those needs. Or were there other, to us less obvious reasons: for example, the loss of the inherent meaning of hieroglyphic signs such a step would have brought about? The most obvious reason was perhaps the fact that the infrastructure of Egypt was most efficiently served by the existing form of writing. Egypt was not primarily a trading nation (like Mesopotamia or Crete); it was predominately inward looking. Egyptian writing was not exported. Even Diringer at one point agrees, somewhat tentatively, that the idea of the alphabet being directly based on Egyptian hieroglyphs is not quite maintainable, though attempts in this direction have repeatedly been made. In many ways Egypt's infrastructure was so finely tuned that, together with the Egyptian form of writing, it collapsed once foreign elements penetrated permanently in the wake of Greek influence and the establishment of Greek Pharaohs.

From 200 BC onwards some unsuccessful attempts were made to write the Egyptian language in the Greek alphabet. After the Roman conquest demotic continued, though the traditional brush gave way to the reed pen. The last firmly dated and badly executed hieroglyphic text so far discovered dates from 394 AD and is inscribed in the wall of the temple of Philae, half a century after Christianity established itself in the Roman Empire. From then on the knowledge (though not the evidence) of Egyptian writing disappeared until Napoleon's foray into the Nile Delta and the eventual decipherment of the Rosetta stone.

Mesoamerica

Even the most dedicated followers of monogenesis find it difficult to apply their theory to the Americas. Elements congenial to the development of writing — an advanced agriculture capable of supporting non-productive specialists, a dependency on taxation and some form of organised labour, a trained priesthood interacting between palace and temple and a centralised and efficient form of administration — existed, according to our present stage of knowledge, in three place: among the Mayas of Yucatan, the Aztec of Mexico and the Incas of Peru. In fact, not only writing but the art of making books was at least a millennium old by the time Columbus arrived in Mexico (Brotherston, 1995).

Mesoamerican writing exhibits many distinctive features, the most important ones being an emphasis on religion and politics. This places it into a different category to systems used in other parts of the ancient world (Mesopotamia, the ancient Mediterranean) and, to some extent, even Peru, where writing was primarily used to facilitate bureaucratic control, either for the purpose of administration or to serve as an accounting system in support of taxation and/or trade. Mesoamerican writing stresses history in relation to divination and ritual. Economic accounts exist but they appear rather late, in fact not before the Spanish conquest. Another distinct feature is the lack of a uniform ability to read language; scripts are more inclined to provide clues and are thus not restricted to just one language. Also, and this is another interesting factor, Mesoamerica scripts were perhaps less read than performed to the accompaniment of song and dance. The written version provided a form of canonical basis from which longer texts could be improvised, often within a public setting (Houston, 1995).

Both pictures and numbers played an important part (see Plate 23). The first appearance of Zapotec writing from the Mont Alban (Oaxacan) region shows mutilated and castrated prisoners together with name glyphs. Shortly afterwards place glyphs appear, an indication that the conflict was no longer between individuals but between regions. The dating system was from the beginning closely related to genealogy, aiming largely at the establishment of dynastic legitimacy. At the beginning of the Christian era calendrical notations, the ability to fix dates in absolute time, gained prominence.

Broadly speaking, Mesoamerican writing can be divided into three groups: the south-eastern part, Oaxacan (including the Maya region) and the highland post-classical period (including Mixtec and Aztecs cultures).

Maya writing

Whereas the Bible had given Western scholars an, at least, biased knowledge of ancient Mesopotamia, the cultural achievements of the people of Mesoamerica reached Europe only in the 16th century AD, mostly through the accounts of Christian missionaries who aided the Spanish conquistadors in their search for acquisition and wealth. Recent surveys have shown that already by around 1500 BC people who might have spoken an ancestral form of the Maya language lived in simple forest villages in the eastern part of Mexico, Guatemala, Belize and El Salvador (Stuart and Houston, 1989). Around 250 BC some fundamental changes seem to have taken place. Within a few centuries the villages gave way to powerful city states with rulers who, according to the earliest glyphic texts, claimed divine status. The Mayas have for long been credited with the creation of writing and the development of a highly sophisticated almanac but it is now becoming increasingly more apparent that much of it had been handed down to them by the Olmecs, whom local tradition name the original inhabitants of the area. They seem to have been the original town and temple builders and the first to construct courts for the famous

Plate 23. A disc depicting a man (in the centre) playing the ritual ball game of the Mayas, hitting the ball with his thigh. The glyphs are read clockwise, beginning from the glyph above the man's head, the inscriptions gives the Mayan date: 9.7.17.12.14.Ix 7 Zotz, which equals 17th of May 591 AD.

game played with a rubber ball from which they took their name (*olli* — Olmec). They are also thought to have used a system of abstract signs that represented supernatural beings and their relation to each other, as well as name glyphs (Houston, 1995). In fact, certain design elements in Olmec clothing and accessories may already represent embryonic script signs (Thompson, 1971).

The most elaborate form of writing was used by the Mayas, who employed two styles of script, a monumental and a written form. The monumental script was hewn in stone, incised in jade or moulded out of a kind of stucco for the decoration of buildings. Visually, the written form of Maya glyphs — painted on deerskin or bark paper — differs considerably from the signs carved during the classical Maya period (300-900 AD). Despite the fact that various Maya languages are still spoken in some parts of Mesoamerica and imaginative efforts at decipherment, probably no more than some 85% of the glyphs can be read and this mostly as far as their meaning and not their pronunciation is concerned (Robinson, 1995). Mayan writing is exceedingly complex (see Plate 24) in the way it uses a mixed system of logography and phonography (see Plate 25). Moreover, the same word (glyph) can be read in several different ways and glyphs can be 'scolded' together so intimately that it is often extremely difficult to divide them into their individual components. Each Mayan city had its own emblem glyphs, there were name glyphs and there were the all-important and highly complex calendrical glyphs.

Pictures and numbers are of equal importance in Maya writing. But unlike in Mesopotamia, numbers are not just tools for practical account keeping. They support more intellectual and abstract concepts, namely that of reckoning time in the shape of a complex calendrical system. By accounting for time, numbers underpinned personal and dynastic history, the movement of cycles and with it essential elements of mythology, ritual and religion, as well as social concepts and commitments.

The Mayas knew the meaning of zero and their mathematical system depended on the use of just three different symbols: a stylised shell for zero, a dot for one and a straight horizontal bar for five. The position of a number symbol determines its value, with values increasing by a factor of 20 from bottom to top in a vertical column. The first and lowest place has a value of one, the next 20; the next 400; the next 8000 and so on. In addition to numbers, the Mayas also used name glyphs for different months. Their understanding of the abstract concept of numbers allowed

Plate 24. Part of a tablet carved after the accession of King Pacal (603-683 AD). The glyph at the uppermost left in the right column stands for King Kuk, the protagonist of the tablet. The next glyph is the Palenque emblem glyph. This part refers to the 20th anniversary of the king's enthronement. The glyph in the upper left indicates the King's father, King Chaac. Maya glyphs are usually read from left to right and from top to bottom in pairs of columns.

Plate 25. A pottery vessel found in the north-eastern part of Guatemala. The glyphs, written in black on a blue background are typical of the Early Classical Period. The glyph on the left end of the lid is written syllabically ka-ka-wa *(meaning 'cocoa')and traces of cocoa have indeed been found in the vessel.*

them to create an almanac based on a high level of mathematical and astronomical knowledge. This calendar was made up of two cycles operating concurrently. One cycle, the sacred years of 260 days, determined the pattern of ceremonial life. It was formed by joining the 20 day names to the numbers 1 to 13. A 365-day cycle of eighteen 20-day months ran concurrently. To designate a particular day, the position in both cycles would be indicated. The combined system (which did not repeat a single date) divided time into self-contained 52-year cycles, with the uncomfortable possibility that the end of each cycle could mean the end of the known world if proper ritualistic precautions were not observed. To indicate days beyond the span of 52 years, another much larger cycle was used. Dates from this cycle, called the Long Count, were inscribed in monuments. Those dates record the number of days that have passed since the 13 August 3114 BC, the beginning of the cycle we presently live in, which will come to an end on the 23 December 2012 AD.

Comparing the use of numbers in Mesopotamia and Mesoamerica provides an interesting insight into the way infrastructures support existing needs and can as such arrive at quite different solutions or different interpretations of comparative realities. In the Ancient Near East numbers, and with them the use of writing, never moved away from the practical needs of society: personal property, the disposal of surplus, trade, the protection of trade, laws to enforce this protection. In Mesoamerica numbers supported time, the legitimacy of dynastic histories, and with it a move into the more abstract sphere of a recognition of zero. Zero, the absence of a definite, differentiated reality, the void, is of no use to traders, it does however becomes a decisive element when we consider ourselves in the power of cycles that have to end in just such a void so that a new cycle (may perhaps) begin.

Aztec script

In 1320 AD the Aztecs, who according to their own tradition came from a land called Aztlan (*aztatl* plus *tlan* 'heron-land'), consolidated their position in northern Mexico.

Their highly advanced civilisation was to a large extent a modification of the inheritance left behind by previous inhabitants. Their most spectacular achievements, the lake city of Tenochtitlan (now Mexico City), dazzled the Spanish Conquistadors, as did their wealth, especially that in precious metals. They had a highly efficient administration which saw in the palace the centre of the Aztec world, a well-developed legal system and excellent method of communication based on runners and post houses every six miles. Their army could match that of ancient Rome. But there was a fatal flaw in their perception of the world. Wars were less a means of conquest than a religious rite designed to obtain prisoners for the all-important sacrifices meant to preserve the order of the universe. In consequence, territorial gains were hardly ever sufficiently consolidated to create a single empire.

One can assume that the Aztecs took over the concept of writing from the Mayas, even if there is little recognisable similarity in the outward appearance of the two scripts. Altogether 20 Aztec manuscripts have survived the zeal of Spanish friars, compared to only four Maya manuscripts. All are made of long strips of bark paper or deer skin, covered with a thin white coat of lime plaster to provide the basis for their highly colourful form of picture dominated script. Structurally the scripts consist of a mixture of logography (sometimes mixed with iconographic elements), ideograph and rebus writing. Whether the ability to produce paper from the bark of the *amatl* tree would eventually have progressed to something similar to Chinese paper-making, and how the script might have developed, is impossible to say. The infrastructure, which supported Mesoamerica's civilisations and its very special form of writing, was brought to an abrupt end in the 16th century AD. The knowledge of writing itself, which was in the hands of trained priestly scribes, was however highly efficient: two days after Cortez had landed in Vera Cruz, the Aztec ruler in Mexico City received a written account of the arrival of the Spaniards, describing their ships, their horses (at this point unknown in Mexico) and their weapons (Barthel, 1972).

Mixtec (see Plate 26) and Aztec manuscripts (wrongly termed *codices*) are remarkably complex and detailed historical documents but they pre-suppose a supplementary knowledge on the part of the reader. The phonetic elements of the Aztec script were in the first post-conquest century used by Spanish officials and missionaries to assist communications in matters of religion and administration. But such attempts were soon abandoned. In the long run the indigenous scripts of Mesoamerica had little chance of survival. By the end of the 16th century the native elite had lost its identity. The system of patronage and scholarship which had long served as the basis for education and cultural advancement vanished and by the 17th century Spanish and the Roman alphabet had replaced all indigenous script forms.

Indus Valley civilisation

The most enigmatic of those early scripts is, however, clearly the still undeciphered Indus script which, in the 3rd millennium BC, supported a large and well-organised urban civilisation in the north-west of the Indian subcontinent. Despite many plausible attempts at a decipherment, we still do not know the meaning of the script signs, the way they related to each other, nor are we fully informed about the ethnic

Plate 26. A section from the Codex Nutall *which describes the sacred history of the Mixtec people, mainly in connection with the exploits of their great military and political leader 8-Deer Tiger Claw, who lived between 1063 and 1101 AD. The Codex was written on deerskin not long before the Spanish conquest. It can be hung up like a mural or kept folded accordion-wise. Vertical guidelines divide each page into three or four rectangles. In general, each rectangle is read from the bottom right-hand corner up to the top of the vertical guideline and then down and up until the next guideline.*

and linguistic allegiance of the people who used this script. We know that both — script and civilisation — vanished sometime around 1600 BC but we do not know the reason for their disappearance. Later Vedic hymns talk of the god Indra as the 'destroyer of cities' and of the dark-skinned *dasus* (considered by some the ancestors of the South Indian Dravidians) he vanquished but these are, as so many things surrounding the enigma of the Indus culture, retrospective speculations, in part inspired by prevalent political needs. Alternative possibilities might include climatic changes, floods, the silting up of the River Indus or some sudden epidemics.

The centre of the Indus civilisation lay in what is now Pakistan, though southern outposts reached as far as Rajasthan and Gujarat — in fact, the area covered was larger than that of Sumeria and Egypt put together. How did this highly sophisticated culture so suddenly arise? We may, with a certain degree of confidence,

Plate 27. Seal from the Indus Valley civilisation with the representation of an animal (a humped bull) and a short inscription above. The inscription (still undeciphered) seems to start at the right hand side.

assume that, as in other parts of the world, it developed out of an earlier Neolithic village culture, perhaps under the influence of trade and all those elements that make trade possible.

From earlier periods we have the evidence of pottery marks, painted pottery, but no writing as such. As in Egypt and in the Americas we might be well-advised to give more consideration to pottery decorations. For example, one of the most prevalent Indus script signs, the picture of a fish, appears repeatedly on early pottery shards; though to connect the fish signs with the (present-day) Tamil word *min*, which can mean both 'fish' and 'star', and to see in it a rebus signifying an astral name is perhaps over optimistic.

The Indus script itself seems to have emerged, after a relatively short transitional period, around 2500 BC. Some 3500 inscriptions have so far been discovered in about 60 different sites. The inscriptions themselves are short and can mostly be found on seals. There are recognisable pictorial signs, abstract signs and lines (numbers?). Many of them show, in addition, representations of (imaginary or real) animals. The suggestion has been made that these picture are indicative of religious beliefs. The most famous example is a masked, horned figure sitting in yoga posture, surrounded by animals, which Sir John Marshall (1938), who excavated the city of Mohenjo-daro, was tempted to call a proto-type of Shiva, one of the most important and controversial deities of the Hindu pantheon (see Plate 27).

Even if we cannot read the script, we can at least try to speculate about the purpose and importance of the seal stone inscriptions. We know that around the time the script appeared, naval transport and overland trade seemed to have greatly increased, creating a number of new settlements along the coast, some as far south as Maharashtra. In fact, the last documented example of the Indus script so far comes from Maharashtra and has been dated to c. 1700 BC. The fact that some 50 seals have been found in the Middle East points towards not only internal but also external trading relations.

Unfortunately, no Mesopotamian seals have so far been found in Indus cities, nor do any cuneiform tablets refer to such trade, at least not in any, to us, recognisable form. Any script based on, or at least related to, trade needs an ability to mark property and a knowledge of numbers and weights. The Harappans, it seems, used a standard system of weights made of stone and based on a binary system with the traditional Indian ratio of 16; i.e. 16 annas = 1 rupee (Durrans, 1982). Scales and instruments for measuring length have also been discovered (Joseph, 1991), showing considerable sophistication.

Did the script serve the palace and the temple? We do not know the connection between both, nor where the centre of gravity lay. The discovery of the citadel in Mohenjo-daro put paid to the original, somewhat romantic idea, of an oligarchy. The great public bath, the storage centres, the uniform layout of the cities which hardly changed for over a millennium, justify speculation about strict administrative control and the consequent need for an efficient infrastructure, served by written information storage. But we still know little more about this script except that there seem to have been some 400 different graphemes, many with allographic variations. There are also many ligatures which may indicate phonetic or semantic compounds. The direction of the script probably ran from right to left, since empty spaces in a line usually appears on the left side of the inscription.

The various attempts at a decipherment of the Indus script — some highly seductive yet still unproven — will be discussed later. But there is one point which has so far received little attention. This is the fact that what have been described as round pottery rattles with small clay pellets inside have been found in many locations (Wheeler, 1968). These so-called pellets are triangular, occasionally also round or square, and made of baked clay, which would indicate that they were in some way considered important. Wheeler regards them as 'model cakes for ritual use either as offerings or grave goods. This interpretation is unproved and unlikely . . . they can be found in great abundance . . . [and may have been] used as equivalents of toilet paper, such as lumps of earth are sometimes used by modern peasants.' The latter seems a highly unlikely explanation. After all, if meant for this particular purpose they would hardly have been baked, making them more expensive to produce and at the very least profoundly uncomfortable. One is more tempted to think of the (also baked) clay tokens found in Mesopotamia from c. 8000 BC onwards — but this too must fall, at least for the time being, into the realm of speculation.

Bibliography

Andrews, S. C. *The Rosetta Stone*. London: British Museum, 1981.

Arkell, A. J. *Prehistory of the Nile Valley*. Leiden: Brill, 1975.

Arnett, W. S. *The Predynastic Origin of the Egyptian hieroglyphs. Elements of the Development of rudimentary forms of Hieroglyphs in Upper Egypt in the First Millennium BC*. Washington: University of America, 1982.

Ascher, M. and Ascher, R. *Code of the Quipu*. Ann Arbor: University of Michigan, 1981.

Bankes, G. *Peru before Pizarro*. Oxford: Phaidon, 1977.

Barthel, G. *Konnte Adam schreiben: Weltgeschichte der Schrift*. Koeln: Du Mont Schauberg, 1972.

Benson, P. and Griffin, G. G. *Maya Iconography*. Princeton: Princeton University Press, 1988.

Bonfante, L. *Reading the Past: Etruscan*. London: British Museum, 1990.

Bricker, V. *Grammar of Mayan Hieroglyphs*. New Orleans, 1986.

Brotherston, G. *Painted Books from Mexico*. London: British Museum, 1995.

Chadwick, J. *Linear B and Related Scripts*. London: British Museum, 1987.

Coe, M. D. *The Maya*. 5th edn., London: Thames and Hudson, 1987.

Coe, M. D. *Breaking the Maya Code*. London: Thames and Hudson, 1992.

Extinct scripts: the infrastructure of palace and temple

Collon, D. *Near Eastern Seals.* London: British Museum, 1990.

Curtis, A. *Ugarit (Ras Shamra).* Cambridge: Lutterworth, 1985.

Danzel, T. W. *Die Anfaenge der Schrift.* Hamburg/Leipzig: Museum fuer Voelkerkunde, 1912.

Davies, N. M. *Picture Writing in Ancient Egypt.* London: University of Oxford Press, 1958.

Davies, W. V. *Reading the Past: Egyptian Hieroglyphs.* London: British Museum, 1987.

DeFrancis, J. *The Chinese Language: Fact and Fantasy.* Honolulu: University of Hawaii, 1984.

Diringer, D. *The Alphabet — the Key to the History of Mankind.* 3rd edn., London: Hutchinson, 1968.

Durrans, B. and Knox. R. *India: Past into Present,* London: British Library, 1982.

Evans, A.J. *Scripta Minoa. The written Documents of Minoan Crete with special Reference to the Archives of Knossos.* Oxford: Clarendon Press, 1909.

Fash, W. L. *Scribes, Warriors and Kings: the City of Copan and the Ancient Maya.* London: Thames and Hudson, 1991.

Fischer, H. G. *The Orientation of Hieroglyphs Part 1.* New York: Metropolitan Museum of Art, 1977.

Gardiner, A.H. and Fleet, T. A. *The Inscriptions of Sinai.* edn. by J. Cerny, 1955.

Green, D. *A concise History of Ancient Greece to the Close of the Classical Area.* rpt. London: Thames and Hudson, 1981.

Hammond, N. *Ancient Maya Civilisation.* Cambridge: Cambridge University Press, 1982.

Harris, R. *The Origin of Writing.* London: Duckworth, 1986.

Healey, J. F. *Reading the Past: The early Alphabets.* London: British Museum, 1990.

Hooker, J. T. *The Origin of the Linear B Script.* Salamanca, Linos, 1979.

Hooker, J. T. *Linear B: an Introduction.* Bristol: Bristol Classical Press, 1980.

Houston, S. D. *Reading the Past: Maya Glyphs.* London: British Museum, 1989.

Horapollo, *Hieroglyphs.* Trans. A.T. Cory. London, 1840.

Iversen, E. *The Myth of Egypt and its Hieroglyphs in European Tradition.* Copenhagen: G. E. C. Gad, 1961.

Joseph, G. G. *The Crest of the Peacock: Non-European Roots of Mathematics.* New York: I. B. Tauris and Co. Ltd., 1991.

Justeson, J. and Campell, L. (ed.), *Phoneticism in Maya Hieroglyphic Writing.* New York: Albany, 1985.

Kelley, D. H. *Deciphering the Maya Script.* London: Austin, 1976.

Kramer, S. K. *The Sumerians: their History, Culture and Character.* Chicago: University of Chicago, 1963.

Lurker, M. *The Gods and Symbols of Ancient Egypt, an illustrated Dictionary.* London: Thames and Hudson, 1980.

Marcus, J. *Emblem and State in the classic Maya Lowlands: an epigraphic Approach to territorial Organisation.* Dumbarton Oaks, 1976.

Marshall, J. H. (ed.), *Mohenjo-daro and the Indus Civilisation.* 3 vols. London: Arthur Probstein, 1931.

Miteilungen der Deutschen Archaelogischen Abteilung Kairo. 1993, pp. 23-68.

Morley, S. Brainerd, G. and Sharer, R, (ed.) *The ancient Maya.* Stanford, 1983.

Neugebauer, O. and Sachs, A. J. *Mathematical cuneiform Texts.* American Oriental Series, vol. 29. New Haven (Conn.), 1945.

Nissen, H. Damerow, P. and Englund, R. K. *Archaic Bookkeeping: early Writing and Techniques of economic Administration in the Ancient Near East.* London: University of Chicago Press, 1993.

Nuttal, Z. (ed.), *The Codex Nuttall: a Picture Manuscript from Ancient Mexico.* The Peabody Museum Facsimile, New York: Dover Publications, 1975.

Robinson, A. *The Story of Writing.* London: Thames and Hudson, 1995.

Schmandt-Besserat, D. *Before Writing, 1: from Counting to Cuneiform.* Austin: University of Texas, 1992.

Schmandt-Besserat, D. *How Writing came about.* Austin: University of Texas, 1996.

Schele, L. and Miller, M. E. *Blood of the Kings, Dynasty and ritual in Maya Art.* London: Thames and Hudson, 1992.

Schenkel, W. *The Structure of the Hieroglyphic Script.* Royal Anthropological Institute News, 15. 1976.

Schmitt, A. *Untersuchungen zur Geschichte der Schrift. Eine Schriftentwicklung in Alaska.* Leipzig, 1940.

Shinnie, P. L., *Meroe: a Civilisation of the Sudan.* London: Thames and Hudson, 1967.

Sethe, K.H. *Vom Bild zum Buchstaben: Die Entstehungsgeschichte der Schrift.* Leipzig: Mit einem Beitrag von Siegfried Schott, 1939.

Stephens, J. L. *Incidents of Travel in Central America, Chiapas and Yucatan.* 1841.

Stuart, D. and Houston, S. D. 'Maya Writing'. *Scientific America,* August 1989.

Thompson, J. E. S. *Maya hieroglyphic writing: an Introduction.* University of Oklahoma Press, 1971.

Walker, C.B.E. *Reading the Past: Cuneiform.* 2nd edn. London: British Museum, 1989.

Wheeler, M. *The Indus Civilisation.* Cambridge: University Press, 1968.

Wilkinson, R. H. *Reading Egyptian Art: a Hieroglyphic Guide to Ancient Egyptian Painting and Sculpture.* London: Thames and Hudson, 1992.

Zauzich. K.T. *Discovering Egyptian Hieroglyphs: a practical Guide.* London: Thames and Hudson, 1992.

5. The common origin of contemporary writing systems

Apart from Chinese and a certain group of specially invented 19th century scripts, all contemporary forms of writing go ultimately back to some Semitic prototype (see Plate 28). These scripts include the Greek and Roman alphabets and those derived from them, Square Hebrew, the Arabic script, the scripts of India and southeast Asia and also that of Ethiopia. All these scripts are basically phonetic or, to use another term, segmental forms of writing, insofar as they aim to represent, primarily, the sounds of languages — with, at times, varying degrees of success. They are sometimes simply referred to as alphabets (or at times syllabic) but they are by no means truly identical. In fact, they represent not just different forms of writing but also, to some extent, different forms of cognitive thinking. Though originally in many cases language-based, they have, mostly for political reasons (religious or secular or both), repeatedly been used outside their original linguistic contexts.

How then do these three systems — consonantal, syllabic and alphabetic — differ from each other?

Plate 28. A chart showing the common origin of most contemporary scripts.

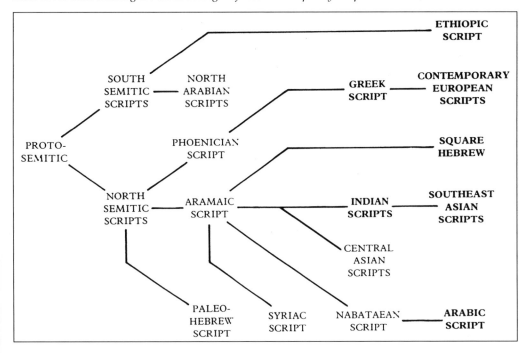

In the case of a syllabic script, the smallest graphic unit is the syllable. A syllable can consist of a consonant plus a vowel plus a consonant (*kam*); a consonant plus a vowel (*ka*), usually referred to as an open syllable; a vowel plus a consonant (*am*); or in certain cases a vowel on its own can have syllabic value. Graphically, a syllable can be represented by one sign or by a combination of a consonant plus an abbreviated vowel sign. The later presupposes the existence of vowel signs whenever they appear initially or on their own.

In the case of consonantal scripts, words are mainly represented by their consonants, which make them especially suited for certain languages; though one should not be carried away by this idea — speed writing, to give just one example, works on a similar principle (*gt* for *get*, and so on). Vowel indications may, and usually do, eventually develop but in most cases they remain auxiliary and optional.

In alphabetic scripts vowels and consonants are of equal value and, in theory at least, each phoneme (the smallest possible sound unit) is represented by one single sign. In practice, this is, of course, no longer strictly true. Most modern languages use, under certain circumstances, two or three signs (*sh*, *sch*, etc.) to represent one sound unit and, in addition, diacritics (*ä,ö,ç*, etc.) may become a necessity. Furthermore, as has already been pointed out, the sound quality of a phoneme can differ considerably not only between different languages but also within the same language.

Semitic scripts

The term 'Semitic' was first used in the 18th century in relation to a group of languages of which Arabic and Hebrew are the most prominent. The term itself refers to an imaginary connection with Shem, the son of Noah. Semitic scripts and Semitic languages share the same characteristics: the root meaning of the word is born by consonants (usually three in number), vowels serve mainly to fashion grammatical forms. Thus the Arabic root k-t-b, depending on the interpolated vowels, can stand for *katib* (writer), *kataba* (he wrote), *kitab* (book), *kutub* (books), *kutubi* (bookseller), *kitaba* (writing), *maktab* (office) or *maktaba* (library, bookshop). The choice of vowels depends on the context and on the grammatical construction of the sentence. This absence of vowel signs was to some extend remitted, at a quite early stage, by the use of consonant signs, such as *j* and *w*, for the representation of long vowels *i (e)* and *u (o)* and by using the sign for the glottal stop *(alef)* for *a*. Though this convention has remained in use up to the present, it was never used consistently. Only relatively late, by the middle of the 1st millennium AD, did languages such as Arabic, Hebrew and Syrian develop additional systems by which vowels could be indicated through diacritical marks; but such conventions were mostly optional.

Semitic scripts go back to phonetic forms of writing which developed in the Near Middle East between 1800 and 1500 BC. They are generally divided into two main branches: North Semitic and South Semitic, with the latter being of lesser importance. One of the advantages Semitic scripts have to offer is the small number of signs necessary for writing: 22 for North Semitic, 29 in the case of South Semitic scripts. Compared to the large number of signs used in ancient Egyptian, the Near Eastern or in Mesoamerican and the even larger number required for writing the contemporary scripts of the Far East, Semitic scripts have the advantage of economy. The reason for this lies in the fact that Semitic scripts are purely phonetic in character: individual signs are meant to represent, not ideas or concepts, but the smallest possible sound units of a particular language. Although phonetic elements played and play an important role in nearly all writing systems, in the case of Semitic scripts this element is used in a more exclusive and consistent manner. Another characteristic are the names given to individual letters and (expect for Arabic) the basic order in which they are represented. The direction of writing, somewhat ambivalent at first, has since c. 1100 BC consistently been right to left.

The question of the origin of the Semitic scripts is one of the most debated subjects that has occupied scholars and amateurs from antiquity to the present day. Was it an independent, unique invention of the Semitic people, an adapted borrowing from one of the prevailing scripts of antiquity — Egyptian, cuneiform, Cretan, Cypriote or Hittite — or did it originate from a set of prehistoric geometric signs (Evans, 1909)? A theory still held in some circles is that of an, at least tentative, connection with Egyptian role models. This theory is largely based on a series of short inscriptions found in Sinai and subsequently also in Palestine, which have been (roughly) dated to a period between c. 1730 and 1580 BC. This (what became known as Proto-Sinaitic) script is thought to have used Semitic words for pictorial signs which some scholars equate with carelessly executed Egyptian hieroglyphs (Gardiner, 1955), the Semitic word providing, by the acrophonic principle, the new value for a particular sign. Thus the Egyptian word for 'house' (*p-r*) stands, when translated into Western Semitic, for *bet* and the first letter of *bet* can then be used to represent the consonant *b* and so forth. This seems a somewhat tortuous theory, especially if one considers that the Egyptians already had the possibility of a consonantal script embedded in their way of writing. Problems of this kind, are generally explained away by the claim that anybody conversant with the full complexity of the whole Egyptian system would have been intimidated by the sheer weight of tradition attached to it. It was therefore easier for less literate (illiterate?) persons (Semitic slaves working in the nearby copper and malachite mines?) to take at random some Egyptian hieroglyphs (which they did not really understand) and use them for writing their own language. Adherents of this theory point out that to this day some languages, for example, Greek or Hebrew, name some of their letters in a fashion which seems to hark back to the objects depicted by the original (Egyptian?) pictorial sign (hieroglyph?); despite the fact that those words are meaningless in either language. Why explain the name of the letter *b* by *bet*, the Semite word for house, when the Egyptian word for 'house' was *p-r*, let alone why rely on those mysterious Semitic semi- or altogether illiterate mine workers? Indeed this particular theory is no longer universally accepted and much has, indeed, always rested on guesswork. Some scholars (Sethe, 1971), while agreeing to Egyptian influence, see this influence less in the outward appearance of the characters or in a faint memory of the hieroglyphic system than in the concept of single consonant signs which did indeed form part of the Egyptian system of writing. Lately it has been argued, with more conviction, that those proto-Sinaitic letters may just have been conventional signs with no direct relation to original pictorial signs and the names given to them nothing but mnemonic devices.

The second question, already discussed at the beginning of this book, is 'who invented the Semitic script?' — providing the term 'invented' is at all appropriate. One single inventor (suggested by Schmitt, 1938) or a group of people? The later theory has again been answered differently by different scholars. One theory names the Hyskos, a Semitic pastoral people who used a Canaanite language (Sethe, 1939) and conquered lower Egypt in about 1670 BC. Another possibility is that of a series of parallel developments in the Syro-Palestinian area which did, however, not exclude variations of mutual influence (Jensen, 1970).

Attempts to create a phonetic script by using cuneiform signs were made at around the same time in northern Syria and Palestine. Inscribed clay tablets, found at the site of the ancient city of Ugarit (c. 1400-1200 BC), document a system which used some 30 different cuneiform signs (27 for consonants and 3 for vowels). This script has variously been described as consonantal or alphabetic. Different theories have also been put forward as to the relationship between the cuneiform and the linear forms of phonetic writing. In the opinion of some scholars (Diringer, 1968), cuneiform phonetic scripts presuppose the existence of North Semitic; but much is still speculative and much we simply do not know.

The revolutionary achievement of Semitic scripts lies less in their (linear) appearance than in the implied ability to isolate individual sound elements and represent each sound by a distinct sign. The question about their exact origin will probably remain speculative. The reasons for their emergence and success, however, are more easy to detect. There was the cosmopolitan nature of the coastal towns, the decline and final disappearance of the old hieratic/theocratic Egyptian and Mesopotamian social order and new forms of international trade. These elements warranted not so much a more 'democratic' form of writing (Diringer, 1968) but one able to speed up transactions. One could say that just as the *scriptorium* gave way to the printing press, the typewriter to the word processor, so the 'mixed' forms of writing, only to be acquired after lengthy studies and basically reserved for a particular social class, made way for quicker and easier to learn segmental forms of writing, mostly for purely practical considerations.

North Semitic scripts

North Semitic scripts are generally thought to have emerged from the above Proto-Sinaitic/Proto-Semitic/Proto-Canaanite. They have been divided into various branches; the two most important ones, directly or indirectly responsible for the development of most contemporary scripts being Phoenician and Aramaic.

Phoenician

The Phoenician script, which became fully established around 1050 BC, can claim the distinction of being the direct ancestor of the Greek alphabet. It seems to have evolved in a direct line of descent from early North Semitic consonantal script forms sometime around the 13th century BC. During the long period of its existence it remained

Plate 29. Aramaic inscription found on a basalt pillar in northern Syria near Aleppo. The text, which includes the name of an Aramaic king, is a peace treaty concluded between two local kingdoms. Mid-8th century BC.

remarkably consistent, any variations, even in its colonial sub-divisions such as Cypro-Phoenician (c. 10th-2nd centuries BC) and the Carthaginian or Punic script with its secondary branches (the last Punic inscription dates from the 3rd century AD), being purely external. The number of letters (22) and their phonetic value remained unchanged, as did the direction of writing: horizontal, running from right to left.

The Phoenician script served the infrastructure of a widely flung trading empire which created independent city states but never made the mistake of stabilising or, better, destabilising itself into a centrally administered political power. Apart from being traders, the Phoenicians were brilliant navigators who reached the coast of Cornwall, in all likelihood circumnavigated Africa and possibly sailed as far as India.

Aramaic

The most vigorous offshoot of the Phoenician script was Aramaic (see Plate 29) which came into existence around the 11th/10th century BC. Whereas the Phoenician script, despite its wide use among trading communities, had basically been a national script, Aramaic soon acquired a truly international character. In the 7th century BC, after the Aramaic city states had lost their independence to the Assyrians, the Aramaic language, written in the Aramaic script, became the *lingua franca* of the Assyrian Empire. In the period of the Persian Empire (c. 550-233 BC) Aramaic was the official language and the principal script of diplomats and traders between Egypt and northern India. Its association with India had far reaching consequences and led to the

Plate 30. *Square Hebrew, one of the offshoots of the Aramaic script, developed around the 5th/4th century BC. According to Jewish as well as Christian traditions, Ezra, the 5th century reformer of Judaism, adopted this script for the writing of the scriptures, which gave it the necessary seal of approval. Square Hebrew became the Hebrew script as such and from the 2nd century BC onward it was widely used by most Jewish communities. Its appearance has changed little, despite the fact that after the Babylonian exile more and more Jews began to live outside Palestine. It is to this day the main script for religious and secular Hebrew literature and with the creation of the State of Israel it has gained new political status. A Hebrew leather scroll of the Book of Ecclesiastes written in a Yemeni hand; 15th/16th century AD.*

development of a large number of (syllabic) scripts in south and southeast Asia.

From the 8th century BC onwards Aramaic became more cursive and more simplified: the top of certain letters, such as *b*, *d* and *r* (originally closed) became open, a tendency towards a reduction of strokes in certain letters appeared, final angles became more rounded and ligatures were introduced. After the collapse of the Persian Empire the Aramaic language, and the Aramaic script, both up to then fairly homogeneous, split into several local dialects and corresponding script variations developed. The main variants were Jewish (Square Hebrew), Palmyrene, Nabataean (Arabic) and Syriac; there was in addition also a Mandaic script used by the Mandaeans, a gnostic Jewish-Christian sect. The continued tendency towards corrosiveness in some of these scripts (notably Syriac and Nabataean) led to the emergence of final forms of letters and of definite conventions about how individual letters should be joined.

Hebrew

At first the Hebrews simply used the Phoenician script unaltered but by the 9th century BC a distinct script form appeared in an inscription found in the Moab. This early (Paleo)-Hebrew script was, however, a purely national form of writing, more or less restricted to the people of Judea; in the course of time it was also favoured by certain Jewish sects, such as the Samaritan who retained it for their (hand-written) literature.

After the 6th century BC this script was abandoned in favour of Aramaic. To give legitimacy to the new convention its introduction was ascribed to Ezra, who is supposed to have brought it back from the Babylonian exile. By the 2nd century BC a somewhat modified form of Aramaic was used by most Jewish communities. This script, which became known as Square Hebrew (see Plate 30), spread eventually throughout the Jewish Diaspora and is still the standard Jewish book hand. Out of the 22 Hebrew letters, five (*kaf, mem, nun, pe, tzade*) have dual forms, one when standing initially or medially and another when in the final position. During the Middle Ages two cursive hands developed alongside Square Hebrew: the rabbinical (after the scholar Rashi, d. 1105) used by medieval Jewish savants and another which became responsible for the creation of many local variations in the Levant, Morocco, Spain and Italy.

Hebrew did not develop any calligraphic traditions comparable to Chinese, Arabic or the various Western styles of lettering. There were not Jewish kingdoms, no courts, and with it no possibility to establish consistent scriptorial traditions. But writing was highly valued: it kept Judaism alive during the long years of the Diaspora and to this day every Jew should (in theory) be able to write his own Talmud. But it is the meaning of the text, not the beauty of the script, that counts. The Hebrew script did, however, provide Jews with an infrastructure but it was an infrastructure supporting their faith; it only acquired political connotation with the creation of the State of Israel.

Like all Semitic scripts Hebrew is purely consonantal, though some letters (*aleph, he, vav* and *yodh*), generally referred to as *matres lectiones*, can be used for the representation of long vowels. But once Hebrew was replaced by Aramaic as the language of daily use and the knowledge of biblical Hebrew began to decline, the need arose for a system of vocalisation to ensure the correct pronunciation of the biblical texts. Vocalisation by means of punctuation marks, consisting of little dots and dashes placed above or below a consonant, was probably introduced in the 5th or 6th century AD, with the older Syrian vowel indication system acting as model. One of the three main vocalisation systems, the sublinear Tiberian, arose after the 8th/9th century and is still in use today.

Syriac

Another offshoot of Aramaic developed in Edessa in the 1st century AD. In its early stages it showed a strong resemblance to Palmyrene. Both scripts have a tendency to join letters together and most letters are written differently according to whether they stand alone, are at the beginning or at the end of a word, or are joined on both sides to another letter.

An important event which encouraged the maturing of the Syriac script was the fact that Edessa became the focus for the spread of Christianity to Semitic-speaking countries. When in the 3rd century the Bible was translated from Greek into Syriac (the local Aramaic dialect), the difficulty of transcribing Greek words, written in the alphabet, into a Semitic consonantal script encouraged moves towards a reasonably consistent and effective vocalisation. The three main systems eventually used were: (1) Nestorian, the earliest, which consisted of a combination of the consonants *w* and *y* and a dot placed above or below or two dots placed above or below the consonant to be vocalised; (2) the Jacobite system, created c. 700 AD, which used small Greek letters placed below or above the lines and (3) a later system consisting of a combination of diacritical vowel marks and small Greek letters.

Over the centuries, variation of Syriac, mainly based on the choice of vocalisation, came into being. The three most important ones were Estrangela (the earliest extant manuscript dates from 411 AD), Nestorian and Jacobite; the two latter ones developed as a result of a heretical split between Syrian Christians.

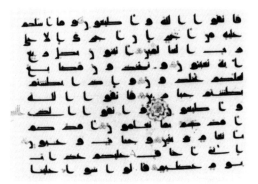

Plate 31. A page from a Koran written in Kufic; 9th/10th century AD. Kufic, a monumental style named after the city of Kufah, is a script of great elegance and beauty. Between the 9th and 12th centuries it was the main style for writing the Koran.

As the Nestorian Church grew in importance, missionary monks, travelling eastward along the old trading routes, brought the knowledge of their script to the Kurdistan highlands, central Asia and China. Marco Polo described the trade routes from Baghdad to Beijing being lined with Nestorian chapels. A knowledge of Nestorian Christianity and the Syriac script also reached the Turki and Mongol tribes of central Asia, Turkistan and the Sogdians.

In the 7th century Nestorian monks appeared in southwest India (now the State of Kerala) and gave a new impetus to the Christian communities already in existence. To reproduce the local Malayalam language in the Syriac script, eight more signs, borrowed from the syllabic Malayalam script, were added. Today a modified form of the Syriac script is still used for the liturgy of the local St Thomas Christians. Altogether the Semitic consonant script was to prove, if necessary, highly adaptable, turning into the alphabet in Greece and into syllabic forms of writing in Ethiopia and India.

Arabic

Arabic, the final offshoot of Aramaic, is today, together with the Roman alphabet, the most widely used form of writing. It is generally accepted that the Arabic script originated in the 4th/5th century AD from the form of writing used by the Nabataeans, the people who created the first well-defined (northern) Arab kingdom around Petra (now in Jordan).

The Nabataeans employed two script variations, one monumental for inscriptions and another, more cursive, which developed into the cursive forerunner of modern Arabic. Before the coming of Islam in the 7th century the Arabs relied largely on oral traditions for the transmission of their rich literature but the revelation of the Koran created the need for an extension of literacy (see Plate 31) and a more secure form of documentation.

The Arabic script consists of 29 letters made up of the original Semitic consonant signs, plus seven additional characters designed to represent the finer shades of pronunciation required by the Arabic language. Graphically these letters are made up of 17 basic outlines plus diacritical points to distinguish otherwise identical basic signs. Short vowels can be indicated by vowel marks written above and below the consonant preceding the vowel. Some Arab traditions name al-Khalil (d. c786) the inventor of this vocalisation system which gained prominence in the 8th century but its roots go back to much earlier, probably towards Syriac models. Vocalisation is to some extent less important than in Hebrew since Arabic has remained a living language. But the sacred nature of the Koran requires exactness of transmission and to this day vocalisation is employed consistently in Koranic texts.

South Semitic scripts

This group of scripts was less influential and it is also less easily traceable. It remained confined to Arabia where it seems to have been used mainly by the Minaens and Sabaeans. Surviving inscriptions are, despite much effort, still difficult to date, with the earliest thought to go back to c. 500 BC. Around 600 AD the script(s) became extinct — with the exception of Sabaean, which spread into Africa and became the direct ancestor of the classical Ethiopic and modern Amharic scripts. Sabaean (or South Arabian) inscriptions are written in a beautiful and well-proportioned style, individual letters are carefully arranged and executed, often (especially after 300 BC) in hollow relief.

The question of the origin of the South Semitic scripts and their exact connection with North Semitic is still under discussion. Some 7th/8th century BC inscriptions seem to indicate a line between Proto-Canaanite and South Arabian (Healey, 1990) but on the whole it is doubtful that South Semitic scripts descended directly from the North Semitic ones. One view (Diringer, 1968) sees in Proto-Sinaitic a possible link between Proto-Semitic/Canaanite and South Semitic.

Ethiopic

The Ethiopic script, still in use today, goes back to a form of writing the Semitic-speaking Sabaeans brought with them from South Arabia when they crossed the Red Sea c. 2500 years ago to establish a kingdom with Axum as its centre. The indigenous language of Ethiopia (or Abyssinia) is non-Semitic, belonging to the Cushite group of languages. The earliest evidence of a decidedly Ethiopic form of writing comes from the 4th century AD, the time when Christianity was introduced to the country by Greek-speaking, Syrian missionaries. After the fall of the Axumite Empire, in about the 9th century AD, classical Ge'ez declined and was replaced by Amharic as a spoken language.

Today Ethiopic is clearly a syllabic script. It uses some 27 consonantal signs and seven indication of vowels in the manner of Indian syllabic scripts; i.e. all consonants are perceived with an inherent short vowel (*a*), unless otherwise indicated. The reason for the change from a consonantal to a syllabic script (and the direction of writing which now runs left to right) has invoked much speculation: was it the invention of just one person, a general script reform or the influence of foreign models — Greek or, more likely, Indian?

The alphabets

For well over 3000 years the alphabet has been the primary form of information storage in Europe and in all regions where European influence has made itself felt. When speaking of the alphabet, most Western people automatically think of the Roman or Latin alphabet. The Roman alphabet was, however, only a later variation of the original Greek alphabet, which in turn was itself an adaptation of the Phoenician consonant script. Moreover, various segmental forms of writing existed even earlier,

Plate 32. An early Greek inscription from Ephesus, 6th century BC, recording omens derived from the flight of birds.

albeit as part, or at least in relation to, other, more dominant systems. Leaving aside the 24 consonant signs embedded in the Egyptian script, an alphabetic script form existed in Ugarit, on the north coast of Syria, in what is now Ras Shamra, in the 14th century BC. The city itself was a great international trading centre and no less than ten languages and five different scripts were used at Ugarit — not an ideal situation for furthering trading interests. Neither was the dominant script, Akkadian cuneiform. The alphabetic script which developed (perhaps within the merchant communities) consisted of a set of only 30 cuneiform-like signs which were written on tablets and, from surviving evidence, dealt mainly with administration, commercial correspondence and governmental records. However, these and other early experimental alphabets were in many ways *Sackgassen*, serving only a temporary and strictly limited purpose within a particular but ultimately quite different power agenda.

The Greek alphabet

On the basis of available evidence it is now generally assumed that the Greeks came into contact with the Phoenician form of writing sometime between 1100 and 800 BC, probably in one of the many Phoenician trading posts, either in Asia Minor, Syria or perhaps even on some of the Greek islands. With no script of their own, the Greeks had already made two previous attempts at borrowing a writing system, both of them syllabic: the Cypriote script and Linear B from Crete. The reason why both attempts were short-lived (and in the end unsuccessful) is usually put down to the fact that a syllabic script is ill-suited to represent an Indo-Aryan language like Greek. But this seems a somewhat forced explanation. After all, the Sanskrit-derived North Indian languages manage perfectly well with syllabic scripts. Moreover, the Phoenician consonant script was, if anything, even less suited to represent an Indo-Aryan language. Even the fact that for the first time the Greeks went beyond a mere borrowing and made a number of important adjustments, beginning with the use of the Phoenician consonantal signs for which Greek had no corresponding sounds, to represent vowel (*a*, *e*, *i*, *u* and *y*), does not fully explain the overwhelming success of the new writing system. There were other adaptations but the decisive reasons were no doubt more complex than straight linguistics.

It has been suggested that the earliest surviving Greek inscriptions (see Plate 32), dating from around the 8th century BC, are not so much commercial as personal and quasi-literary documents (Brown, 1998). Economic documents could of course have existed on more perishable material; after all, Linear B was mostly inscribed in clay. However, the romantic notion that the beginning of the Greek alphabet was stimulated by Homer's epics is rather unlikely or at least so far totally lacking in evidence. The Greeks were not world traders but they acquired early on considerable political awareness. It is more likely that the need of the newly developing Greek city-states for an infrastructure that did not depend on trained scribes but on the active interaction of all free male citizens did play a decisive part.

To begin with, a number of local script variations arose to fit the dialects spoken in different parts of Greece but in about 403 BC the Athenians passed a law which made

Plate 33. An inscription relating to a religious rite involving the sacrifice of lambs and calves; c. 4th-6th century AD. The script bears some resemblance to the one used for the 4th century Codex Sinaiticus.

the use of the Ionian alphabet compulsory for all official documents. Eventually, the Ionian alphabet superseded all other local variations and after this the Greek alphabet underwent no further radical alterations. Why was the alphabet so successful and for so long and over such a variable linguistic area? It had, after all, been primarily designed for writing the Greek language. The fact that it was strictly phonetic did not make it automatically suitable for other languages. Indeed, whenever the Greek alphabet was used for another language, further modifications had to be made. We are therefore perhaps on safer ground if we go back to contemporary political considerations as the most likely initiative. As we shall see later, the continuing success of subsequent alphabetic developments were in turn linked to changing power structures and political fortunes (see Plate 33).

In the first Christian millennium BC a number of alphabets came into use (mainly among non-Hellenic peoples) in Asia Minor but none of them gained lasting importance. In Egypt the situation was somewhat different. Alexander's conquest, the establishment of a Greek dynasty of Pharaohs and the foundation of Alexandria as a centre of Greek learning provided a power base for the introduction of both the Greek language and the Greek alphabet. Early attempts to write Egyptian in the Greek alphabet had not been particularly successful. But by the 4th century AD, with the old Egyptian way of life having finally declined, Christian, Gnostic and Manichaean missionaries began to work among the Egyptian speaking element of the population. They translated the Scriptures into Coptic (from *qobt-gyptios* — Egyptian) which in the process became a literary speech.

Coptic used a modified form of the Greek alphabet. It consists of 32 vowels and consonant signs of which 25 were taken from Uncial Greek and seven (some claim nine) from demotic Egyptian. The Islamic conquest in 641 AD introduced Arabic to the country but Coptic remained in use until the 9th century. Christian communities continued to use it for another four centuries as their written and spoken language, and for much longer for liturgical purpose.

The Roman alphabet and the role of the Etruscans

Sometime between 800 and 700 BC Greek settlers, attracted by Italy's rich mineral

resources, began to move westward, bringing their Euboean form of the Greek alphabet with them. There it was adopted, subject to some minor modifications, by the Etruscans for writing their own (still largely unknown) language (see Plate 34).

There still remains some mystery about the Etruscans themselves. The question of their origin and language has been the object of speculation since

Plate 34. Three lines of Etruscan letters inscribed on the body of a pigeon, c. 3rd-4th century BC.

Herodotus (c. 450 BC); today's scholars seem to agree that both developed in Italy itself (Bonfante, 1990). The Etruscans, though by no means isolationists, centred their political power base on influential city states. According to Roman tradition, Etruscan kings ruled the most important Italian cities, including Rome, from the end of the 7th century BC until around 510 BC when Rome became a republic. The Romans soon began to write their own language (Latin) in the alphabet they had learned from the Etruscans. By the 1st century BC the Etruscans ceased to be an independent power and were assimilated by the Romans who, in the process eliminated nearly all traces of Etruscan literature, even a proper knowledge of the Etruscan language itself. It was in every way a highly successful act of cultural genocide. All that has survived from the Etruscans who, as far as writing is concerned, acted as bridge between Greece and Rome, is a large number (c. 13,000) of rather short inscriptions, mainly of a funerary nature and thus ill-suited for a reconstruction of the original Etruscan language. This despite the fact that we are perfectly able to read those inscriptions. Rather a good example how, in the final instance, the ability to write and read is not necessarily enough to preserve a particular language and a particular culture in the face of a different and politically more powerful agenda — almost total elimination can in fact be achieved over a relatively short period. The Roman or Latin alphabet, documented from the 7th/6th century BC onwards, gradually supplanted all other Italian scripts and became in due course the script of the western half of the Roman Empire.

The oldest Roman alphabet contained 21 letters and used at first (as did Greek) a right to left or boustrophedon direction of writing. Externally, the difference between the Roman and the Greek alphabet is slight, showing itself mainly in a tendency to replace angular lines by curves. The Semitic-based names of the Greek letters were replaced in favour of the familiar *abecedarium*. Subsequent developments limited themselves to an increase in the number of letters (26 instead of the original 21), alterations in the shape and sound quality of certain letters and, eventually, the development of distinct calligraphic and national styles.

The success of the Roman alphabet does, however, owe less to any inherent superiority of the script itself than to the fact that legionaries and administrators introduced it to all corners of the Roman Empire, which at one time stretched from the Euphrates to Britain. Very soon the alphabet became one of the most important elements of the infrastructure necessary to control ever larger territories. But the Romans were first and foremost conquerors and administrators: they had little interest in acting as teachers to

Plate 35. An early Christian epitaph recording the name of Staturninus, a Roman citizen of apparently high rank in the first line. The capital letters of the Roman alphabet have changed little from the way they are being used today. c. 4th century AD.

nations who seemingly had no writing system of their own. This role was taken up, after the fall of Rome, by Christian missionaries who not only christianised (see Plate 35) but, one could say, also alphabetised the rest of Europe, religion, as so often, taking over what remained basically a political agenda. After the 16th century, with the creation of overseas colonies and a steady growth in commercial interests, the alphabet spread even further. It was introduced not only to people who had no script of their own but often also forced upon those who already had perfectly functional writing systems — without much consideration for local interests. The alphabet was certainly a success story but the success did not rest on linguistic considerations nor on the fact that it was easy to use (which in the case of many languages was often not the case) but that it remained, for some two millennia, one of the most important tools in the hands of dominant political, religious and economical powers.

The question of Runes and Oghams

What exactly are Runes and Oghams? A good deal of speculation still surrounds these two European scripts which were mainly found outside Greece and Italy: Runes appeared — between c. 200 and 1200 AD — in a wide geographical area, reflecting a range of (some still only little known) Germanic languages (Robinson, 1995), in Sweden, Norway, Denmark, Iceland, Greenland, the Faroes, parts of Scotland and in Ireland. They have also been found inscribed on objects in Eastern Europe in an area stretching from Germany to Russia and down to the Danube and, owing to Viking expansion, as far down as the Baltic Sea. Ogham inscriptions on the other hand seem to restrict themselves to the Celtic-speaking parts of the British Isles and date mainly from a period between the 4th and 7th centuries AD.

The basic Runic alphabet has 24 letters (the appearance of the letters can vary according to different traditions) arranged in a particular order known as Futhark (see Plate 36), so called after the first six letters. Occasional bilingual inscriptions (in Runic and in the Latin alphabet) have added somewhat to our understanding of the script. As in the case of Etruscan writing, we can read Runes but, owing to our limited knowledge of early Germanic languages, much remains cryptic. Runes were never a literary script; existing records are mainly found on memorial stones and the very name (*run* or *rune* meaning 'secret' in Old Irish, Old Saxon and Middle High German) indicates connections with cult and secret writing.

It is important to note that both Runes and Oghams are closely connected with preceding oral traditions. Ogham, the 'tree alphabet' (the characters bear the names of trees), resembles tallies in the way strokes and points are arranged along a horizontal

Plate 36. The runic alphabet, or futhark, *so called after the first six letters.*

line. The Oghams were mainly used by the Irish and in areas of Irish influence between the 4th and the 6th century AD, though their existence may go back to the Iron Age (Brown, 1998). The fact that they consist of 20 characters in families of five has encouraged theories about the Oghams going back to a (secret?) finger alphabet used for signalling by Celtic Druids.

The form and appearance of these two scripts has been variously discussed (e. g. Jensen, 1970; Barthel, 1992, etc.) but the questions of their origin remains to a large extent still unanswered. Did they arise out of a knowledge of the Roman/ and or Greek alphabet or are they primarily two indigenous, non-Roman scripts representing the response of sophisticated oral societies to Greek and Roman script-based traditions (Brown, 1998)? Were the Runes a form of writing brought to Britain by Anglo-Saxon invaders? Did the Oghams represent an encoding of the Roman alphabet by means of notches cut into stone slabs (Henderson, 1967)? Or were they a primary, perhaps secret, form of finger spelling used by the Druids, a professional priestly class guarding well-disciplined oral tradition, which only later, under the influence of a knowledge of the Roman alphabet, converted themselves into writing?

Bibliography

Barthel, G. *Konnte Adam schreiben: Weltgeschichte der Schrift*. Koeln: Du Mont, Schauberg, 1972.

Bauer, N. *Zur Entzifferung der neuentdeckten Sinai Schrift und zur Entstehung des semitischen Alphabets*. Halle, Gesellschadft der Wissenschaften in Goettingen, 1918.

Baumstark, A. *Geschichte der Syrischen Literatur*. Bonn: E. Webers, 1922.

Bender, M. L. et al. *Language in Ethiopia*. London: Oxford Press, 1976.

Birnbaum, S. A. *The Hebrew Scripts. Part I; the Text*. Leiden: E. J. Brill, 1971.

Bonfante, L. *Reading the Past: Etruscan*. London: British Museum, 1990.

Brown, M. P. *Writing and Script: History and Technique*. London: British Library, 1998.

Cook, B. F. *Reading the Past: Greek inscriptions*. London: British Museum, 1987.

Diringer, D. *The Alphabet - the Key to the History of Mankind*. London: Hutchinson, 1968.

Driver, G. R. *Semitic Writing: from Pictograph to Alphabet*. London: Oxford University Press, 1948.

Elliott, R. W. V. *Runes: an Introduction*. Rpt. Manchester. 1959.

Gardiner, A. H. and Peet, T. E. *The Inscriptions of Sinai*. London: Egyptian Exploration Fund Memoirs, 1955.

Gelb, I. J. *A Study of Writing: the Foundations of Grammatology*. London: Routledge and Kegan Paul, 1952.

Harris, R. *The Origin of Writing*. London: Duckworth, 1986.

Healey, J. F. *Reading the Past: the Early Alphabet*. London: British Museum, 1990.

Henderson, I. *The Picts*. London: 1967.

Jensen, H. *Signs, Symbols and Scripts: an Account of Man's Effort to Write*. London: Hutchinson, 1970.

Logan, R. K. *The Alphabet Effect: the Impact of the Phonetic Alphabet on the Development of Western Civilisation*. New York: 1986.

Mercer, S. A. B. *The Origin of Writing and our Alphabet*. London: Lusac and Co., 1959.

Moltke, E. *Runes and their Origin: Denmark and elsewhere*. Copenhagen: Museum of Denmark, 1985.

Naveh, J. *Early History of the Alphabet: an Introduction to West Semitic Epigraphy and Palaeography*. 2nd edn., Jerusalem: Magnes Press, 1982.

Naveh. J. *The Development of the Aramaic Script*. Jerusalem: Magnes Press, 1970.

Naveh, J. *Origin of the Alphabets*. London: Cassell, 1975.

Page, R. I.. *Reading the Past: Runes*. London: British Museum, 1987.

Petrie, W. F. W. *The Formation of the Alphabet*. London: British School of Archaeology in Egypt, 1908.

Robinson, A. *The Story of Writing*. London: Thames and Hudson, 1995.

Rosenkranz, B. *Der Ursprung des Alphaberts von Ras Schamra*. ZDMG, Bd. 92, 1938.

Sampson, G. *Writing Systems*. London: Hutchinson, 1985.

Saskia, R. de Melker (ed.), *The Image of the World. Jewish Tradition in Manuscripts and Printed Books*. Amsterdam: Peeters, 1990.

Schmitt, A. *Die Erfindung der Schrift*. Erlangen: Academia Fridericiana, 1938.

Sethe, K. *Die neuentdeckten Sinaischrift und die Entstehung der Semtischen Schrift*. Goettingen: Nachrichten der Goettinger Gesellschaft der Wissenschaften, 1917.

Ullendorf, E. *Studies in Ethiopian Syllabary*. Africa xxi:3. (1951).

Wright, W. *A short History of Syriac Literature*. rpt., Amsterdam: 1966 (1st. edn. London, 1894).

6. The special place of certain writing systems

The scripts of India and China differ considerably not only from each other but also from all other forms of contemporary writing. Chinese is still predominately a mixed script based on ideographic/logographic/phonetic concepts and has a repertoire of signs which reaches upwards to 50,000. Indian scripts are strictly syllabic with a maximum of about 50 different signs. The Chinese script has existed in a unbroken line for over four millennia. Indian scripts, on the other hand, are the only ones firmly based on preceding, strictly scientific oral traditions about concepts of linguistics, phonology and grammar. Writing in India did not replace oral traditions, it simply wrote them down.

In the case of China we do not know how, where or when this script originated. Any claims of some connection with the ancient Middle East, at times brought forward by adherents of the monogenesis of all writing, rest, so far, on unfounded speculations. Similarly, the insistence that Chinese is not based on pictographic/logographic but on phonetic principles is more a result of misguided post-colonial guilt than verifiable facts. Interestingly, the number of Chinese picture signs increased with time, a phenomenon quite opposite to other pictorial-based script organisations. If Chinese would really be a syllabic script — as some authorities claim — then this alone would make it (for a syllabic script) an amazingly ineffective one. The fact that the many homonymous (monosyllabic) Chinese words make it necessary to refer to different written characters for clarification hardly adds to the credibility of the argument.

Neither China nor India have achieved or, at least until very recently, tried to achieve universal literacy. In India oral literacy was definitely an exclusive property — in China all literacy was for long restricted to a governing elite. We must, however, not ignore the fact that, even though in the West we not only most earnestly aimed at universal literacy (at least during the last two centuries), we have never quite achieved it. Furthermore, there are claims that we are now getting increasingly further away from this aim. The reasons for this are hardly to be found within the field of linguistics. Indian scripts are superbly suited to represent Indian languages. Chinese, on the other hand, seems exceedingly difficult, yet modern Chinese children master it as easily as their Western contemporaries master their alphabet. In fact, the problem of dyslexia is much more part of an alphabet-based literacy than of the seemingly much more difficult Chinese way of writing.

Indian forms of writing
Hinduism was by its very nature an oral phenomenon. India's literary traditions pre-date the use of writing by a good millennium. To no other civilisation does the dictum

81

that orality implies ownership apply more stringently than to ancient India. From at least 1500 BC onwards, Vedic literature was composed orally by individual Vedic priests. It was transmitted by generations of priestly families, who passed it on, by word of mouth, assisted by a complex mnemonic system specially devised for this purpose (Losty, 1982). Orality and ownership are political concepts; the knowledge of these Vedic hymns presented the true, underlying infrastructure of society and since the existence of the universe was bound up with their exact transmission, those hymns were an instrument of spiritual as well as political power. No ceremony was valid, or indeed permitted, without the presence of an officiating Vedic priest whose services had to be appropriately rewarded by material goods.

The hymns were looked upon as *shruti* (hearing) of the precisely pronounced sequence of a large body of verbal utterances in the mind's ear of primeval sages; the language of these utterances was a form of Sanskrit (*devabhasha* — the language of the gods). The Vedas had to be transmitted, word perfect, to achieve the result desired by the sacrificing priest. This made Sanskrit a sacred language, the word for sacred speech being *vak*. 'By sacrificing [the priest] walks the tract of *vak* [speech].' In consequence, from about the 1st millennium BC onwards the Vedas became the subject of intense and systematic phonetic, etymological, grammatical and exegetic concern. Long before the introduction of writing, Indian grammarians had developed a concept of letters (*akshara*), consonants (*vyanjana*) and vowels (*svara*) and by the 5th century BC they had scientifically analysed the phonetic system of the Sanskrit language. Vowels come first, followed by consonants grouped together on the basis of their articulation. All consonants are perceived syllabic, containing a short inherent *a* if not otherwise indicated; in other words, they are not unpronounceable and nebulous phonemes. Vowels are written in their full form only if standing on their own or initially; in conjunction with a consonant they are abbreviated to auxiliary signs placed before, after, above or below the consonant in question.

By around 700 BC a standardised and ordered letter system of Sanskrit had already come into existence (*akshara-samamnaya*), which not only recognised the distinction between vowels and consonants but also the concept of *sandhi*. *Sandhi* means 'putting together'. Ancient Indian grammarians had already discovered that words and morphemes, when combined with each other, may undergo phonological modification. The Sanskrit grammarian Panini (c. 350 BC) used various Vedic oriented oral treatises to formulate aspects of grammar. His grammar provides such a concise analysis of the grammatical structure of the (Sanskrit) language that Western grammarians have been greatly influenced by it during the last two centuries. In other words, our present knowledge in this field owns much to an ancient oral tradition that reached us from a culture long since gone and in no way similar to our own. Indian scripts are indeed the only ones which truly make 'speech visible'. They are much more strongly anchored in phonetic traditions than the alphabet, which is, after all, only a haphazard, need-driven, adaptation of an alien writing system.

Most non-Indian as well as Indian scholars still assume that a knowledge of writing was brought to India by Semitic traders sometime in the 7th or 6th century BC, possibly even earlier. We have no definite proof as to what this Semitic prototype

Plate 37. Kharoshthi, rather cursive and phonetically somewhat less strictly controlled than Brahmi, has long been considered a purely commercial and clerical script. But the recent appearance of a collection of birch bark scrolls dating from the 1st century AD recording a section of a Buddhist Canon in Gandhari language has re-opened a number of questions.

was, though Aramaic is, mostly for historical reasons, still considered a likely candidate. Orthodox Hindu society, however, considered the idea of committing their eternal revelation (the legitimate property of certain Brahmanical sub-castes) to some transient and easily corruptible, as well as easily accessible, form of writing material not only irrelevant but more or less blasphemous. The earliest dated record of a Sanskrit inscription comes from 150 AD. This is several centuries later than the Prakrit inscriptions of the Emperor Ashoka. Both the Buddha and the Mahvira had not only broken away from the sacrificial cult of the Vedas, rejecting caste, ritual and power based on secrecy and occupational exclusiveness, but also used Prakrit (instead of Sanskrit), the language of the people, to record their teaching. It is not without interest to note that movements (religious or secular) which derive their authority from a human founder have usually favoured a written, not a remembered, infrastructure.

The earliest palaeographical evidence of a decidedly Indian form of writing is the often quoted edicts of the Emperor Ashoka (272-231 BC). These inscriptions served a double purpose: to proclaim how, after a series of ferocious wars, the emperor had created a more or less unified India (an achievement not repeated until 1947) and to announce his conversion to Buddhism. The edicts are written in two different but already well developed scripts, Kharoshthi and Brahmi.

Kharoshthi, short-lived and kept within a well-defined geographical area, has long been considered a purely commercial and clerical script. Written from right to left and rather cursive in appearance, it seems to point more clearly towards a Semitic origin. One (not fully

Plate 38. Fragments of an Ashoka pillar, inscribed with Brahmi characters; 3rd century BC.

substantiated) interpretation claims that the name itself is derived form the Aramaic *harattu* (writing/engraving). Kharoshthi documents have been found in the northwest of India and in central Asia on coins, wooden tablets or rough pieces of leather dating between the 3rd century BC and the 3rd century AD. In central Asia the script seems to have survived, sporadically, for another four decades. However, in 1994 the British Library acquired a collection of birch bark scrolls dating from about the 1st century AD. Written in Gandhari, the language then used in northeast Afghanistan and northwest Pakistan, they were found in a coarse clay jar and record a section of a Buddhist canon belonging to the Dharmagupta School (see Plate 37). This is the first example so far discovered of Kharoshthi having been used for a religious text and though the script still lacks some of the clear phonetic distinctions of Brahmi, it poses a number of new questions (Solomon, 1999). For example, were the earliest Buddhist texts transmitted to China based on this otherwise unknown Gandhara canon? Was Kharoshthi more widely used for Buddhist texts? And why are books never mentioned in the otherwise detailed descriptions listing the possessions of Buddhist monks?

The second script, found on the edicts of the Emperor Ashoka, was Brahmi (see Plate 38), by then already well developed and probably the most scientific script in existence. At first also written from right to left, it settled, after a short boustrophedon spell, into a definite left-to-right direction. Brahmi is one of the most important and influential scripts. In the course of time it was to play an important role in the development of writing in south and southeast Asia. Directly or indirectly, no less than some 200 different scripts can claim descent from Brahmi; in fact, nearly all contemporary Indian scripts, with the exception of those imported by Islam, are in one or the other way derived from it.

At present India recognises about 14 official languages, written in 19 different major scripts (see Plate 39). Linguistically and theoretically, the population of India can broadly be divided into two main groups: the Indo-Aryan speaking people of the north — descendants (though much intermixed) of the original Indo-Aryans who moved into the northwest of India c. 1500 BC — and the Dravidian people of the

ગાંધીયુગમાં આપણા વિવેચનનું લક્ષ્ય પાછળથી કાવ્ય પરથી
ખસીને કવિ તરફ ગયેલું લાગે – ખાસ કરીને ઉમાશંકરમાં. કવિની
સાધના, કવિની શ્રદ્ધા, કવિના સર્જનવ્યાપાર – આ બધા વિશે
GUJARATI

বদলে রইলো এই ঘড়ি। একটা অদ্ভুত ঘড়ি। এই ঘড়িটাই শব্দ ক'রে
তাল দিতো গানের সঙ্গে-সঙ্গে। একটা যন্ত্র ঘুরিয়ে দিলে প্রত্যেকটি
টিকটিক আওয়াজ রীতিমতো জোরে তবলার বোলের মতো টকটক
BENGALI

ସେଇବେଳେ କବ ଲେଖୁଥାନ୍ତ କମ୍ପା ଧାନମନ୍ତ ଥାନ୍ତ ।
ଅନେକ ସୂଚନା ମିଳିକ ସେ, ସେବେ କୌଣସି ଉଚ ମହଲରୁ
ଡାକୁ ସିବାପାଇଁ ଡାକର ଆସେ, ସେ ବଡ଼ ଅପ୍ରସ୍ତୁତ ବୋଧ
ORIYA

சுதந்திர புருஷர்களாய் இந்த மண்ணில் வாழ்ந்த முன்னோர்
களின் நினைவு தோன்றி அவர்களைப்போல் நாமும் சுதந்திரப்
பிரஜைகளாய் வாழ வேண்டும் என்ற தீவிரம் நமக்கு
TAMIL

രതിയുടെ ദുഃഖം കനിഞ്ഞു. കാരണമില്ലാതെ ശരീരം
വിറച്ചു. നെഞ്ചിൽ ചൂണ്ടക്കൊക്ക കൊളുത്തി വലിക്ക
ന്ന അനുഭവം. എന്താരള്ളപ്പെട്ടൂ രേഖ്യുന്നാണിയാാം.
MALAYALAM

ಹೋಗು ನೆನೆನಸು ಮಾಡುತ್ತಿ ."
ನಾನು ಉಀರಲ್ಲಿ ತುಂಬ ಅಸ್ಮಿವಂತ ಮುದೆಕ. ನನ್ನ ಒಬ್ಬನೇ ಮಗ
ಇವನ ಕೈಗುಣದಿಂದಲೇ ಬದುಕೆದ್ದ. ಆ ಸಂತೋಷ ಒಂದು ಕಡೆಗೆ. ನನ್ನಸ್ಸು
KANNADA

రామఫలాూ్ల మెక్ సల్క్రాంతి లక్ష్మి త్రైన్పన విధంగా
తీయు తే ఫులు పవవధువుల హృదయాంతరాళ రాళాల శారా
డాయు. కొ గ్ తల్లప్పు అత్తనరిఖ్ అభ్ఙంగన స్నానాలు
TELUGU

ඈ නීමෙ. එවිඩ සහිත්‍ය කාලවෙන් කල හැති කල යුත සංස්
කාතික විප්ලවය සරච්ක වන්නේ. සම්ප්‍රදායිකව අරඹ්‍ශ
කල යුත්තේ ඇත්ත වශයෙන්‍ම අඩික ආර්ථික දිඝ්ණ්ල නිසා
SINHALESE

south, who linguistically and ethnically belong to an altogether different and not yet fully understood background.

Most contemporary north Indian scripts can be traced back to the so-called Gupta script which developed in the 4th century AD. Of the four south Indian, Dravidian scripts, three (Kannada, Malayalam and Telugu) faithfully follow the Brahmi-derived model. Only Tamil, the script of the most important Dravidian language, does not fit as neatly into the same mould. Instead of the 36 or more basic syllabic consonants, Tamil has only 18, using the same sign for voiced, unvoiced, aspirated and unaspirated consonants — the pronunciation being determined by the position of the consonant within the word. In addition, the Tamil script has no sibilants (retroflex *sa*, dental *sa* and *sha*), no signs for the two palatals (*ja* and *jha*) and no aspirant (*ha*). It also lacks ligatures, which in other Indian scripts help to identify consonants without the inherent *a*. In fact, Tamil exhibits elements of scriptorial economy similar to those we encounter in the Cypriote and some other Mediterranean syllabic scripts. Ancient Tamil grammarians took great care to counterbalance this deficiency by framing rules, not only for correct pronunciation, but also for euphony. Unlike other Indian languages, Tamil is singularly unsuited for writing Sanskrit and another script, Grantham, was specially devised for this purpose. The earliest records of Tamil date from about 200 BC. Epigraphically Tamil becomes identifiable from the 8th century AD onwards, the same time when another variant of the Tamil script, Vatteluttu, appears in wider use. Vatteluttu is a distinctly cursive script, more used for speed than inscriptions. In many ways the relationship between Tamil and Vatteluttu is reminiscent of the one between Brahmi and Kharoshthi. Vatteluttu too exhibits the paucity of signs which characterise Tamil. It is not outside the realm of possibility that Vatteluttu goes back to some earlier and quite independent (trading?) connections between south India and the West — perhaps via Phoenician traders.

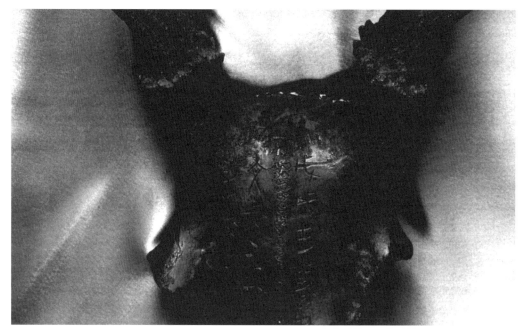

Plate 40. A rare example of an oracle bone inscription from the Shang Period, incised into the horned skull of a deer. The deer had been killed by the king whilst hunting and the inscription asks whether an offering of the deer should be made during a ceremony for the repose of the king's ancestors. When consulting the oracle, the officiating priest would apply a hot poker to the reverse side of the bone and use the cracks as model for the inscription.

Language, and with it script, are important and contentious political issues in India. The various states created in 1947 are, at least theoretically, based on language areas. Nehru's attempt to make Hindi, written in the Devanagari script, the official national language/script of India has never met with any recognisable success, especially not in the Tamil-speaking Dravidian south.

Not only did the (as always, sometimes arbitrary) division into linguistic states cause violent disturbances in some parts of the subcontinent at the partition in 1947, even today any pronouncement from the central government in Delhi about Hindi being the national language is usually greeted with civil unrest in Tamilnadu, especially in Madras.

The most remarkable difference between Indian scripts and other writing systems is the fact that for once they truly make speech visible — it is difficult to be dyslexic in an Indian language written in an Indian script. Unlike the alphabet, Indian scripts are designed to fit Indian languages and are firmly based on a long and distinguished period of purely oral traditions. This has various implications not only for writing but for literacy as such. And with it, on the correct way of teaching literacy, which even today, certainly in traditional Sanskrit schools, treats oral literacy as a precondition of written literacy.

Chinese forms of writing

Nothing definite is known about the precise origin and the exact age of the Chinese writing system which, subject to a variety of stylistic developments, is still in use today. Until the beginning of the 20th century the earliest available examples were signs scratched into animal bones or pieces of tortoiseshell used for the purpose of divination (see Plate 40). Ironically, these so-called oracle bones, first discovered in the province of Henan and considered to date back to the Shang period (c.1776-1122 BC or 1500-1028, according to some scholars), had made their first appearance several decades earlier. A peasant (or so the story goes) had found what he believed to be 'dragon bones' and brought them to an apothecary who was convinced that, suitably ground and prepared, they would provide a new form of medicine. Fortunately, a councillor from the court of the Chinese Emperor recognised in one of the inscriptions the name of a Shang emperor and further destruction was consequently prevented. In 1987 scholars from the Institute of Archaeology in Beijing announced that similarly inscribed bones had been discovered during the previous year in Sian and had been dated 3000-2500 BC (Mote and Hun-Liam Chu, 1988).

This early form of writing used over 3000 characters of which half can be read with reasonable certainty today. Though the characters were not yet fully standardised, the script itself seems to have reached a reasonable stage of development. What about earlier stages? It seems that as in Egypt, Mesoamerica, probably also Peru and the Indus Valley, we would be well advised to pay more attention to preceding pottery decorations and weaving patterns. In 1928 systematic excavations of Neolithic sites revealed highly suggestive marks on ceramic vessels and fragments. Some of the earliest examples found in the province of Shaanxi have been (radiocarbon) dated to a period of c. 4800 to 4200 BC. Other Neolithic sites have yielded similarly decorated pottery and some scholars see in those signs the earliest beginnings of the Chinese writing system.

Looking at a piece of Chinese writing one is immediately struck by the fact that this is a script unlike any other so far known to us. The assumption that it is basically a pictographic/ideographic concept script has in recent years been challenged by some scholars such as, for example, DeFrancis (1984) and others, who are trying to prove that Chinese is basically a morphemic (perhaps even syllabic) system; but such challenges are often based on rather subjective thinking. Even more suspect is their attempt to enlist the support of an ancient legend quoted by Xu Shen in the earliest surviving Chinese dictionary *Shuowen jiezi* (Explanations and Interpretations of Characters) complied in 120 AD. This story described how Cang Jie, the court recorder of the legendary Yellow Emperor (trad. 2697-2597 BC), looking at the marks left by the tracks of birds and animals, realised that the basic elements of writing were marks unconnected with the forms or ideas (pictures) of the things they stood for. Whatever this charming legend tries to tell us, it is difficult to see in it proof that the Chinese script was basically, and from the beginning, syllabic.

Since so many elements and facts that created Chinese writing are still unknown to us, it is perhaps best to say that the Chinese script does not primarily represent the sounds of a particular language but the concepts by which language as such can be

	Old form	Modern
child	孕孓	子
tree	朱	木
gate, door	門	門
arrow	矣夨	矢
word, to speak	舌	言
rain	㲃雨	雨
dog	犭	犬
large snake	乙	巴
hand	龵	手
field	田	田

Plate 41. *Some ancient and modern Chinese characters shown side by side. In all of them the original pictorial element is still clearly visible.*

represented. Many of the characters (words) have their roots in pictures derived from nature and this pictorial origin is very often still clearly visible (see Plate 41). Unlike systems based on the Phoenician consonant script (Arabic and the Greek/Roman alphabets), Chinese characters do not represent meaningless sound units but words and with them, by implication, ideas and concepts.

Though the Chinese script does without doubt include phonetic elements (as did those of Egyptians and Mesoamerica), it is at least curious to note that this particular, contemporary script still exhibits so overwhelmingly one of the greatest disadvantages attached to iconic writing, namely the large number of signs necessary to represent all possible linguistic, practical and cultural needs. It is also interesting that unlike in other scripts (e.g. Mesopotamia), their number increased over time. Thus the 3000 or so characters of the Shang period had increased to 9000 by 100 AD, to about 18,000 by 500 AD and to 27,000 by 1000 AD. By the 19th century the number had reached almost 49,000. Comprehensive modern dictionaries number some 50,000 different characters, arranged around radicals or categories, 214 in number. Chinese characters consist to a large extent of radicals and a (phonetic) complement made up of a particular number of strokes — though characters can also be formed by radicals alone or a combination of radicals. Generally, a radical acts similar to the way determinatives operate in Egyptian and cuneiform writing: it indicates the overall sphere of meaning. For example, radical 85 alone means 'water'; combined with a phonetic complement consisting, in this case, of five strokes, the now emerging character stands for 'to anchor'.

Since the Chinese language is strongly based on syntax and less on what we would call grammar, it is (at least in theory) possible to look up each character and to understand (up to a point) a Chinese text without being proficient in the language itself. This of course has always been the great strength of the Chinese script. In a vast country with different dialects and different people all ruled from one centre, it offered the ideal infrastructure for administrative control. The claim that the Chinese script, owing to its unique construction, could also be read by those not conversant with the Chinese language was first made in 1569 by a Dominican friar working in China. This opinion has recently been challenged, though often in a somewhat tortuous fashion. For example, we are told that it is not the inherent character of the Chinese script but the survival of various dictionaries which have made this possible. On the other hand,

Plate 42. A four-legged bronze vessel dating from the time of the early Western Zhou Period (c. 1050-771 BC). Such vessels were used by record-keeping officials, an important post, responsible for ritual prayers at festivals and letters of appointment given by the king to his vassals. Inscriptions in sunken characters (many of them clearly pictographic) could be cast in bronze vessels by inserting a section in the mould on which the characters were shown in relief.

the different appearance of characters (see Plate 42), which has sometimes been quoted to create doubts about the script's unity, are in fact simply calligraphic styles. This often considerable visual difference of individual characters is not a Chinese prerogative. One has only to look at Islamic calligraphy to see how the Arabic script can be made to look quite different during different periods, in different geographical areas, for aesthetic as well as political/religious reasons, without being anything other than Arabic. It is also interesting to note that despite the fact that there are many different languages and dialects in China, 70 per cent of Chinese speak Mandarin ('the common speech'). Indeed, those connected with the powerful and prestigious administration have always used and understood Mandarin — rather like the administration of the Austro-Hungarian Empire used German written in the Gothic script. Today's Chinese can read and (under certain preconditions) understand the classical text without an exact knowledge of their original pronunciation. This may become more clear to us if we consider that even those English people who (wrongly!) use an English pronunciation for Latin can still understand the meaning of the text (providing they have been taught Latin in the first place).

Though a knowledge of all 50,000 characters is only required for reading the classical texts and some 4000-7000 (some claim only 2000) characters are considered sufficient for everyday use, it still seems a cumbersome instrument for storing and disseminating information. But ease of access to a writing system, and its close correlation to a particular language, has not always been the deciding factor for making a script successful (or even useful).

From the later part of the 19th century onwards, various attempts have been made to simplify, even altogether replace Chinese by romanised forms of writing. The first attempt at romanisation, mainly concerned with serving the needs of foreigners, was the Wade-Giles system, introduced by Francis Wade in the second part of the 19th century and modified by H.A. Giles in 1912. In 1928 the 'National Language Romanisation' was worked out by the linguist Zhao Yuanren and others. In 1930 a romanised (*Sin Wenzi*) 'New Script' was devised in the then USSR, specially for Chinese immigrants. In 1935 a scheme of simplifying characters was adopted by the Nationalist Government (an attempt to abolish Chinese characters altogether, which had Mao's support, having failed). In 1949, at the foundation of the Peoples' Republic, the Communist government addressed the task of modernising and unifying the Chinese language as well as the Chinese script and 1956 saw the adaptation of 'Modern Standard Chinese'.

In 1958 the Chinese government made a decisive effort to oust the foreign Wade-Giles transliteration scheme and replace it by Pinyin, the 'Phonetic Alphabet' — this romanisation (or, if we like, transliteration) is much closer to the spirit of the Chinese script and language but it gained acceptance mostly outside China. In the USA the Library of Congress stuck, for much longer than the British Library, to the outmoded Wade-Giles system owing to the opposition of some ageing academics who looked upon Pinyin as a Communist-friendly move. On the other hand, during the Cultural Revolution some xenophobic Red Guards saw in Pinyin a way of kow-towing to Western imperialistic concepts, even tearing down street signs written in Pinyin. But on the whole, the Chinese, though feeling less need to transliterate their own script for their own use, did teach school children who did not know Mandarin to write Chinese first in Pinyin (Brown, 1998) in an attempt to decrease illiteracy, especially in villages and factories — thus (however unwittingly) creating a further level of stratified functional literacy.

In 1964 a revision of the Chinese script increased the number of simplified characters (for everyday use) to 2238; in 1977 a plan was put forward to add another 883 simplified characters but this suggestion was eventually withdrawn. In other words, the Chinese mode of writing has, subject to some modifications and simplifications, so far survived all foreign and indeed also most indigenous attempts to change it. It is still an important element of China's culture and of the political infrastructure; indeed, modern information technology — the use of computers — has made its use in many ways not more but less problematic. Reform movements are by definition political tools; they do, however, quite often produce the most unexpected results.

Bibliography

Abercrombie, D. *Elements of General Phonetics*. Edinburgh: University Press, 1967.

Allen, W. S. *Phonetics in Ancient India*. Oxford: University Press, 1953.

Allen, W. S. *Sandhi: the Theoretical, Phonetic and Historical Basis of Word Junctions in Sanskrit*. S-Grabenhoge: Moulton, 1962.

Billeter, J. F. *L'art Chinois de l'ecriture*. Geneve: Shira, 1989.

Bonkhorst, J. *On the History of Paninian Grammar in the early Centuries following Patanjali*. JIP.II, 1983.

Brown, M. P. *Writing and Script: History and Technique*. London: British Library, 1998.

Buehler, J. G. *On the Origin of the Indian Brahmi Alphabet*. 3rd edn., Strasbourg: Trubner, 1892.

Caldwell, R. *The comparative Grammar of the Dravidian or South Indian Family of Languages*. 3rd edn., New Delhi: Oriental Books Reprint Corporation, 1974.

Dani, A. H. *Indian Plaeography*. Oxford: Clarendon Press, 1963 (rpt. Delhi, 1986).

DeFrancis, J. *The Chinese Language: Fact and Fantasy.* Honolulu: University of Hawaii, 1984.

Karlgren, B. *Sound and Symbol in Chinese.* rev. edn., Hong Kong/London, 1962.

Kratochvil, P. *The Chinese Language Today.* London: Hutchinson, 1968.

Kiparsky, P. *Panini as a Variationist.* Poona: University Press, 1979.

Losty, J. P. *The Art of the Book in India.* London: British Library, 1982.

Mote, F. W. and Hun-Liam Chu. *Calligraphy and the East Asian Book.* Princeton, 1988.

Padoux, A. *Vac: the Concept of the Word in Select Hindu Tantras.* trans. J. Gontier. Albany: State University of New York, 1990.

Robinson, A. *The Story of Writing.* London: Thames and Hudson, 1995.

Sastri, G. B. *The Philosophy of Word and Meaning: some Indian Approaches with special Reference to the Philosophy of Bhartrhari.* Calcutta: Sanskrit College, 1959.

Shapiro, M. C. and Schiffmann, H. *Language and Society in South Asia.* Delhi: Motilal Banarsidas, 1981.

Solomon, R. *Ancient Buddhist Scrolls from Gandhara. The British Library Kharoshthi Fragments.* London/Washington: British Library, 1999.

Staal, J. *Universals: Studies in Indian Logic and Linguistics.* Chicago: University Press, 1988.

Thieme, P. *Panini and the Vedas: Studies in the Early History of Linguistic Science in India.* Allahabad: Globe Press, 1935.

Upasak, C. S. *The History and Palaeography of Mauryan Brahmi Script.* Patna: Nava Nalanda Mahavira, 1960.

Verma, T. P. *The Palaeography of Brahmi Script.* Varanasi: Siddharta Prakashan, 1971.

7. The political success of unsuitable writing systems

The success of a particular writing system does not necessarily depend on its ability to reproduce speech as accurately as possible. It is more often motivated — directly or indirectly — by political expediency. Such motivation can be secular or religious or both, since religion is simply another form of politics. The process of conversion (religious or secular) removes the individual from the security of his or her intellectual and emotional background and negates most of what has so far been the basis of identity. To retain the impetus of conversion, this vacuum has to be filled, as soon as possible, by a new set of concepts, a new social order, new moral aims, a new language — a new script.

A common script is a strong tool not only for unification but also for enforcing and, where appropriate, preserving political dominance. Both the Chinese and the cuneiform script of Mesopotamia enforced the concept of unification. The spread of English and the alphabet (and later that of the Russian language and the Cyrillic script) were based on the same principles. In an imperialistic/colonial situation the impetus for understanding the instructions of the new administration rests with the ruled, not the rulers. Under certain circumstances, not only a particular writing system but even a particular calligraphic style can be used, almost like a corporate logo, to signify ownership. When after the disintegration of the Roman Empire the alphabet was taken to western Europe by Christian missionaries, it soon lost its uniform character and split into a number of so-called 'national hands' (Brown, 1990). In the 12th century one particular calligraphic style — Gothic — emerged, which, after the introduction of printing, became the main system used in Germany. In German speaking areas calligraphic traditions based on Gothic were used long after the English round hand had become the preferred business script in other parts of the world. In the states absorbed by the Austro-Hungarian Empire local people were obliged to learn and use this script (together with the German language) if they wished to gain posts in the administration.

Traders confront a quite different situation: their success depends largely on being understood. Though they may act as script disseminators, they are not interested in imposing a particular script, especially one that is difficult to learn. This may have been one of the reasons why phonetic scripts developed on the eastern shore of the Mediterranean in the second millennium BC, then a highly cosmopolitan area, a meeting-place between Egypt, Mesopotamia, the Aegean and parts of western Asia. The international character of the coastal towns required a knowledge of several languages, making great demands on the scribes (especially those in the employ of traders), who had to be conversant with a number of different writing systems. A typical example are the Phoenicians, who had no territorial or imperial ambitions but took their script as part of a viable trading commodity to a widely scattered area.

On the other hand, the retention of a writing system can also be motivated by a desire to protect the vested interests of a particular group, especially if the script is complex and time-consuming to learn. Egyptian, Mesoamerica and Mesopotamian scribes, as well as the Chinese-educated elite in Korea and Japan, had little interest in supporting script reforms which, in the long run, would only have weakened their own place in society. Similarly, if the use of a particular script had become synonymous with a particular political power elite, extended literacy would only endanger the power structure. On the other hand, the retention of a particular writing by a disadvantaged and discriminated group can provide a means to preserve its essential cultural identity within an often hostile environment, something that happened to Hebrew and the Jewish communities during the long years of the Diaspora.

A change in script can also reflect changing political fortunes. In the 2nd century BC Vietnam was incorporated into the Chinese Empire; this brought the Chinese language, the Chinese script and Chinese administration to the country. But for a considerable time Chinese education was denied to the Vietnamese people to prevent the development of a class of officials able to administer their own country (Le Thanh Khoi, 1955). After the Trung rebellion (39-43 AD) local people were given access to Chinese education but only a small number of Vietnamese became well versed in writing Chinese; historically we know of altogether only five names (DeFrancis, 1977). The removal of political domination in 939 AD did little, however, to diminish Chinese cultural influence; in fact, it encouraged more Vietnamese to study Chinese, which they had learned to associate with domination and power. In the 17th century Christian missionaries devised a romanised scheme for the publication of their religious texts. Unlike political aims based on exclusiveness, religious influence (without a strong backup of a secular power) depends on conversion and the spread of information. After all, both the missionaries and the traders have something to sell. French colonial rule led to a diffusion of this new script (ironically called 'national language', *quoc ngu*) throughout the country and by 1910 it was made compulsory. Like the Chinese, the French had great faith in the civilising properties of their own script and language. This, at one point, led to the suggestion that a knowledge of both should be rewarded by French citizenship (Aymonier, 1890).

Another interesting example, mirroring changing fortunes accompanied by changes in the political/religious attitude, comes from Turkey. In 1928 Mustafa Kemal Ataturk (1881-1938) replaced the Arabic script by a modified Roman alphabet in an attempt to break the power of the religious establishment and create a secular state out of the old Ottoman Empire. The strength of his own position and the prevailing political climate, which then generally favoured 'modernisation', ensured the success of his reform. But despite the fact that it also dramatically raised the literacy level of the country (Arabic has only three letter signs for the eight vowels of Ottoman Turkish), we now witness the beginning of a swing in the opposite direction. In today's world the old Western/ Christian/alphabet-writing powers are no longer so dominant; Islam is experiencing a tremendous revival and the pendulum might well swing back towards Arabic.

The thesis that the nature of linguistic organisations determine the type of writing system that can adapt and survive in a given linguistic community appears in the face

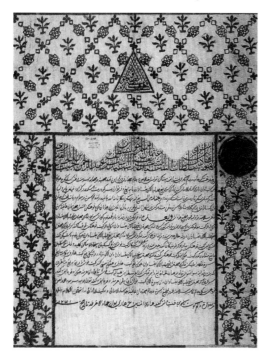

Plate 43. Letter from the Sultan Syarif Uthman of Pontianak to Baron van der Capellen, the Dutch Governor-General in Batavia, dated 18 December 1825. The text is written with silver and gold on English paper in Malay language in the Jawi script.

of available evidence rather doubtful. It is certainly true that in one or the other way languages have made a contribution to writing. But this contribution is often quite limited to a change of characters, modifications added to make the script more readable in another language, the creation of modified signs for sounds or tonal variations. The so-called invention of the Greek alphabet was in reality nothing more than a modification of the Phoenician consonant script — just as the Jawi script of Malaysia is in fact Arabic with four additional characters representing sound elements essential to the Malay language (see Plate 43). Such modified systems are less dependent on language than on the political/religious power of the group using (or introducing) them.

Languages may modify a system but they are in themselves seldom powerful enough to create (or even more important, retain) a new system. This manifests itself quite clearly in relation to the 19th century African and American script inventions: despite an initial success they soon disappeared, since they served communities without true political power.

The Chinese derived scripts of Korea and Japan

Korea and Japan provide good examples of how an almost totally unsuitable writing system can, quite voluntarily, be accepted and retained. One might argue that this willingness was perhaps understandable since neither Korea not Japan had scripts of their own and that culturally as well as politically China was a powerful factor. However, this does not in itself explain why such a complex system as Chinese remained in use, even after both Korea and Japan had successfully created their own, far more suitable forms of writing.

The fact that the Chinese script had by then become associated with the ruling elite and was as such perceived as a sign of power and intellectual superiority, safeguarding clearly-defined vested interests, overruled linguistic considerations.

In Korea national elements eventually triumphed but in Japan the Chinese script has become so assimilated that it is more or less considered part of Japanese culture.

Korea

In 109 AD the Han Emperor Wu Di conquered the northern part of the Korean peninsula which, at the time, was ruled by several independent kingdoms. Though the political balance soon readjusted itself in favour of Korea with the emergence of three independent kingdoms, the cultural contact with China, once initiated, continued by land as well as by sea. This brought, in due course, Buddhism, Confucianism and the Chinese form of writing to the peninsula. By the time of the unification of Silla in 668 AD, Chinese characters had become the official script of the court and were used as such by the educated, powerful elite of the country. But the basic unsuitability of the Chinese script for transcribing the very different grammatical features of Korean soon led to repeated attempts to find more acceptable alternatives.

At first Chinese characters were probably just read in Korean but around the 5th/6th century a system called *Idu* developed and was used until the 19th century for recording factual information by government officials. Certain Chinese characters, which had meanings corresponding to those of certain Korean grammatical particles or auxiliary verbs, were used in the context of a sentence to write Korean grammar. After 750 AD *Idu* was also used for describing morphemes of the Korean language. After the 9th century another system called *Hyangch'al* was used for lyrical poetry and verses written in Chinese script. Here nouns and verb stems were written in Chinese characters, using a process of bilingual identification. *Hyangch'al* disappeared in the 15th century. The third system, *Kugyol*, attempted to give a complete and accurate representation of the underlying Korean sentence. It was especially used for Buddhist scriptures and Confucian philosophical works. It used part of a Chinese character for phonetic purpose to transcribe Korean morphemes and annotate a given text.

Eventually, in 1446, the great reforming king Sejong (r. 1418-1450 AD) promulgated an alphabetic script called Hangul which consisted of 11 vowel and 17 consonant-signs. The individual characters showed simple, often

Plate 44. Hunmin chongum. *King Sejong's explanation of the Korean script; a modern facsimile of a block-print. The simplicity of the Hangul characters stands in clear contrast to the complexity of the Chinese script.*

rectangular shapes and were a perfect medium for writing Korean (see Plate 44). However, the new script met with fierce resistance from Confucian scholars who opposed the extension of literacy as strongly as they revered Chinese language, writing and culture. In consequence, Hangul did not replace Chinese but was simply used side by side with Chinese characters as an aid to pronunciation, for grammatical terms and to clarify ambiguities. The ability to read and write Chinese continued to be seen as a sign of social and intellectual elevation. The new system was thought fit only for popular literature and novels meant for the consumption of women and persons of low rank.

During the Japanese occupation (1940-5) the Japanese authorities greatly encouraged the use of their own language as a medium for publication. Under this threat Hangul became at last a truly national issue. Today a mixed script (Chinese and Hangul) is still used in the south of the country. In the north all writing — and all calligraphy — is done in the indigenous alphabet. The 9th of October is, however, celebrated throughout Korea as Alphabet Day, in acknowledgement of King Sejong's achievement (Eckert, 1990).

Japan

A knowledge of the Chinese system of writing reached Japan via Korea. No definite records exist about the time Chinese characters were first used but at the beginning of the 4th century Japan invaded Korea and successfully held some of the territory until 562 AD. In consequence, the thus far tentative contact between Japan, Korea and China increased. In the 6th century Buddhism became the official state religion of Japan, with the result that a certain (though still relatively small) section of society was now 'Chinese-educated'. From then on Japanese scholars went regularly to China for further studies. In 645 AD a centralised administration, based largely on Confucian ideas, was installed which lasted until the end of the Heian period (12th century). Chinese writing techniques were adopted wholesale: the brush, ink, the ink-stone and, after 600 AD, the manufacture of paper.

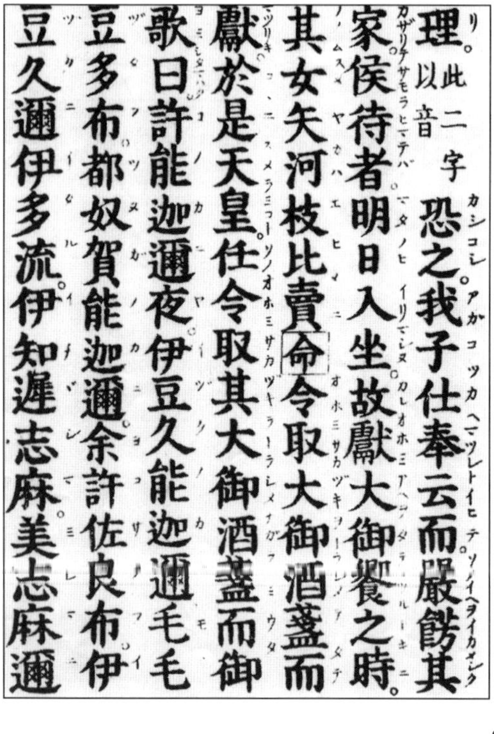

Plate 45. A 19th century block print copy of Kojiki, an ancient history of Japan, completed in 712 AD. Though the actual text is written in Chinese characters (kanji), the Japanese pronunciation of the words has to be indicated by kana signs beside the Chinese character.

The political success of unsuitable writing systems

How then did the Chinese script, designed for a largely monosyllabic form of speech, adapt itself to the polysyllabic, agglutinative Japanese language full of formal words? Basically, as in Korea, by a number of complex compromises. *Kanji* (Chinese characters) could be used phonetically for reading Japanese, especially proper names. But the Japanese syntax is vastly different from Chinese, a difficulty which had to be overcome by adding special notations to indicate the order in which characters should be read. The next step was the modification and simplification of some phonetic characters to form a syllabary (*kana*) with fixed phonetic values (see Plate 45). Between the 8th and the 10th centuries two such syllabaries evolved. One, *katakana*, a square formal type of script, was formed from isolated parts of Chinese characters which could be used for more formal works (official documents, lexical works, etc.). The other *hiragana*, a round flowing script, was derived from the cursive form of (whole) Chinese characters; it was mainly used for more informal writing. The number of syllables was eventually reduced to 47 and Japanese could from then on have been written using only those characters. In the 11th century Chinese Buddhist studies of original Sanskrit texts created, in addition, the so-called *Kunrei* system, which is reminiscent of the way Indian scripts are arranged.

But as in Korea, *kana* did not replace Chinese. Though much poetry and some very fine prose literature was produced during the Heian period (794 AD-1192 AD), it was composed mainly by women authors; the two most famous being Murasaki Shikibu (*The Tale of Genji*) and Sei Shonagon (*Pillow Book*). Chinese was too deeply entrenched as the prestigious form of writing to make its abolition feasible. In addition, borrowing from Chinese continued side by side with *kana* and by the end of the Heian period a mixed Chinese/Japanese script, known as *kana-majiri*, evolved, which is still in use today.

Is the alphabet likely to replace *kana-majiri* or even *kana*? Talk about reforms of the Japanese script have been going on since the 1880s, much of it based on ill-placed feelings of Western superiority and a total misunderstanding of the place writing systems hold within a particular culture. To give just a few examples: there was Sir George Sansom who, in 1928, glibly stated 'there is no doubt it [the Japanese system of writing] provides for some a fascinating field of study, but as a practical instrument it is surely without inferiors'. Or, more recently, J. Marshall Unger: 'in a broad sense, over the centuries, Japanese scripts have "worked". Japanese culture has not flourished because of the complexity of its writing system, but it has undeniably flourished in spite of them.' The most amusing, or embarrassing (depending at how one looks at it) remark was, however, made by a group of American educationalists, who after the end of the last war warned MacArthur that as long as the Japanese did not abolish their 'Chinese-derived ideograms' they could never hope to achieve technological parity with the West (Diringer, 1968).

In the 1980s the Roman alphabet found its way into Japanese writing, mainly through advertising. Advertisements, especially those connected with imported goods, sometimes mix *kanji, Romanji* (letters of the Roman alphabet) and *kana*. But the idea that the alphabet has acquired prestige in Japan similar to that once given to Chinese,is probably premature Euro-centric optimism — or the result of Japanese courtesy when answering the questions of foreign researchers. The Japanese have always been adept at taking from other cultures what suited them at a given time for a given purpose, without sacrificing their own originality. Computers are now able to cope with Chinese writing in a way typewriters never could. In addition, the fact, that the Japanese have always held hand-written documents in greater esteem than printed texts played an important role in speeding up the development and acceptance of the fax.

Indian script forms in Southeast Asia, the Himalayan countries and Central Asia

By the 3rd century AD Buddhism had become the state religion of India. Unlike Hinduism, which was strictly exclusive (one is born a Hindu, one cannot become one), Buddhism relied, like other revolutionary creeds promulgated by one individual, on the ability to increase its ranks by propaganda and conversion. For such a movement, written texts are more effective than oral traditions. In the middle of the first Christian millennium Buddhism lost ground in its own homeland but spread to the Himalayan region in the north and westward to the many different countries (and different linguistic communities) of southeast Asia — none of them having a script of their own.

Southeast Asia

In the course of the first Christian millennium Indian traders, colonists, military adventurers, Buddhist monks and missionaries brought their language (Sanskrit), their script (a South Indian Grantham variation of Brahmi) and their religion (Hinduism/Buddhism) to the countries of southeast Asia. The Indian system of writing, which had been carefully fashioned on the basis of ancient phonetic (oral) traditions to fit the characteristics of Indian languages, had now to cope with four entirely different language groups: Sino-Tibetan, Thai, Malayo-Polynesian and Austro-Asiatic. This called for modifications and compromises. But in most cases change was limited to the usage and number of syllabic vowel and consonant signs, which were either enlarged, diminished or interchanged; sometimes diacritical marks were added for the representation of the tonal range of a particular language. The basic internal structure of the Indian script, the arrangement and construction of the syllabic units, the way vowels were represented (either initial or auxiliary) and the phonetic arrangement of characters remained largely the same, as did the direction of writing (from left to right). Visually the contemporary scripts of southeast Asia may look very different from each other and from the various scripts that evolved in the course of their development but this difference is largely external.

The development of southeast Asian scripts is closely connected with the complex pattern of southeast Asian history. The majority of modern mainland scripts such as Burmese, Cambodian, Thai can be traced back, directly or indirectly, to scripts introduced by Hindu colonists who, early in the first millennium AD, created the first independent Hindu kingdoms in Fu-nam and Champa (now southern Vietnam). In the case of Burmese, the (later) import of manuscripts from Sri Lanka written in Pali introduced additional elements. In fact, at one time, southeast Asian scripts were wrongly labelled the Pali branch of Indian scripts. But the Burmese script goes back to

Plate 46. The oldest so far discovered Thai text inscribed on a stone monument erected by King Ramakamhaeng (Sukhothai dynasty 1279-1300), in 1292. The Thai script is modelled after the ancient Khmer script.

an inscription dating from c. 1000 AD to a script form adopted from the Mon script which in turn derived from South Indian Grantham.

The present form of the Thai script (see Plate 46) too has its origin in South Indian Grantham but in 1283 the so-called Sukhotai script is thought to have been created by a local king of that name in an attempt to strengthen national feelings. In 1357 and 1680 further, though quite minor revisions, were made by two other Thai rulers. The present Thai script is a modification of the 13th century Sukhotai style plus 2 more characters added in 1736.

Most of the scripts used at one time or the other on the various islands of southeast Asia are linked to India, indirectly, via the so-called Kavi script which prevailed in Java between the 9th and the 15th centuries. It is now generally thought that Kavi is not, as has sometimes been suggested, a new invention or introduction (directly from India) but a later development of a script used for Sanskrit inscriptions during the middle of the first Christian millennium.

This script differs only slightly from South Indian (Pallava?)-Grantham and shows similarities to the Cambodian script of the time. Kavi was directly responsible for the growth of modern Javanese and it also stimulated the development of the greatly simplified scripts of the Batak, Redjang and Lampong of Sumatra. In all three scripts the number of signs is greatly reduced, to 23 in the case of Lampong and to a mere 19 in Batak and Redjang. Apart from the left-to-right direction, Batak is also written in vertical columns beginning at the lower left hand side. Visually this script looks totally different from its Indian ancestors but it nevertheless follows the same internal pattern.

It seems fairly certain that the two scripts of Celebes, namely Buginese and Macassarese, were equally derived from Kavi, perhaps through the intermediary of Batak. Kavi may also have been responsible (directly or indirectly) for the ancient and by now extinct Philippine scripts (Diringer, 1968) which first became known in 1521 when the Spanish reached the Philippine islands.

Plate 47. A folio from the Kanjur, *the Tibetan Buddhist Canon written in then* dbu-can *(head-possessing) style of the Tibetan script.*

The Himalayan kingdoms

The origin of the Tibetan script has long been closely associated with the reforming king Song-tsen-gam-po who ruled the country between 620 and 645 AD. Having unified the various tribes of the region, he created a kingdom which spread its influence from China to India. He also introduced paper and ink from China, writing from India and he is generally credited with laying the cornerstones of Tibetan orthography. To accommodate the peculiarities of the Tibetan language, the creation of six new signs and a number of modifications were necessary. Tradition claims that the Indian script model was brought back to Tibet in 632 AD by a minister of the court whom the king had sent to India to study Buddhism and the Sanskrit language. But in reality the Indian forms of writing may well have reached Tibet via Buddhist monasteries in Chinese Turkistan or Kashmir.

Nowadays scholars are no longer so sure about the precise origin of the Tibetan script, the region from which it came and the exact period of its introduction. What is remarkable is the fact that the script remained standardised and more or less unchanged from the 7th century onwards. As such it became a vital part of the kingdom's infrastructure which united and sustained Tibetan civilisation over a large and thinly populated area.

Almost from the beginning two different styles seem to have existed side by side: *dbu-can* (head-possessing), mainly used for religious texts (see Plate 47), and a more cursive form called *dbu-med*, which was considered suitable for correspondence and administrative records. *Dbu-can* produced some highly stylised 'seal-scripts' from which the Mongols chose in due course the so-called Passepa script for their own language. In addition, variations of the Tibetan scripts, such as, for example, Lepcha, developed in the neighbouring Himalayan countries.

Central Asia

In the first millennium AD Indian cultural influence reached as far as central Asia. The export of Buddhist manuscripts introduced the Gupta script to this area, where it became instrumental in the development of various scripts which served not only Sanskrit but also Iranian and Tocharian dialects. Descendants of the Gupta script remained in use until after the 10th century. Buddhism and Buddhist manuscripts took the Siddhamatrika script to China where, under the name of *siddham,* it introduced a knowledge of the Indian syllabic form of writing and a phonetic arrangement of letters. *Siddham,* incidentally, also became the basis of a special and intricate style of Chinese calligraphy. In the wake of Buddhism this knowledge spread from China to Korea and Japan and became a contributory factor in some script reforms.

The success of cuneiform

The system of writing that developed in Mesopotamia (later to be known as cuneiform) in support of business transaction was well suited to the agglutinative Sumerian language. But when after c. 2800 BC the Semitic Akkadians (Babylonian/Assyrians) began to establish their dominance in the area this so far highly effective form of writing had to accommodate the structure of their very different Semitic language for which it was ill-suited. Unlike the Koreans and Japanese, the Akkadians made no significant innovations or alterations but adapted the cuneiform script for the representation of their own language simply by using a number of additional modifications and compromises which, if anything, should have made writing and reading even more difficult. Yet by all accounts this complex and cumbersome script not only provided an effective infrastructure for administration and trade but, in due course, it also served as vehicle for works of literature (*The Epic of Gilgamesh*), astronomy, mathematics, medicine, dictionaries, translations, law (*The Code of Hamurabi*), etc. In fact, the cuneiform script was one of the most successful systems ever devised and was used for a period of well over three millennia. It was chosen to represent some 15 different languages of a widely diverse linguistic nature. In some cases only the technique of cuneiform was used, not the system itself. For example, Hittite, an Indo-Aryan language, overcame difficulties by using Sumerian logograms to express certain words and by borrowing the style of making wedge-shaped signs but not the actual cuneiform signs themselves. Ugaritic used a limited number of cuneiform signs to create what could be called an alphabet. Cuneiform also formed the basis for Old Persian, a script created under the rule of Darius (521-486 BC) for royal monuments, using cuneiform signs in a consonantal manner.

In fact, during the 2nd millennium BC Babylonian-Assyrian, written in the cuneiform script, became the language and the script of international diplomacy and was used as such from Persia to Anatolia, from the Caspian Sea to the river Nile. It was only after Alexander's conquest (c. 331 BC) that the use of cuneiform became gradually more restricted, until it was eventually superseded by Aramaic. The last cuneiform document so far discovered was written in 75 AD. By then the old order that had created Pharaonic Egypt and the Near Eastern city states had declined, making way for an altogether different way of life, a different infrastructure and, with it, the need for different forms of information storage and communication.

There are some interesting differences in the way various scripts can adapt themselves to new demands. Whereas in Southeast Asia the visual shape of the Indian proto-type changed to an extent that the new script variations often looked totally different, their internal structure remained practically unchanged. In Japan and Korea definite attempts were made to create indigenous and eminently suitable forms of writing, which however failed to succeed. The cuneiform script on the other hand, visually unprepossessing and difficult to read, was adopted by various linguistic groups and in the process changed into, for example, consonantal/Semitic or alphabetic/Ugarit. But the external appearance of the script remained more or less the same. Societies will accept what best suits their needs. In Korea and Japan the Chinese script had acquired enormous cultural prestige and those conversant with it were unwilling to endanger their position by allowing for a wider spread of literacy. Even those anxious for upward mobility saw an entrance into the established elite a better way to achieve status. Cuneiform, on the other hand, had from the beginning been a trading commodity, with few cultural or political pretensions. Indian scripts in turn rested on centuries of oral tradition which had provided them with a well thought out phonetic structure. Amazingly, the strength of this phonetic basis was such that it easily survived not only total changes in outward appearance but also the varying needs of different linguistic demands.

The Arabic script and the Roman alphabet

The Roman alphabet and the Arabic script are today the two most widely used forms of writing. Both base their success on religion and politics but it is only in Islam that those two elements form a total and coherent symbiosis without any division between the sacred and the profane. According to tradition, the Koran was orally transmitted to the Prophet in the Arabic language, thus making both script and language a divine gift. This not only necessitated immediate and far-reaching script reforms, creating in the process one of the finest calligraphies the world has ever known, but it also imposed Arabic on many non-Semitic languages of Europe, Asia and Africa. Within a century after the Prophet's death (632 AD) Islamic influence extended from Spain to India and eventually further east towards the borders of China. Since the Koran should be read and studied in Arabic, every Muslim, whatever his nationality and daily speech, should to this day be able to read and write Arabic.

Christianity made use of the Roman alphabet in a similar way. But Christianity never quite achieved total unity between state and church, despite the efforts made by the papacy. In a way, Christianity simply took over the mantle of imperial Rome, imposing a prophetic religion on what had up to then been a highly organised and highly successful political empire. But the Romans had neither been teachers nor missionaries; their aim had always been an efficient administration, not a message that transcended secular political needs. Here the Christian missionaries could add a powerful new element, that of promises only to be fulfilled in a non-verifiable afterlife. Together with the Bible, the alphabet was introduced, first to the rest of Europe and later, with economic power added to political domination, also to Asia, Africa and to the Americas. In the process the alphabet frequently replaced indigenous (and often more efficient) forms of writing, endangering, at times even destroying, local languages and cultural traditions.

Work on the decipherment of the Maya script had already begun in the 16th century when the script was first discovered. But despite many imaginative attempts and despite the fact that Maya languages are still spoken in parts of Yucatan, we can still only read a limited number of glyphs. This is to a large extent the result of proselytising friars who reached the Americas in the wake of the Spanish conquest. They not only imposed their own religion, their own language and their own script but in the process destroyed inscriptions and manuscripts, as well as omitting terms referring to Maya religion and ritual from their otherwise praiseworthy dictionaries.

This process has not always been totally successful or even produced the same results. In India, for example, despite the political power of first the East India Company and, after the mutiny, that of the British government, as well as T. B. Macaulay's (1800-1859) dictum that one shelf of books in a good European library was worth more than the whole of Oriental literature, English and the alphabet never eradicated indigenous languages and script forms. Though English was introduced as the language of teaching and administration, newspapers and other publications printed in Indian languages, in Indian scripts, began to flourish; in fact, by 1900 all Indian scripts appeared in print. The credit for this seeming contradiction goes at least in part to Portuguese missionaries who, on reaching Goa in 1556, set a widely followed example by cutting founts in Konkani and Tamil. More anxious to spread their faith than to underpin the power of politicians and traders, those missionaries were in a quite different situation to the friars who followed Columbus to the Americas.

Bibliography

Aymonier, E. *La langue francaise et l'enseigment en Indochina.* Paris, 1890.

Brown, M. P. *Writing and Script: History and Technique.* London: British Library, 1998.

Burney, J. and Coedes, G. *The Origin of the Sukhodaya Script.* Jss 21, 2:87-102.

Buzo, A. *Early Korean Writing System.* Transaction of the Royal Asiatic Society Branch 55, 1980.

Casparis, J. J. de, *Indonesian Palaeography: a History of Writing in Indonesia from the Beginning to c. AD 1500.* Leiden: E. J. Brill, 1975.

Danvivathana, N. *The Thai Writing System.* Hamburg: Helmut Buske Verlag, 1987.

DeFrancis, J. *Colonialism and Language Policy in Viet Nam.* The Hague: Mounton, 1977.

Diringer, D. *The Alphabet - the Key to the History of Mankind.* London: Hutchinson, 1968.

Eckert, C. J. *Korea Old and New: a History.* Seoul: Korean Institute, 1990.

Fried, M. H. *The Evolution of Political Society: an Essay on Practical Anthropology.* New York: Random House, 1967.

Gallop, A. R. and Arps, B. *Golden Letters, Writing Traditions of Indonesia.* London: British Library, 1991.

Hale, A. *Research on Tibeto-Burman Languages.* New York: Mounton Publishers, 1982.

Huffman, F. E. and Im Proum. *Transliteration System for Khmer.* CORMOSEA, Newsletter 8. 1974.

Huffman, F. E. *The Cambodian System of Writing and Beginning Reader.* New Haven: University of Yale, 1970.

Jones, R. B and Khin, U. *The Burmese Writing System.* Washington: American Council of Learned Societies, 1953.

Kolers, P., Wrolstad, M. and Bouma, H. (eds.) 'Processing Visible Language', pp.67-82. I. Taylor. *The Korean Writing system: An alphabet? Syllabary? A Logography?* New York, 1980.

Kratochvil, P. *The Chinese Language Today.* London: Hutchinson, 1968.

Kuo, W. *A Workbook for Writing Thai.* Berkeley: University of California, 1979.

Lee, S. B. *The Origins of the Korean Alphabet.* Seoul: National Museum of Korea, 1957.

Le Thanh Koi. *Le Vietnam, historie et civilisation*. Paris, 1955.

Ledyard, G. K. *The Korean Language Reform of 1446: the Origin, Background and History of the Korean Alphabet*. Berkley: University of California, 1966.

Logan, T. *The Alphabet Effect. The Impact of the Phonetic Alphabet on the Development of Western Civilisation*. New York: 1986.

Miller, R. A. *The Tibetan System of Writing*. Washington: American Council of Learned Societies, 1956.

Miller, R. A. *The Japanese Language*. Chicago: University Press, 1967.

Morison, S. *Politics and Script*. Oxford: University Press, 1972.

Pedersen, H. *The Discovery of Language: Linguistic Science in the Nineteenth Century*. Cambridge: Harvard University Press, 1931.

Pigeaud, T. G. T. *Literature of Java, vol. i. Synopsis of Javanese Literature, 900-1900 AD*. The Hague: Martinus Nyhoff, 1967.

Roop, D. H. *An Introduction to the Burmese Writing System*. New Haven: Yale University Press, 1972.

Seeley, C. *A History of Writing in Japan*. Leiden: Brill, 1991.

Unger, J. M. *The Fifth Generation Fallacy*. New York: University of Oxford Press, 1987.

Vaid, J. and Park, K. *The Role of Script and Phonology in Lexical Representation: Korean Data*. Presented at Annual Meeting of the Psychonomics Society, Chicago, 1988.

8. Script inventors and script inventions

Nearly all civilisations have legends attributing the origin of writing to the intervention of some divine or semi-historical beings (see Plate 48). Basic to all these myths, concepts and stories is a profound sense of the existential importance of writing to political power and with it the ability to establish, maintain and control tradition and order. The ancient Egyptian considered the ibis-headed god Toth not only the scribe of the gods and the 'master of papyrus' but also the inventor of writing. He was also thought to be the administrative keeper of the established order and as such protector against rebellion. Mesopotamia, with its frequently changing power structure, assigned this role to a variety of deities, foremost perhaps to Nabu the god of wisdom but also to his consort Tashmetum or to Nidaba or Enlil. The Mayas regarded one of their most important deities, Isthmian, the son of the creator god, as the inventor of writing and also of books. The Ogham script, which appeared among the Celtic speaking people of the British Isles between the 4th and the 6th century AD, names the legendary Dogma Mac Elathan or the God Ogmios as possible inventors. The Abanaki Indians of North America believe that the Oonagamessok, a special group of deities, presided over the making of petroglyphs and explain the gradual disappearance of these rock engravings by the fact that the Oonagamessok became angered by the lack of attention accorded to them after the coming of the white settlers (Mallery, 1893).

Up to the 20th century ideas concerning the origin of writing polarised around two main traditions: one, less influential in the long run, based on Greek, the other on Judaeo-Christian concepts. Both had their own vested interests, promoting the idea that writing was somehow sacred and consequently of divine origin. The sacred origin of writing (and language) is also central to Islamic thinking but it is one of the special

Plate 48. Cang Jie, the Court Recorder of the legendary Yellow Emperor (trad. 2697-2597 BC) is traditionally credited with the invention of the Chinese script. While nearly all civilisations claim divine or semi-historical figures as the inventors of their scripts, Cang Jie has, quite recently, been given more credence as script inventor by some Western scholars, despite his somewhat nebulous past. In addition, the description of the way his invention took place, which appears in the first etymological dictionary of Chinese characters dating from c. 120 AD (some 2 millennia after the period in which Cang Jie is supposed to have lived), has been taken as proof that the Chinese script had never been pictographic.

features of Islam that it does not deal with vague generalisations but with one particular language and one particular script, namely Arabic.

Greek and Roman traditions give diverse accounts of the origin of writing, as well as of the political and cultural motivations promoting its creation. Prior to Diodorus' *Bibliotheca Historica*, Greek history and philosophy offered rather meagre information. Even Homer, who knew about the multiplicity of languages existing in the world, made just a somewhat vague reference to 'grim, deadly signs' written on folded tablets (Il., 6. 168-60). Most remembered, and most frequently quoted (though often out of context), is Plato's opposition to writing as an instrument designed to encourage forgetfulness.

Much has been written on the Greek attitude to writing. To give just a few, more history-linked examples: classical Greek tradition attributes the invention of the Greek alphabet to the Phoenician King Cadmus who brought the 16 'Cadmean' letters from his homeland to Boeotia. During the time of the Trojan war Palamedes is supposed to have added four more letters until finally the poet Simonides of Ceos (556-468 BC) added a final four — and so on.

It was, however, the Judaeo-Christian traditions which embedded themselves most deeply into Western thinking. Until well into the 20th century, the concept of monogenesis remained predominant and on the whole unquestioned. At its basis lay the attempt to justify the theory that Hebrew was the original language (and by implication the original script) of the Garden of Eden. This lack of distinction between language and script ranged from such ideas as Adam naming all creatures (Genesis 2:19-20), the declaration of Philo of Alexandria (s. 25 BC–50 AD) that Moses had learned the alphabet (!) from the Egyptians (Eusebius, *Ppraep. Ev.*), to the story of the tower of Babel. In other words, Moses superseded Greek traditions, which were in themselves based more on stories, mythologies and hearsay than any coherent thought. By the Middle Ages the idea of monogenesis was so deeply entrenched in the minds of even the most distinguished Western thinkers (e.g. Thomas Aquinas, Roger Bacon, etc.), that it remained dominant for the next five centuries. The first to raise doubts was Leipniz (1646-1716), who stated that, far from Hebrew being the basis of all languages, it was in itself only the descendant of a much older and much richer form of speech. But Leipniz remained a lone voice. As late as the first half of the 20th century scholars like A. Schmitt could confidently call the invention of writing a *Urerfindung*, made just once, by just one person, in just one place.

Doubts created by such events as the decipherment of the Egyptian hieroglyphs were relatively smoothly overcome by making Egyptian writing dependent on the Mesopotamian *Urerfindung*. The threat posed by the obvious originality of Chinese was defused by vague talk about the descendants of Cain and the lost tribes of Israel. Similar threats posed by the Mayan system were neutralised by further talks about the lost tribes of Israel or by vague references to the possibility of enterprising ancient Egyptians having sailed to America and somehow given the impetus for the development of Mesoamerican culture. Diego Landa, the first bishop of Yucatan on the other hand, was fully convinced that the Mayan form of writing was simply an alphabet.

Moving away from the realm of legend, traditions and mythology towards recorded history, we repeatedly find the names of rulers, kings, statesmen, writers and reformers, Buddhist monks and Christian saints associated with, if not the invention of writing, then at least the creation of a particular script. Both Cyrus the Great (558-629 BC) and Darius (521-486 BC) have been credited with the invention of Old Persian cuneiform. The Tangut script is supposed to have been invented by a Tangut prince in 1036 AD (Grinstead, 1972), just as modern Thai is thought to go back to Sukhotai, a 13th century Thai prince. But a good many of these so-called inventions were in reality either variations of an already existing script or the result of team work. In addition, all 'inventors' and their teams were at least conscious of the existence of writing. By attributing the invention itself to a historically well-documented and highly prestigious personage, the scripts were given additional credibility and, with it, authority.

Hangul - the script of the people

The unsuitability of the Chinese script for the use of the Korean language, and the fact that from the 7th century onwards Korea was a politically independent and unified state, encouraged a number of moves towards more acceptable alternatives. The three most important ones, already discussed here, were *Idu, Hyangch'al* and *Kugyol.* All three were however (like the Japanese *kana* syllabaries) still largely dependant on Chinese. The inadequacy of these compromises became especially apparent in the 13th/14th century AD, when, under Chinese influence, printing with moveable type was brought to Korea. Eventually, in 1446 AD, King Sejong (r. 1418-1450 AD), the great reforming ruler of the early Chosen dynasty, promulgated a simple alphabetic script called Hangul which was to be 'the script of the people', from the Korean word *ham*, meaning people (see Plate 49). Though the king is generally referred to as 'inventor', Hangul was in reality the result of years of research by the king and a team of assistants. Using Sejong's name as sole inventor gave gravitas and authority to the invention.

Hangul consists basically of 11 vowels and 17 consonant signs. The individual consonants are graphic representations of the way the organs of speech are used to articulate them. Vowel forms consist of different arrangements of one long line joined at right angles at the centre of one or two short lines. Syllables are formed on the basis of consonant plus vowel plus consonant. Though a knowledge of the Indian order and use of letters may have played a part, the simplicity of the system and the shape of letters are decisively original. But Hangul met with considerable resistance from the aristocratic elite who perceived it as a threat to their own position. In consequence, the new script,

Plate 49. An example of the work of the contemporary Korean calligrapher Kim Ki Seoung written in Hangul and first shown at the 30th Exhibition of Calligraphy by Kim Ki Seoung in Seoul, in 1990.

though ideally suited for Korean, did not replace Chinese but was used side by side with Chinese characters as an aid for pronunciation, for grammatical words or to clarify ambiguities — similar to the way *kana* was used to support Japanese.

As in Japan, Hangul was thought fit mainly for the consumption of women and people of low rank. This was contrary to King Sejong's own intentions, as he had already issued in 1434 an edict calling to search for 'men of learning and sophistication, without regard whether they are noble by birth or means, earnestly encouraging them and urging them to teach people to read, even women and girls' (Robinson, 1995).

It is not quite certain how the idea of an alphabetic script and especially the form of the letters, both quite contrary to Chinese traditions, arose. Most likely, many elements combined. We know, for example, that the Koreans were in contact with the Mongols who used two phonetic scripts, Uighur (consonantal) and Phags-pa (syllabic), the latter named after a Tibetan lama who developed it at the request of Kublai Khan. Phags-pa was itself based on Indian models. Indian Buddhism, transmitted to Korea through Chinese translation of the original texts, also introduced a knowledge of the scientific order and the phonetically based arrangement of Indian characters. In addition, the Korean alphabet is in practice always written syllabically, with groups of letters arranged in discreet squares, reflecting the structure of the language.

Scripts invented to aid the spread of Christianity

For Christianity, based on the Bible, writing, and with it a certain amount of literacy, were essential elements for conversion. After the fall of Rome, Christian missionaries took the Roman alphabet, the parchment codex and the quill pen along the old Roman routes to the rest of Europe, to people who did not seem to have a script of their own. Later, as a result of military conquest and the creation of vast trading empires, the alphabet also 'colonised' large parts of America, Asia and Africa. Though at one point only three languages (Hebrew, Latin and Greek) were deemed suitable for translating the Bible, missionaries working actively with communities speaking a number of quite different languages realised that success depended on making their texts more readily accessible to the people.

Prophetic religions (unlike Hinduism or Judaism) depend on attracting converts and to succeed in this task they must make their message comprehensible — like traders, they have something to sell. Being neither secretive nor elitist, they rely on the politics of persuasion. Thus during the first Christian millennium several efforts were made to create variations of alphabetic scripts (Greek and Roman) which could be used more effectively to suit the languages of the new converts. Here language did no doubt play an important role but only as part of a new infrastructure serving political/religions aims.

Islam was in a different position. It did not have to invent new scripts since the faith, the language and the message were one, indivisible unit.

West Gothic and Old English

In the 4th century Ulfila, the Apostle of the Goths', left his post as Bishop of Constantinople to return to the Gothic people in what is now Bulgaria. His aim was to translate the Bible into the West Gothic language. But the only script then known to the

Gothic people was the Runes, which for various reasons Ulfila considered tainted by paganism. In order to fulfil his self-chosen mission he created a new, variant script form based on Greek and Roman alphabets, with a few Runic characters added to it. His translation has the distinction of being the earliest, lengthy text in any Germanic language (Luft, 1898).

A combination of Roman characters and some borrowing from a pre-existing Runic alphabet also formed the basis for another script variation. Soon after St Augustine and his Roman missionaries had reached Kent in the 6th century, they convinced the then ruling Anglo-Saxon king that as legitimate heir of Rome he needed a written law-code (Brown, 1998). To prepare this code not only called for an extension of literacy but also for a new script variation. This script, usually referred to as Old English, combined the Roman alphabet with some Runic characters. Both scripts — West Gothic and Old English — raise some questions: was writing solely a Greek/Roman and, with it, Christian contribution or had some form of (written) literacy already been in existence among the Germanic people themselves?

Armenian and Georgian

Sometime between 404 and 406 AD, St Mesrob (c. 361-440 AD) created a system of writing for the Armenian people with the active encouragement of Catholicos Sahak. This new script, which consisted of some 36 letters, was largely based on the Greek alphabet. At first only capital letters were used but in the 13th century a more cursive form, called *notrgir,* developed. Tradition ascribed the creation of the Georgian alphabet to the same St Mesrob, who is thus also thought to be responsible for devising an alphabet for the Albanians of the Caucasus (Lang, 1980). The main Georgian styles of writing are *mkhedruli* (lay hand), still used today, and the old ecclesiastical script which employed 38 letter signs.

Cyrillic and Galgolitic

The origin of the two most important Slavonic alphabets, Galgolitic and Cyrillic, is to some extent connected with the rivalry between Constantinople and Rome, which goes back to the division of the Roman Empire by Diocletian in the 3rd century AD. In the 9th century, after the establishment of a Slav principality in Moravia, King Rastislav of Moravia, in an attempt to free himself from the influence of the Roman Church, asked the Byzantine Emperor Constantine for teachers who could instruct his people in the Christian faith in their own language. Despite the opposition of Rome, which considered only Hebrew, Greek and Latin fit for the translation of biblical texts, Constantine sent the two brothers Cyril (d. 869 AD) and Methodius (d. 885 AD) to Moravia. According to the *Vita Cyrilli,* Cyril, after whom the Cyrillic alphabet is named, is traditionally credited with the invention of a script. Whether this script was Cyrillic or Galgolitic has for long been a matter of controversy but the question has now more or less been decided in favour of Galgolitic (see Plate 50). The two alphabets differ considerably in appearance but as far as the phonetic value of letters is concerned, they are more or less identical, using a total of 40 and 43 letters respectively — today's Cyrillic consists of about 30

Plate 50. The Codex Zographensis, *one of the earliest Galgolitic manuscripts of the Gospels, discovered in the 19th century at the Zograph Monastery located on the Athos Peninsula on the north coast of the Aegean Sea. Many old orthodox monasteries existed on the peninsula but in the 13th and 14th century the Zograph and St Mary Monasteries had the special support of the Bulgarian royal household.*

letters. The majority of them are thought to have been derived from contemporary Greek, though other elements may also have played a role.

Of the two alphabets Cyrillic (see Plate 51) is without doubt the more important one. After a number of reforms, it became the national script of the Slavonic people, finding acceptance among Russians, Ukrainians, Bulgarians and Serbs, together with the Greek Orthodox religion. Eventually, Cyrillic became the Russian alphabet as such. With the arrival of Communism, an uncompromising atheistic 'faith', it was used to serve the new political infrastructure, replacing all other scripts in the European as well as those in the Asian part of the USSR and thus becoming the vehicle of information storage for over 60 different languages. This despite the fact that Cyrillic was often ill-suited to represent some of the languages in Central Asia and in the Caucasus — politics overruling, as so often, linguistic considerations. It will be interesting to see what, if any, changes the collapse of the Russian Communist empire might bring about in the future.

The Samuel Pollard system
Once the task of establishing Christianity in Europe was more or less complete, missionaries began to venture further afield. At first they came mostly in the wake of

Plate 51. One of the earliest Cyrillic inscriptions discovered at the banks of the Lake Prespa in (what is now) Macedonia. The area was once part of the independent empire of western Bulgaria. The inscription reads 'Samuil [r.976-1014 AD] built this in 993 in the memory of his parents Nikola and Ripsimia and elder brother David'.

adventurers, conquistadors and emigrating colonists, giving a veneer of respectability to what was in many cases just greed for new acquisitions, more often than not accompanied by slaughter and genocide. The *raison d'être* of the missionaries being that, while the conquerors and colonists looked for earthly goods, they were there to save the souls of the pagan natives.

After the 18th/19th centuries, with well-established trading companies more interested in permanently profitable trade than in quick acquisition, missionaries became less welcome camp followers, since their zeal was likely to upset the often delicate equilibrium. In addition, some of the 19th century missionaries were genuinely interested in spreading what they considered to be the true faith and very often they supplemented these efforts by furthering education and medical knowledge in general.

At the end of the 19th century Christian missionaries working in southwestern China among the non-Chinese Miao people tried at first to preach the gospels in written and spoken Chinese but this soon proved too difficult. Eventually Samuel Pollard and other members of the Bible Christian Mission started to work on a syllabic script for the Miao language, a task completed in 1904 (see Plate 52). The new script consisted of simple geometrical signs and proved so successful that Pollard's system was adopted for other non-Chinese dialects. In addition, similar syllabic scripts, consisting of Roman capital letters differently positioned and imbued with different phonetic values, were devised by the American Baptist Mission in 1915 and the British and Foreign Bible Society in 1930.

Plate 52. Ta Hua Miao; St Mark's Gospel translated into Miao and written in the syllabic script invented by Samuel Pollard; printed in Shanghai in 1906.

At present the Pollard's system is still used and treated with respect by a significant number of Himong people, former residents of Laos, who are now living in California. Unlike other scripts, which were more or less variations of the alphabet (e.g. Cyrillic and Georgian), the Pollard system is truly original (like Hangul); it is also (unlike Hangul) closer to a syllabic than a truly alphabetic script.

The Cree script

Between 1840 and 1846 the English Methodist missionary John Evans, who lived in the Hudson Bay, created a syllabary which was first printed in 1840. His chart displays cognisant values down the left hand side and vowel qualities across the top. Each symbol occurs twice, the second time in broken form, to indicate an added feature of vowel length. In the next couple of years, two more symbols were added. Cree was one of the most successful script inventions and it is still in use. As a consequence, the Cree nation became fully literate within ten years; in fact, the Cree people could boast a higher level of literacy than contemporary French and English communities living in the same area.

This quick acquisition of literacy reflected the organisation of Cree culture. Structured horizontal, political decision-making was carried out by consensus and mutual support. Nobody actually gave orders to regulate their nomadic lifestyle. Children learned their skills from their parents; there was no need for teachers and schools outside the family group. Thus 70 to 80 years ago Cree-speaking people had one of the highest literacy rates in the world. This rapid transmission from orality to written information storage occurred despite the fact that there was a total lack of institutional literacy (Taylor and Olson, 1995). Little, however, was printed except Christian literature, which provided the main teaching tool. Children were taught by parents; schools were mission schools. But with the introduction of full-time Western-style schooling, younger people began to abandon tribal traditions and with it lost their script in favour of the dominant Roman alphabet. To a very limited extent the script is still used in the Baffin islands.

Scripts as part of a self-respect movement

A number of predominantly phonetic scripts originated in the 19th and the beginning of the 20th centuries in parts of Africa, Asia and — most notably — America, among indigenous communities. Those scripts were in many ways part of a self-respect movement that tried to create its own infrastructure. Though nearly all of them were based on some awareness if not an actual knowledge of the alphabet (in some cases also of the Arabic script), they were not mere imitations but genuine attempts to demonstrate abilities equal to those of Western settlers, traders, teachers, missionaries and administrator. Barnett's theory of cultural change (1953) states that an element in a new configuration must identify with elements in a familiar configuration before it can be accepted by society. The inventor himself must be part of the culture to show that the innovation is an extension of a cultural pattern already in existence. There is, however, one further point to be considered. Even if the inventor's own society accepts the invention as legitimate, the sheer weight of power vested in an alien but dominant group can severely restrict the success of the invention. In nearly all the cases we shall now discuss the new scripts were well thought out, often the result of lengthy experiments, yet in the final instance only few survived and those too became subject to severe limitations.

In northern America, where the original inhabitants found themselves increasingly threatened by white immigrants who took their land, killed their buffaloes and destroyed their way of life, various attempts were made to find means which equalled the 'talking leaves' of the white people. It was felt that this alien form of information storage and information transmission, which enabled white settlers to send messages over vast distances, was part of their success. As a result, a number of gifted indigenous people tried to devise their own forms of written communication.

Alaska Script

The Alaska script has, at one time, received much attention (Schmitt, 1940), which in turn led to a good deal of (non-verifiable) speculation about the development of writing as such. The script is generally considered to have been invented in the Kuskokwim territory of the Alaskan Eskimos. There were in fact several closely related developments that followed each other in quick succession. The most important script innovation was the one connected with the labours of the Eskimo Neck (Uyako), who lived in the area between 1860 and 1924. This particular script seems to have come to the attention of Christian missionaries who, for better or worse, failed to find it suitable for the translation of their own literature. Neck, working with a group of assistants, based his efforts on some picture writing (Jensen, 1970) then in existence among the Eskimos. Gradually he moved, via what could be called logography and the introduction of phonetic elements, towards a form of syllabic writing. Whatever the outcome — in the end the script did not achieve wider acceptance — Neck's efforts were not a mere imitation but a genuine, original attempt to create a script on the basis of indigenous conventions.

Plate 53. Sikway (c. 1760-1843) surrounded by examples of the script he created. The picture is copied from a contemporary portrait painted by Charles King Bird. Though Sikway had contact with white settlers, he did not know English and his script invention was a genuine attempt to find an equivalent to the 'talking leaves' of the white people.

Cherokee

One of the most important 19th century script inventions, as far as America is concerned, was made by the Cherokee Sikwayi (see Plate 53). Initially, Sikwayi created a logography where one character stood for one word. But when, after only one year, the number of characters had increased to several thousands, he began to divide words into syllables. Eventually, after a good deal of experimentation and enlisting the help of English spelling, he arrived at 200 characters, which were later reduced to just 80. Both Schmitt (1940) and Gelb (1963), who considered such script inventions a mirror of the way writing had originated and developed, saw in Sikwayi's script proof of their own theory, namely, that there exists a logical progression which invariably leads from picture writing and logography towards a syllabic script. They also felt that this justified another of their assumptions: once a script has reached a syllabic stage it has arrived at a *Sackgasse* from which it is impossible to progress towards the ultimate gaol of all true writing — the alphabet.

The new script was quickly learned by many Cherokees, first in North Carolina (the place of its origin), and later in Oklahoma, the area to which most Cherokees emigrated after 1830. Newspapers and official documents were printed with type designed in Boston. About 90 per cent of Cherokees became literate. But eventually this script too fell into disuse and was replaced by English and the alphabet. As in the case of other 19th-century script inventions, the Cherokees lacked the political power to maintain their own (written) communication system in the face of increased pressure from the more and more firmly established white settlers. Recently, in the framework of promoting the indigenous people to 'native' or 'original' Americans, some attempts have been made to revive the Cherokee script but this is in the final instance more a manifestation of guilty romanticism than an genuine effort to promote the existence of a different infrastructure.

Chukchi

Apart from the Alaska script, another Arctic script was invented by the Chukchi shepherd Tenevil in 1920. Specimens, consisting of 14 wood-panels inscribed by Tenevil himself and of basically autobiographical content, can now be found in the Arctic Institute in St Petersburg. Little else is known of this script, which remains basically logographic, though there exist some speculations that Tenevil based his invention on a previous (unknown) picture script (Jensen, 1970).

Bamum

In Africa, too, several attempts were made to create an indigenous form of writing. Between 1903 and 1919 King Njoya, together with some of his dignitaries, created a script for his own people. It has sometimes been suggested that the king had initially been influenced by contacts with literate Europeans and Arabic-speaking Haussa traders. However this may be, the new script proved highly original. It started with some, by now little-known, picture signs (Jensen, 1970) but soon introduced phonetic elements in the form of a rebus transfer. At the same time, the number of signs were reduced, from 450 to 80. The system as well as the number of characters remained constant but after the death of King Njoya (1932) the script itself gradually disappeared.

Vai

Vai is one of the most important indigenous West African forms of writing. It was used by the Mende group of the Vai people who lived on the coast of upper Guinea in what was then the Republic of Liberia (Jensen, 1970). Outside Africa it first came to the attention of linguists in 1849 through the publication of an American engineer by the name of F.E. Forbes. The script is supposed to have been invented between 1829 and 1839 by Momoru Doalu Bukere, though subsequent research suggests that his contribution was perhaps limited to the phonetisation of a much older picture script.

One theory suggests that in his early youth Momoru Doalu Bukere came into contact with missionaries who taught him the Bible and with it also some English. However, he seems to have been unable to understand the basic concept of either script or language. Later, when he was employed by slave traders, he was sent to deliver a letter and was greatly surprised that his master knew something he had done in quite a different place — which was in fact the message in the letter he himself had delivered. Tradition tells us that after a dream (an established way of claiming inspiration) he decided to create a script as powerful and effective as that of the white people, which would enable the Vai to communicate over great distances in a similar fashion.

Momoru Doalu Bukere invented signs for sounds, probably based on what he remembered about the alphabet, but his sounds represented syllables not alphabetic phonemes. For the purpose of conveying phonetic elements he used a form of rebus but more as an afterthought than as a truly creative device. It is possible that he had at one time come across the Arabic script but suggestions of this notions are partly (though not solely) based on the direction of the Vai script. The new script spread quickly but, predictably, failed to gain overall dominance. In the event the Vai people now use three different scripts, each connected with a different social activity: Arabic in connection with religion, the indigenous Vai script for letters and occasionally also for commercial records and the Roman alphabet for administration.

Mende

At the beginning of the 20th century, the Mende, a group closely related to the Vai, possessed a script of their own which was discovered in the course of expeditions through their territories in the 1930s (Jensen, 1970). Like the Vai script, it was basically syllabic, using about 190 different signs. The invention is ascribed to an African tailor by the name of Kisimi Kamala, who created it within three and a half months. The fact that the script is written from right to left has led to suggestions of an Arabic influence or at least vague knowledge of the Arabic script on the part of the inventor. But it is equally possible that he took his inspiration from the Vai script.

Nsibidi

Nsibidi (from *sibidi* 'to play', 'to bewitch') was first discovered in 1905 among the Ibo of southern Nigeria. It is an iconographic script, using pictures and concepts, but it can also express abstract concepts. Nsibidi belongs in the realm of secret or enigmatic writing and was used, at least in principle, only by members of the secret Nsibidi society (Weule, 1915). Some signs were also understood by outsiders and some were supposed to have magic qualities. Nothing is known about the origin of this script. This encouraged some rather fanciful speculations, one of them claiming connections with Egyptian hieroglyphs. There exists, however, a charming local legend about how the script was originally taught to the appropriate people by baboons who came and sat round their camp fires.

Somali

In 1960 the newly independent Somalia found itself in need of a script which could be used for its various languages. Since Islam was the official religion, Arabic seemed appropriate. Against this was held that English and Italian were widely spoken in the country, which suggested the use of the alphabet as an appropriate script form. A government committee established to solve the problem put forward 18 different solutions: four suggested Arabic, three the Roman alphabet and 11 a special 'Somali' script form.

The leading Somali script was eventually the Osmanian alphabet, so named after its inventor Osman Yusuf, the son of the Somali Sultan Yusuf Ali. It blended ideas from Italian, Arabic and Ethiopic. The use of distinct consonants and vowels signs and the direction of the script followed what the inventor termed 'the Italian mode'. The order of letters and the long vowels imitated Arabic and the general look of letters showed Ethiopic influence. This was without doubt an imaginative attempt to please all interested groups but a rather cumbersome way of solving the problem of writing and literacy.

In 1961 two scripts were officially selected: Osmanian and the Roman alphabet. In 1969 the government was overthrown and one of the stated aims of the new administration was a resolution to debate the country's writing system. In 1973 the Osmanian system was abandoned and the Roman alphabet became the official script (Robinson, 1995). This is, at least to the onlooker, a somewhat amusing story. It does, however, stop being amusing when one considers the time, effort and resources used for arriving at what would from the beginning have been a simple solution. On the other hand, without going through the process, the solution might never have been acceptable. Politics are seldom connected with common sense.

Bibliography

Barnett, H. G. *Innovation: the Basis of Cultural Change.* New York: McGraw Hill Book Company, 1953.

Berry, J. W. *Human Ecology and Cognitive Style: Comparative Studies in Cultural and Psychological Adaptation.* New York: Sage/Halsted, 1976.

Brown, M. P. *Writing and Scripts; History and Techniques.* London: British Library, 1998.

Dalby, D. *The indigenous Scripts of West Africa and Surinam; their Inspiration and Design.* African Language Studies 9, 1968.

Darell, R. (ed.). *Canadian Languages in their Social Context.* Edmonton: University of Alberta Press, 1973.

Dunning, R. W. *Social Change among the Northern Ojibway.* Toronto: University of Toronto Press, 1959.

Ellis, C. D. *Spoken Cree.* rev. edn., Edmonton Pica Pica Press, 1983.

Fishman, J. *Language and Nationalism: Two integrative Essays.* Rowley: Newbury House, 1969.

Gelb, I. J. *A Study of Writing: the Foundations of Grammatology.* 2nd edn. London: Routledge and Kegan Paul, 1963.

Goody, J.C. (ed.), *Literacy in Traditional Societies.* New York: Cambridge University Press, 1968.

Grinstead, E.D. *Analysis of the Tangut Script.* Lund: Scandinavian Institute of Asian Studies, 1972.

Hair, P. E. H. *Notes on the Discovery of the Vai Script, with a Bibliography.* Freetown/London: Sierra Leone Review, 1963.

Helm, J. (ed.), *Handbook of North American Indians.* Washington: Smithsonian Institute, 1979.

Jensen, H. *Signs, Symbols and Scripts: an Account of Man's Effort to Write.* London: George Allen and Unwin, 1970.

Lang, D. M. *Armenia, Cradle of Civilisation.* 3rd edn., London: Allen and Unwin, 1980.

Ledyard, G. *The Korean Language Reform of 1446: the Origin, Background and early History of the Korean Alphabet.* Amsterdam: Berkley University, 1966.

Lee, P. H. *Source Book of Korean Civilisation.* 2 vols., New York: Columbia U.P., 1996.

Luft, W. *Studien zu dem Aelteren germanischen Alphabet.* Guetersloh, 1898.

Mallery, G. *Picture-Writing of the American Indians.* Washington, 10th Report of the Bureau of Ethnology, 1893.

McLean, J. *James Evans — Inventor of the Syllabic System of the Cree Language.* Toronto: William Briggs, 1980.

Pickering, J. *Ueber die indianischen Sprachen Amerikas. Aus dem Englischen des Nordamerikaners Herrn John Pickering uebersetzt und mit Anmerkungen begleitet von Talvj.* Leipzig, 1834.

Pinnow, H. J. *Die nordamerikanischen Indianersprachen, ein Ueberblick ueber ihren Bau und ihre Besonderheiten.* Wiesbaden, 1964.

Rayfield, D. *The Literature of Georgia. A History.* Oxford: Clarendon Press, 1994.

Robinson, A. *The story of Writing.* London: Thames and Hudson, 1995.

Salia, K. *History of the Georgian Nation.* Paris: Nino Salia, 1983.

Schmitt, A. *Die Alaska Schrift und ihre schriftkundliche Bedeutung.* Marburg, 1951.

Schmitt, A. *Untersuchungen zur Geschichte der Schrift. Eine Schriftentwicklung in Alaksa.* Leipzig: Mit Mitarbeit des Missionars John Hinz, 1940.

Taylor, I. and Olson, D. R. (eds.), *Scripts and Literacy. Reading and Learning to Read Alphabets, Syllabaries and Characters.* Dortrecht: Kluwer, 1995.

Weule, J. K. *Vom Kerbstock zum Alphabet: Urformen der Schrift.* Stuttgart, Frankh'sche Verlag Handlung, 1915.

9.   Rewards and problems of decipherment

Decipherment offers more than the ability to read a new script; it opens a window into an unknown part of human history and with it allows us to re-evaluate the present. Up to the 19th century the history, languages and scripts of Egypt and ancient Mesopotamia were largely unknown quantities. Homer and Greek, Hebrew and the Bible were, even for the most educated person, the earliest records of what was then considered true human civilisation. This is all the more surprising since the monuments and scripts of ancient Egypt were clearly visible to all who travelled through the area. The ancient cities (then admittedly just piles of rubble), as well as important names of Mesopotamian rulers, were known through the Old Testament — even if, in most cases, portrayed in an unfavourable light. There were also the reports of Herodotus, although until the 19th century they were considered somewhat closer to legends than historical facts (admittedly, some of them are). Interestingly, Marco Polo (1254-1324) seems to be suffering exactly the opposite fate: some evidence suggests that his fabled descriptions of China are to a large extent hearsay, picked up in the course of his travels through Persia and Mongolia (Wood, 1995).

Decipherment of the scripts of Egypt and Mesopotamia introduced different concepts (and possibilities) of writing and revealed the existence of political infrastructures radically different to our own. Similarly, the decipherment of Brahmi and Linear B widened our understanding of phonology and, in the case of the latter, introduced us to the fact that the Greek language existed in written form long before the alphabet developed from a Semitic consonant script. The story of the decipherment of these ancient scripts is one of human endurance and intellectual devotion. It has also had its share of jealousy and intrigues, which invariable accompany that type of obsessive ambition which, given the right combination of circumstances, leads to success.

Certain prerequisites are necessary to make decipherment possible: inscriptions of the same text in more than one language, a knowledge of the language for which a script has been used and, last but not least, texts of reasonable length. The story of the decipherment of the Egyptian as well as of the cuneiform script has been the subject of long and detailed discussions and we will here only review it very briefly. Overall, the decisive element of success was the existence of reasonably long passages of the same text, written in different languages and scripts. In a way we can say that Egyptology begins with the discovery and the subsequent acquisition of the Rosetta stone (see Plate 54) by a member of Napoleon's army in 1799. The stone, following the changing fortunes of war, is now in the British Museum. It consists of a slab of black basalt inscribed with the same text in two Egyptian scripts (hieroglyphic and demotic) and a Greek translation written in the Greek alphabet. In 1822 Jean Francois Champollion succeed in breaking the code and opening the way for what would become a flourishing study of ancient Egyptian culture. A good deal of groundwork had,

118

Plate 54. For anybody with an ambition to decipher an as yet unknown script the Rosetta stone provides an almost perfect tool: the same inscription is written in two languages, Egyptian and Greek; the Greek section (at the lower part) can therefore be read without too much difficulty. The two top sections are written in two variations of the Egyptian script: hieroglyphic and demotic. Important names in the Egyptian part are surrounded by oblong cartouches, and since those names can easily be read in the Greek text, they presented an invaluable point of entry into the Egyptian sections.

however, already been done before that date by other scholars, foremost by Thomas Young, whose work diaries are now in the British Library. Young realised that the demotic script consisted of phonetic (which he still perceived as alphabetic) as well as non-phonetic signs and, even more important, that hieroglyphic and demotic, so different in appearance, were only variations of the same script. He also recognised that groups of signs enclosed by elongated oblongs (cartouches) represented royal names and since those names were repeated in the Greek text, he was eventually able to identify the correct value of several signs. Between 1814 and 1818 Young worked hard on enlarging his knowledge. He also communicated his discoveries to Champollion who, however, never acknowledged them officially. In the eyes of the general public, Champollion is still the hero of the story and his devotion to the task was indeed single-minded. Despite having studied Coptic (our only guide to what may have been the pronunciation of the ancient Egyptian language), he clung for several years to the belief that the hieroglyphs were symbols without any phonetic value. This had up to then been a quite commonly held opinion, probably re-enforced by Horapollo, whose book (a 4th century AD Greek translation of a treatise on hieroglyphs) interpreted them as symbolic icons without any scriptorial value (e.g. the picture of goose equals the sun because the sun produces warmth just as the goose shows more maternal feelings than any other bird and so on). For Champollion the turning point came when he discovered that the number of signs in the hieroglyphic text outnumbered the words in the Greek translation three to one and that obviously several hieroglyphs were needed to construct one word. In 1822 Champollion wrote his now famous *Lettre a M. Dacier relative a l'alphabet des hieroglyphes phonetiques* to the Paris Academy, which established his position.

Several scholars and some gifted amateurs, scholar-travellers, even spies (Norman, 1992) had laboured on the decipherment of the cuneiform script since that day in 1771 when the Abbe de Beauchamp dismissed the many clay bricks inscribed with wedge-shaped signs as simply 'too many of them for any of them to have any particular value'. The most decisive moment was without doubt Sir Henry Rawlinson's daring transcription of Darius' tri-lingual inscription (in Old Persian, Elamite and Babylonian) on the sheer rock face of Behistun some 150 feet above ground level. The final act was played out in May 1857 by the decision of the Royal Asiatic Society to invite four scholars (Rawlinson, Hincks, Talbot and Oppert) to submit their translations of the Tiglathpileser cylinder (see Plate 55) text in sealed envelopes. When opened, the translations showed similarities 'so great as to render it unreasonable to suppose the interpolation could be arbitrary or based on uncertain grounds'.

Other ancient scripts were successfully decoded in the course of the 19th century. One was the Indian Brahmi script, decoded by James Prinsep between 1834 and 1839, which introduced new concepts of phonology and grammar into Western linguistics. A number of scholars worked on not one but several different scripts, with varying degrees of success. But no other decipherment matched the excitement following that of the Egyptian hieroglyphs and the cuneiform script and none brought about quite the same public interest and acclaim. There was just one exception: the decipherment of Linear B in 1953 by the British architect Michael Ventris who, building on the work of

Plate 55. The Tiglathpileser cylinder finally decided the decipherment of the cuneiform script. With several scholars claiming to have achieved success, the mathematician William Henry Fox Talbot sent his own translation of the cylinder to the Royal Asiatic Society in London, with the request that Rawlinson and Hincks should likewise submit their translations in sealed envelopes. The Society invited a fourth scholar, the Orientalist Jules Oppert, to join in the contest. The four sealed envelops were finally opened on the 29th of May 1857 by two specially appointed examiners, who concluded that the resemblance of the different translations was 'so great as to render it unreasonable to suppose the interpretation could be arbitrary or based on uncertain ground'.

the archaeologist Sir Arthur Evans and the American classical scholar Alice Kober, recognised that the tablets were not written in an unknown Cretan language but in Mycenean Greek (Ventris and Chadwick, 1958). Ever since Evans's day, and even before, Crete had held a romantic fascination and the fact that most of the tablets dealt with commercial information and not philosophy or literature not only brought some disappointment to those with a more romantic disposition but also showed just how vital and dominant trade related information had been in the ancient Near East and the Mediterranean.

What then of the scripts which are still, totally or at least in part, undeciphered? They fall basically into three broad categories: known scripts in an unknown language, unknown scripts in a known language and unknown scripts in an unknown language. Even if the script is fully and the language at least partially known, decipherment may elude us — a situation amply illustrated by the mystery surrounding the Etruscan language. Despite a large corpus of inscriptions and the fact that we can read the script, we are still unable to reconstruct, or indeed even adequately classify, the Etruscan language. The explanation is almost certainly a politically motivated attempt at the part of Rome to deny its

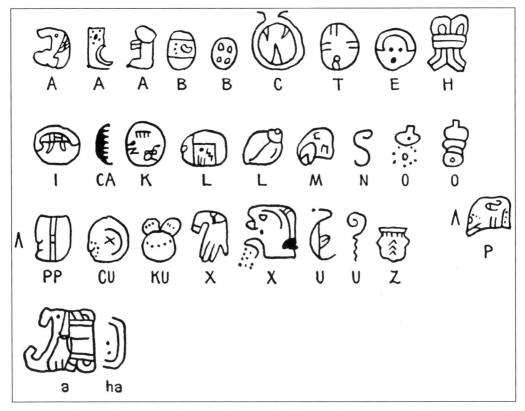

Plate 56. Bishop Landa's Maya 'alphabet' as shown in his Relacion de las Cosas de Yukatan. *A typical example of cultural misunderstanding.*

Etruscan ancestry by erasing its predecessors' language within the relatively short period of just a few centuries.

Ignorance of language has also greatly hampered our understanding of the Oghams, the Runes and the enigmatic Pictish symbol incised on stones in pre-9th century Scotland. The Picts — Caesar referred to them as 'the painted ones' — seem to have represented a fusion of indigenous prehistoric Celtic Iron Age people, using an unknown pre-Indo-European language (Brown, 1998). The disappearance of those languages and the system of information storage they used was probably partly the result of religious politics. From the Middle Ages, when Christianity was firmly established, we sometimes come across stones with Ogham inscriptions but they are often either erased or at least neutralised by having the sign of the cross placed next to them.

If we look for an example of an as yet not fully deciphered script, used for what is a still existing language group, we find it in the Maya glyphs of Mesoamerica. Here too religious politics, bent on the suppression of an indigenous culture, have played a part. Despite many efforts, a full decipherment of the Maya glyphs still eludes us. Even though the first attempts had already been made in the middle of the 16th century by

Diego de Landa (1524-1579), later bishop of Yucatan, who combined a passion for forcible conversion and the destruction of pagan monuments and books with a keen interest in Maya inscriptions and local culture. True to his background, Landa perceived the glyphs as alphabetic, which led to some hilarious misunderstandings between him and his informant, who thought the Spaniard was simply asking for the Maya equivalent of the Spanish names of the letters. Thus *a* became the Maya *ac*, represented by the head of a turtle, and *x* (pronounce *xay*) became *xe* meaning 'to vomit', which Landa's informant duly portrayed for the benefit of the good bishop (see Plate 56).

Over the years the Maya glyphs have attracted many serious scholars. In 1933 and 1952 two Russians (Knorosov and Whorf) tried to read them phonetically and since then J.E.S. Thompson has taken the work a good deal further. But Maya glyphs present a number of intricate problems — apart from the fact that many terms of the language have been lost, for the most part as a result of Spanish word collectors who excluded religious terms from their dictionaries (Thompson, 1972). In addition, the same word can be written in a number of different ways, which makes deconstruction of a symbol into its composite parts far more difficult than the division between a Chinese radical and its phonetic elements. Another difficulty arises from the fact that phonetic elements (syllables, vowels and alphabet-like signs) seem to be arbitrarily intermixed with pictograms, ideograms, synonyms and a rebus-like system. Religious zeal and an alphabet oriented, Euro-centric approach have lost us the ability to find the key to a rich cultural heritage, perhaps for ever.

A good example of the almost insurmountable problems surrounding the decipherment of an unknown script written only in short inscriptions, in an unknown language, is the much discussed Indus script. Until the beginning of the 20th century little was known about this sophisticated civilisation that had flourished in the northwest of India (now Pakistan) some four to five millennia ago. Though we have learned much in the meantime, we are still ignorant about the population's ethnic affinities, their language and despite many efforts and several claims to the contrary, we still cannot read the script.

So far about 400 different signs have been identified and there exists now a tentative agreement about the direction of writing which has been perceived as running from right to left, mainly because empty spaces regularly appear on the left side of a line. But nearly all the inscriptions so far discovered are on seals, the average length of an inscription consisting of not more than five or seven signs, the longest numbering about 20.

In India, more than anywhere else, questions relating to language and script have become the subject of political controversy. Not just controversy but a dangerous one, as the disturbances following the creation of linguistic states after 1947 showed. Many scholars (especially those from the subcontinent) have divided themselves into two different camps. One insists the language was a form of Sanskrit, which is highly unlikely since Sanskrit did not even exist when the Indus Valley civilisation flourished, nor were the Indo-Aryans, who later used a form of this language, anywhere near the geographical area occupied by the city dwellers. The other theory claims connections with the Dravidian-speaking people now living in the south of the subcontinent. In both cases the Indus script is seen as the ancestor of Indian writing as such (Krishna Rao, 1982). All such theories founder on the time factor: the long hiatus between the extinction of the Indus Valley script (c. 1600 BC) and the first documented evidence of a definitely Indian script in the 3rd century BC. In the same way, 2000 years separate the unknown language of the Indus people from the first recorded evidence of a Dravidian tongue.

Despite the fact that speculations like those put forward by the so-called Finnish team in the 1960s (Parpola, 1969/1994), which, for example, identified the picture of a man carrying a yoke with the plural suffix -*kal* in modern Dravidian (derived from *kalai* — bamboo pole; *kallai* — collection, bundle) look seductively convincing, it is highly unlikely that the language itself would have remained practically unchanged for well over three millennia.

Another theory, which surfaces from time to time, tries to connect the Indus script with another undeciphered form of writing found on the so-called *rongo-rongo* (speaking wood) boards of Easter Island (Barthel, 1956; Bahn and Flenley, 1992). This theory rests mainly on the fact that a substantial number of Indus signs look almost identical to those found in Easter Island. But graphic similarity alone is hardly ever a reliable proof of identity. We have only to remember the interest aroused by the discovery, at the turn of the 20th century, of pieces of flint dating from c. 12,000-8000 BC in a cave near the Spanish border. Some of the flints were decorated with signs deceptively similar to some letters of the alphabet, which initiated a good deal of spurious speculation (Jensen, 1970). It is, of course, not totally impossible that a knowledge of certain script signs (though not necessarily their meaning) travelled from India over the span of three millennia and a vast geographical distance as far as the Easter Island but this is hardly a speculation one can use as proof in whatever direction.

Apart from being able to read a particular script, decipherment provides insight into the way political and social infrastructures function at a given time, in a given society. It enables us, for example, to understand the resistance to any extension of literacy whenever scribal arts were in the hands of a privileged class — be they Egyptian scribes or Chinese-educated Koreans opposed to King Sejong's alphabet. We can also begin to appreciate the way certain groups function within society. The *rongo-rongo* boards of Easter Island brought, according to tradition, to the islands by king Hotu Matua in the 12th century AD, acted probably, at one time, as a memory aid for a priestly and/or royal caste, just as the Moso script of the Naxi people of southwestern China and the *kekinowin* of the North American Indians allowed the priest and his chosen successors to retain their (orally remembered) ownership of certain texts. Sometimes such secrecy has from the beginning a special purpose, as in the case of cabalistic practices. In other cases a script and the infrastructure it supports have disappeared and the remaining mnemonic devices simple support vague memories of past conventions. Secrecy is also the main reason for all forms of cryptography created to protect information connected the workings of governments or, especially in times of war, military strategies; in more peaceful time they can also serve commercial interests. The capacity for breaking codes is very similar to that of deciphering forgotten scripts. But since in the case of codes we have a secret script supporting a known language, all codes can sooner or later be broken.

Bibliography

Albright, W. F. *The Proto-Sinaitic inscriptions and their decipherment.* London: Oxford University Press, 1966.

Barthel, T. S. *Grundlagen zur Entzifferung der Osterinselschrift.* Hamburg, Abhandlung aus dem Gebiet der Auslandskunde, 1958.

Bonfante, L. *Reading the Past: Etruscan.* London: British Museum, 1990.

Brown, M. P. *Writing and Script: History and Technique.* London: British Library, 1998.

Chadwick, J. *The Decipherment of Linear B.* Cambridge: University Press, 1958.

Chadwick, J. *Linear B and Related Scripts.* London: British Museum, 1987.

Coe, M.. *Breaking the Maya code.* London: Thames and Hudson, 1992.

Evans, A. *Scripta Minoa. The written Documents of Minoan Crete with special reference to the Archive of Knossos.* Oxford: Clarendon Press, 1909.

Grinstead, E. *Analysis of the Tangut Script.* Lund: Scandinavian Institute of Asian Studies, 1972.

Horapollon, *Hieroglyph.* Trans. G. Boas, New York: Pantheon Press, 1950.

Knorosov, Y. V. and Gurov, N. R. *Review of the Finnish Decipherment of Proto-Dravidian Inscriptions.* Florida: Coconut Grove, 1970.

Mahadevan, I. *What do we know of the Indus Script? Neti neti (not this, not that).* Madras: Institute of Asian Studies, 1989.

Mahadevan, I. *The Indus Script: Texts. Concordances and Tables,* New Delhi: Memoirs of the Archaeological Society of India, 1977.

Norman, J. *Ancient Voices: Decoding Ancient Languages.* New York: Barnes and Noble Books, 1992.

Parpola, A. (et al). *Decipherment of the Proto-Dravidian Inscriptions of the Indus Civilisation.* Copenhagen: Scandinavian Institute of Asian Studies, 1969.

Parpola, A. *Deciphering the Indus Script.* Cambridge: University Press, 1969/1994.

Robinson, A. *The Story of Writing.* London: Thames and Hudson, 1995.

Roy, A. K. and Gidwani, N. N. *Indus Valley Civilisation: a Bibliographical Essay.* New Delhi, 1982.

Shinnie, P. L. *Meroe: a: Civilisation of the Sudan.* London: Thames and Hudson, 1969.

Thompson, J. E. *Maya Hieroglyphs without Tears.* London: British Museum, 1972.

Thompson, J. E. *The History of the Maya from earliest times to the Present Day.* London: Scribner's Sons, 1931.

Trozzer, A. M. (ed.), *Landa's relacion de las cosas de Yukatan. A Translation edited with Notes.* Cambridge, MA, 1941.

Ventris, M. G. F. and Chadwick, J. *Documents in Mycenean Greek. Three hundred selected Tablets from Knossos, Pylos and Mycenae, with Meaning Vocabulary.* Cambridge: University Press, 1956.

Walker, C. B. F. *Reading the Past: Cuneiform.* London: British Museum, 1989.

Wheeler, M. *The Indus Civilisation.* 2nd edn., Cambridge: University Press, 1960.

Whorf, B. L. *The phonetic Value of certain characters in Maya writing.* Cambridge, MA: Peabody Museum, 1933.

Wood, F. *Did Marco Polo go to China?* London: Martin Secker and Warburg Ltd., 1995.

10. Calligraphy — a corporate logo?

What exactly is calligraphy? Since the term itself derives from Greek *graphein* (to write) and *callous* (beautiful) it is often simply identified with beautiful writing as such. But calligraphy is a good deal more. Unlike beautiful writing, it is not just an arbitrary result of some individual effort. It depends largely on the interaction of several, essential, elements: the attitude of society to writing; the importance and function of the text; definite, often mathematically based rules about the correct interrelationship between lines and space; mastery and understanding of the script, the writing material and the tools used for writing. It also demands not only motivation but a definitely perceived need for a visible declaration of cultural unity. Whereas writing supports the infrastructure of a particular society, calligraphy makes a definite statement about the sum total of its cultural and historical heritage. As such it can become subject to political and nationalistic/religious expressions and pressures. In addition, calligraphy unites the scriptorial with the pictorial. A calligraphic passage, or even a single Chinese character, provide information not only through their scriptorial meaning but also communicate on a more direct and archetypal level through their inherent pictorial powers.

According to this definition only three civilisation have produced true calligraphy: the Chinese (and those who use the Chinese script), the Arabs (and those who use the Arabic script) and Western civilisation based on Roman letters, Roman laws and the Christian church. Though visually vastly different, the purpose of calligraphy is in all cases the same: to act as a 'corporate logo' for the whole extended group.

The position of the calligrapher reflects the attitude of society to his craft and the level at which it is practised. In the West, the calligrapher has always been 'in service' - whether to a human master as in Rome, the monastic order to which he had dedicated his life or, eventually, simply to the customer who paid him. The Islamic calligraphers was 'in service' too, but in the service of God and the divine revelation. Only in the Far East did the calligrapher exist in his own right. His work was first and foremost creative (though within strictly defined lines); it did not propagate any secular or religious order but was the expression of his own inner self.

Chinese calligraphy

Chinese calligraphy has from the beginning been closely connected with painting and the pictorial nature of the Chinese script. Painter and calligrapher use the same tools (brush and paper) and are bound by the same aesthetic principles (the division of space by visual symbols). In addition, the multitude of characters (up to 50 000) and the fact that one character can be made up of as many as 36 different strokes allow for a wide range of variations. But though closely interrelated, calligraphy has always been considered the higher art form, and throughout history artists would rather be remembered for their calligraphy than for their painting.

Calligraphy — a corporate logo?

So far, the earliest available examples of Chinese writing go back to the Shang Period (c. 1776-1122 BC) — according to some more recent information from the Institute of Archaeology in Beijing, to an even earlier date. This script, clearly pictographic in character, was followed by some later styles, but Chinese calligraphy as such began during the Han period (206 BC-220 AD). It coincided with the emergence of several congenial factors. One was the invention of the brush (see Plate 57), ascribed to Meng Tian (d. 209 BC). although some kind of brush was probably used much earlier. The other important element was the invention of paper, traditionally attributed to the efforts of Cai Lun in 105 AD, though fragments of earlier examples have recently been discovered. The third important factor was the unification of China in the 3rd century BC under the Qin. To emphasis the new hegemony of the empire, a distinct style of calligraphy was called for. The first Qin emperor is supposed to have instructed his prime minister to collate all existing styles of writing and design a new script, a script that was not only able to meet the growing

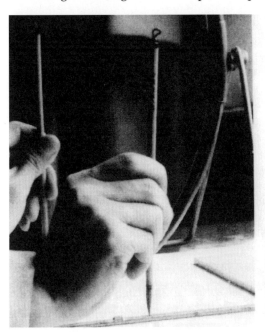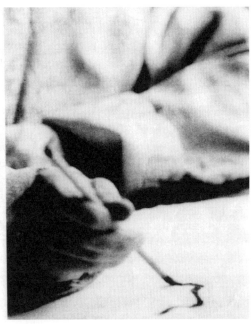

Plate 57. The traditional Chinese brush is about 23-30 cm long; brushes are classified according to the type of animal hair used. For writing the brush must be held vertically and unsupported between thumb and index finger, the middle and ring fingers resting on the holder as guides. The fingers are closed only lightly; Chinese calligraphers claim that it should be possible to hold an egg in the hollow of one's hand whilst writing. Whereas Western and Islamic calligraphers achieved results largely by the way they trimmed the nib of their pens and by the angle at which the pen was held during writing, the Chinese calligrapher relies on rhythm. The brush is lowered, raised, drawn towards the writer, flicked away. Not just the fingers but the hand, the arm, the whole body, indeed the whole personality of the calligrapher must be involved in the process of writing.

demand for more records but was, in addition, able to make a definite statement of the new unity (see Plate 58).

The resulting style, called Xiaozhuan, or Small Seal script, remained in use until the 3rd century AD. Written with the tip of a brush, at first on bamboo or wood slips, each character seems to be executed within an invisible square (see Plate 59). Unfortunately, the new script could not be written with speed — one of the primary reasons for its creation — and another court official is credited with having invented Lishu, which was better suited for this purpose. Lishu also had possibilities for further development and came into its own after the introduction of paper. Because of the speed with which the brush could now move over paper, the thickness of individual lines began to vary, enabling the calligrapher to give them artistic shape and expression. Between 200 and 400 AD three variations of Lishu came into existence: Caoshu (fl. 200-400 AD), Xingshu (fl. from the 3rd century AD to the present); and Kaishu. Kaishu (see Plate 60) became the 'standard' script used for government documents and correspondence, as well as the all important civil service examinations. It is to this day used for writing Chinese as such. But despite its discipline, Kaishu also allows for a maximum of individuality, each line, square or angle, each dot, the structure and the composition of the characters can be shaped according to the will of the calligrapher. The greatest exponents of this style were Wang Xizhi (c. 321-379 AD) and his son Wang Xianzhi (344-388 AD); together they have decisively influenced Far Eastern calligraphy ever since.

Throughout Chinese history calligraphy has been the prerogative of a small, aristocratic and scholarly elite. It is, however, nevertheless deeply anchored in the consciousness of the Chinese people and efforts during the heyday of Communism and the Cultural Revolution to denigrate it as an activity of 'old people' and 'a craze [mainly practised in] the cities' (Beijing Academy of Social Science, 1989) — both, one is given to understand, equally undesirable — have not been successful. Nowadays, calligraphy is again given due official attention, it is taught in schools and gifted pupils receive due encouragement. There are also officially accepted calligraphers who experiment with new styles (something that would not have been possible under the old order where following one's master was considered the highest achievement) and who travel to the West to display and teach their art.

Korea

The Chinese conquest of northern parts of Korea in 109 AD introduced the Chinese language, script, literature and religion to the country. By the time of the unification of Silla in 668 AD, Chinese characters had become the official script of the court. But Chinese characters were ill-suited to transcribe the Korean language and various efforts were made to find acceptable aids for accommodations. Eventually, in 1446, King Sejong promulgated a simple alphabetic script called Hangul which, however, for various social and political reasons, failed to replace Chinese — it also failed, until much later, to create its own calligraphy.

The many foreign invasions have left only few calligraphic fragments predating the sixteenth century but the practice of stone engraving (originally imported from China) provides additional information. It seems that the Unified Silla dynasty (668-935 AD)

Plate 58. Shi Huang Di (259-210 BC), the first Qin emperor ordered his prime Minister Li Si (221-107 BC) to collate the existing writing systems and design a new script capable of meeting the growing demand for documented records. Li Si's response, the creation of the so-called Seal Script, did however prove ill-suited for writing with speed (the main requirement for serving the expanding administration). This is an 18th century example of the style. Chinese calligraphers (similar to Chinese painters) were not encouraged to use their own individuality; they were praised if they could copy the style of existing masters to perfection.

Plate 59. The basis of Chinese painting and calligraphy is space and the division of space by visible objects. Standard Chinese characters seem to be written within an imaginary, subdivided square. When a text is prepared for engraving and printing, the calligrapher will first divide a blank sheet into columns and spaces, with a centre line in the lead column known as variegated space (hua ko) to use as a guide for writing the characters within each space.

was much influenced by (Chinese) Tang models. Contemporary Korean calligraphers based themselves especially on the style of Ouyang Xun (557-641 AD) and that of You Sinan (558-638 AD), who favoured a square, angular form. Around 1350 the style of another Chinese calligrapher, Zhao Mengfu (1254-1332 AD), came into fashion. The resulting *zhao* style retained an enduring influence on Korean calligraphy.

The 20th century saw the emergence of two new trends: in one the influence of Japanese calligraphy from 1920 onwards was again derivative but the other, that started to emerge after the 1960s, concentrated on Hangul. It created for the first time a genuinely Korean form of calligraphy, moving away from centuries of dependency on Chinese conventions and Chinese ways of looking at reality.

Japan

In 307 AD Japan invaded Korea and thus came into contact with Chinese culture. With no script of their own the Japanese accepted the Chinese script, Chinese writing techniques (brush, ink and ink stone) and, after 600 AD, the use and manufacture of paper. But Japanese was, like Korean, ill-suited for the use of Chinese characters and

Plate 60. Chinese translation of a Buddhist sutra *written in fully developed Kaishu script, dating from 700 AD. Kaishu originated around the 4th century AD and is still the standard script for writing Chinese. It was used for government documents, for public and private correspondence dealing with important matters and, eventually, also for printing. The regulations of the civil service examination, enforced during the Tang period (618-907 AD) and abolished only in 1905, stated that each candidate must have a good hand in the regular style. Every Chinese who wanted to become a scholar and enter the civil service (the one depended on the other) took great care to perfect this style and since the civil service examinations were (at least in theory) open to all, this provided an opportunity for upward mobility.*

between the 8th and the 10th centuries two syllabaries evolved: Katakana and Hiragana. The possibility that Japanese could from now on be written in Chinese characters in the syllabic *kana* script or in a combination of both greatly increased the range of calligraphic possibilities and allowed for the creation of uniquely Japanese elements.

Japanese calligraphy begins noticeably in the Nara period (710-794 AD). Some Chinese monks who had come to Japan were not only Buddhist scholars but also accomplished calligraphers. In consequence, a good many Japanese, including some of the early Buddhist emperors, became masters of *kanji* (Chinese script). At first, calligraphy based itself on Tang models and on the work of the 'two Wangs'. A leading role was eventually played by the Japanese monk Kukai (774-835 AD) who, after having studied in China, not only brought back calligraphic specimens but also established an awareness of the theoretic aspects of calligraphy as a major art form. In the course of time various styles using *kanji* developed, all of them based on earlier Chinese counterparts.

This Chinese-based tradition (*karayo*) monopolised Japanese calligraphy until the Heian period (794-1185 AD). At the end of the 9th century Japan officially terminated the embassies to China and Japanese calligraphers began to interpret Chinese models instead of simply imitating them. The final break was made by Kozei (972-1029 AD) and by the 11th century the new Japanese *(wayo)* tradition had established itself. It was followed by courtiers and calligraphers for the rest of the Heian period. Japan's greatest artistic achievement is without doubt the Hiragana calligraphy (see Plate 61) that originated among the women authors of the Heian period. It not only put women into the forefront, it also introduced erotic elements into the practice of calligraphy — a letter written by a prospective lover in a poor handwriting automatically eliminated him or her from serious consideration. Heian models of calligraphy retained their dominant position throughout the Kamakura period (1185-1333 AD) but during the following centuries growing mannerism led eventually to stagnation.

Another, highly original, style of calligraphy was (and still is) practised by the adherents of the Zen sect, established by the monks Esai (1141-1215 AD) and Dogen (1200-1253 AD). The style, which evolved in Zen monasteries especially after the 14th century, is called Bokuseki (traces of ink). The Zen calligrapher does not adhere to traditional aesthetic values but places the ability to communicate an inner state of mind above mere technical considerations. Calligraphy becomes a direct channel of communication between the writer and the onlooker.

Despite its early reliance on Chinese role models, Japanese calligraphy is highly original and highly valued. It is closely connected with that particularly Japanese

Plate 61. Hiragana calligraphy was also referred to as 'women's calligraphy'. It was a style of great elegance, offering sometimes eccentric variations to demonstrate a lady's virtuosity (and with it her suitability as a marriage partner) with the brush.

institution, the tea ceremony. Today it is not only taught in schools but anybody in a position of authority will feel deeply ashamed if his handwriting does not pass muster. Prices for a good piece of calligraphy start around £4000 and masterpieces, sold during one of the large and prestigious exhibitions regularly staged in big cities, change hands for anything up to £1 million.

Islamic calligraphy

Islamic calligraphy begins with the Koran and the need for its precise and appropriate transmission. In the 7th century the Arabs did possess a script called Jazm but it was ill-designed and not widely used. The earliest written copies of the Koran used calligraphic variants of Jazm and were named after the towns where they had originated, such as Anbar, Mecca or Medina. These early Mecca-Medina scripts led to further stylistic developments such as Ma'il, Mashq and Naskh. The most distinguished style, Kufic, developed in the newly conquered territories of Kufah and Basra; it was to have profound effects on Arabic calligraphy. Kufic (see Plate 62) is a bold, elongated and straight-lined script and for the next 300 years it became the sole script for copying the Koran. By the 10th century two variations had emerged: Eastern (or bent) Kufic, developed in Persia, and Western Kufic, which originated around Tunis and became the inspiration for the various scripts of North and West Africa and also Andalusia. After the 13th century Kufic vanished from general use and became predominately a decorative element.

At the same time, a large number of cursive scripts, meant originally for everyday use and commerce, emerged — most of them short-lived and lacking distinction. Eventually, the Baghdad calligrapher Ibn Muqlah (886-940 AD) re-designed these scripts to make them suitable for writing the Koran (see Plate 63). He laid down a comprehensive system of calligraphy based on the 'rhombic dot' (formed by pressing the pen diagonally on paper), the 'standard' *alif* (a vertical stroke measuring a specific number of 'standard dots') and the 'standard' circle, with a diameter equal to the standard *alif*. Ibn Muqlah's reform was successfully applied to the *sittah*, the six major styles: Thuluth, Naskhi, Muhaqqaq, Rayhani, Riqa and Tawqi; similar status was eventually accorded to Ghubar, Tumar, Ta'liq and Nasta'liq. Cursive scripts were further perfected by two famous calligraphers, Ibn al Bawwab (d. 1022 AD), who elevated Naskhi to a major Koranic script, and Yaqut (d.1298 AD), who gave prominence to Thuluth and refined the way the reed pen was cut.

As the sphere of Muslim influence extended from Spain to the Philippines and from central Asia to Tanzania, several new regional styles developed. In the western part of the Islamic empire, which included the countries west of Egypt and, until 1492, also parts of Spain, a distinct style called Maghribi (see Plate 64) developed in Kairouan (Tunisia).

In the 16th century Persian calligraphers evolved a style of great elegance, called Nasta'liq, out of a combination of Naskh and Ta'liq; this script was used mainly for secular literature. With the spread of Persian influence to India, Nasta'liq was introduced to the Islamic part of the subcontinent and eventually also to Afghanistan. During the 14th century a minor Indian style called Bihari evolved that used colour to

Plate 62. A 14th century manuscript by Al-Bukhari As-sahih, *from a collection of Hadith (sayings of the Prophet), written in an ornamental form of Kufic. After the 13th century Kufic lost its monopoly for the writing of Koran texts and became influential in creating ornamental elements of Islamic calligraphy.*

great effect. After the defeat of the Mamluks in 1517, Turkey began to extend its influence over most of the Arab world. From then on Islamic art and calligraphy became increasingly associated with the Ottoman Turks who, apart from using existing styles to great effect, also developed some of their own, such as Diwani and Jali.

As in the case of other countries that had been under colonial rule, the 20th century for Islamic countries has been a time for the re-evaluation of many values. Contemporary Islamic calligraphy, now flourishing in North Africa, the Middle East and Southeast Asia, shows a strong sense of ethnic, religious and national identity. There are well-known developments associated with various schools of calligraphy and there are also (as has always been the case with Islamic calligraphy) a good many patrons.

Apart from traditional forms of calligraphy, there is in addition a rich harvest of new ideas and new experiments but such experiments are always subordinated to the calligrapher's essential awareness of his Islamic identity.

Western calligraphy

All Western styles of calligraphy have their roots in the Roman system of scripts used in the area of the Roman Empire between the reign of the Emperor Augustus (31 BC-14 AD) and the papacy of Gregory the Great (590-604 AD). An important element in

Plate 63. The 10th century calligrapher Ibn Muqlah laid down a comprehensive system of rules based on the rhombic dot (formed by the pen being pressed diagonally on paper), the standard alif *(made up of a specific number of rhombic dots) and the standard circle (which has a diameter equal to the standard* alif*). The size of the rhombic dot depends on the width of the pen and this, together with the number of rhombic dots used for forming the standard* alif, *account for much of the apparent difference in the various calligraphic styles that followed Ibn Muqlah's principles.*

Western calligraphy is the connection between form and function; in general, scripts are either book hands or documentary hands. Book hands, usually the work of professional scribes, exhibit clarity and are often deliberately stylised; documentary hands cover a wider purpose and range from chancery hands to the workaday writings of official and private persons.

Though Roman calligraphy developed with the use of parchment in the early Christian era, the earliest style, Square Capitals, came originally from stone inscription. Each character is based on the square, the circle and the half-square. The square also provides the 'perfect number', namely ten; the width of the main line of each letter is supposed to measure one tenth of its height (see Plate 65). The finishing line (*serif*) at the top and/or foot, a by-product of the way the letters were cut into stone, accentuate the overall impression of harmony. The most used book script of this period, from which all Latin and vernacular handwritings of Western Europe descend, was called Rustic Capitals. It was a slightly more narrow and condensed script form and better suited for the pen. Like Square Capitals, this was still a majuscule script, which means that all letters are of the same height. A more informal script, Old Roman Cursive, used at first mainly for writing on wax tablets and papyrus, eventually influenced the development of minuscule script forms with descenders going below the body of the letters.

Between the 2nd and 4th centuries AD papyrus was finally replaced by parchment and the old classical scroll format of the book gave way to the new Christian codex. Rustic Capitals developed into simpler letter forms, written with a broad pen, that allowed the thickest stroke to fall at right angles to the line of writing. This led eventually to the development of the New Roman System of Scripts, which boasted two elegant book hands: Uncial and Half-Uncial.

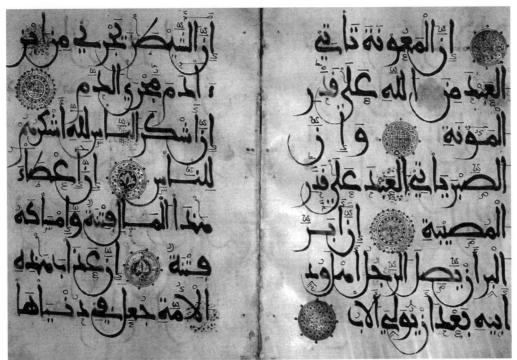

Plate 64. *One of the oldest manuscripts in the Royal Library in Rabat, entitled* Glorious Book of Wisdom: Instruction and Culture. *This text was originally composed by Qadi Abu Abdullah Muhammad (d. 1062). The manuscript is made of gazelle skin and was copied in Valencia, Spain in 1173. The style is the Andalusian version of Maghribi, characterised by a rounding of rectangular angles into curves and semi-circles, especially in the final flourishes of letters which can be extended to touch letters in the next word. Maghribi developed out of Kufic as used in the western part of the Islamic world (northern Africa and Spain). Here the purity of the script was mainly safeguarded by copying established masters and less by strict rules like those laid down by Ibn Muqlah.*

In the period that followed the disintegration of the Roman Empire in the 5th century, Christian missionaries (who, like Muslims, based their faith on the 'book') took the Bible, the parchment codex, the quill pen and contemporary forms of writing along the old (Roman) routes to the northern parts of Europe. Consequently, between the 5th and 14th centuries a number of distinct national hands developed in the various states carved from the disintegrating empire. Just as the Christians had wanted to disassociate themselves from the classical and Jewish scroll format by adopting a new form of the book (the codex), in the same way the various, newly-independent states tried to proclaim their autonomy by instituting new calligraphic script forms to serve as definite and well-defined national logos.

In the course of time many of the great monastic establishments became centres of book production where manuscripts were copied in the *scriptorium;* in the process different localised styles developed — religious politics being added to what had at

LIBERSALOMONIS
IDESTPARABOLAE
EIVSSECVNDVHE
BRAICAMVERITATĒ
TRANSLATAEABEV
SEBIOHIERONIMO
PRBOPETENTECHRO
MATIOETHELIODOR.
EPISHIERONIMVS·

UNCAT epistolaquos iun
git facerdotium immo carta
nondiuidat quosxpi necat
amor. Commentariof in
ofee amof zacchariamma
lachiam quaeposcuitferip
fiffem filicuiffet praeualeau
dinem mittuif folacia fump
tuum natarnof noftrof ecli
bramof fuftentaaif utuobif
potiffimum noftrum defuder
ingenium. Eteccce exlatere
frequenf turbadiuerfa pof
centum quafi aut aequumfit
meuobif efurientib; aliifla
borare. autinrationedatur
accepticui quā prer-uofobngxiuf fim
Itaq; lonza aezrotatione frac
tuf nepaenituf hocanno rea
cerem. etapuduofinutuf effem.
tridui opuf ueftronomini confe
craui. inter praecationemuide
licet trium falomonif uoluminū
mafloth quafhebraeipara

Plate 65. *Regularity, organisation and discipline form the basis of Western calligraphy. These qualities were already apparent in the capital or monumental letters used for the best Roman inscriptions. The basic forms of a letter are based on the square, the circle and the half square.*

Plate 66. *In 796 AD the English cleric Alcuin of York (735-804 AD) accepted Charlemagne's invitation and, as Abbot of St Martin at Tours, took charge of the* scriptorium *to put into effect the emperor's plans for a reform of scholarship, education and the standard for making books throughout his Western empire. This* Biblia Sacra Latina, ex versione vulgate *of Alcuin is thought to have been presented to Charlemagne in the early 9th century. The folio is written in an earlier style which was later superseded by the Carolingian script in which the rest of the book is written. Capitals are used for the headings.*

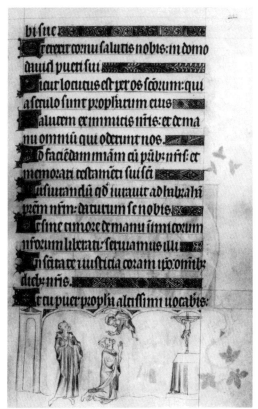

Plate 67. An example of the highest grade of Gothic script (textualis prescissa). Despite the generous proportions of the script, the spacing illustrates why the Gothic script was often referred to as Black Letter (the density of the script seems to turn the page black) or Textualis (a variety of forms on one and the same page can make it look like a piece of woven material). Queen Mary Psalter, c. 1310-1320 AD.

one time only been nationalistic politics. The new scripts were minuscule quatrolinear book hands, written between four lines to accommodate ascenders and descenders. Together with the interchange between capital and small letters in later styles, this became an important element in the formation of Western calligraphy, introducing possibilities for variations in the otherwise limited number of letter forms.

In the 6th and 7th centuries enterprising Irish missionaries introduced Christianity, literacy and the cursive Half-Uncial script to Ireland and soon two distinct Celtic hands emerged: Insular Half-Uncial and Insular Cursive minuscule. When in due course Irish missionaries founded monasteries in Britain (Iona) and on the Continent (Luxeuil, Corbie, St Gall, Bobbio), Anglo-Celtic Insular hands were introduced to a much wider audience. Books produced during this period are amongst the finest achievement of Western calligraphy and manuscript illumination, the two most outstanding examples being the Book of Kells (probably copied in Iona in c. 800 AD) and the Lindisfarne Gospels (written on the island of Lindisfarne around 698 AD).

In 796 AD the English cleric Alcuin of York (735-804 AD) became Abbot of St Martin's at Tours and responsible for the monastery's *scriptorium* (see Plate 66). His most lasting legacy was the creation of a new style, Carolingian (or Caroline) minuscule, a script of great clarity and harmony which was to serve courtly and monastic establishments alike. During the 9th century this new style spread rapidly throughout Europe and from the 10th century onward was also used in England for Latin texts. Soon, however, letters became more compressed, reducing the cost of book production, and by the 12th century a complex hierarchy of formal and cursive scripts developed, variously referred to as Gothic (see Plate 67), Black Letters or Textualis. This script, though never universally admired, nevertheless dominated most parts of

Europe between the 12th and the 16th centuries, in some German-speaking areas for much longer.

After the 12th century the Church began to lose its monopoly, as far as writing, education and book production was concerned, to the newly-established secular scribal workshops which functioned on a more commercial basis. Distinct secretary hands developed in France, England and Germany, and a new range of cursive scripts began to supplant the original book hands for all but the most formal manuscripts. Eventually, in the 18th century, commercial and administrative necessities gave way to the introduction of Copper Plate Writing, a slightly lifeless but highly serviceable script.

The last major calligraphic development before the introduction of printing was the Humanistic system of scripts which started in Florence in association with an essentially literary movement called Humanism. In the 15th century a style referred to as Antiqua was widely used by profession scribes. As the need for speed turned to more cursive forms, yet another style, Italic, developed.

The 20th century has seen new, and in many ways remarkable, developments in the realm of calligraphic traditions. The roots of these development go back to the Arts and Crafts Movement of the 1880s, the work of William Morris (1834-1896) and, most of all, Edward Johnson's (1872-1944) rediscovery of the way medieval calligraphers used their pens. With this came a renewed interest in calligraphy, both in Europe and, perhaps even more so, in America: exhibitions, publications, the foundation of professional societies, teaching at art schools and universities and growing circles of gifted amateurs and fine professional scribes.

Most remarkable and promising for the future is, however, the manifestation of a certain symbiosis that has been developing since the middle of the 20th century between the three major traditions. Some Western calligraphers have begun to take an interest in Eastern conceptions of art and calligraphy. Arabic calligraphers, many of them having studied at Western universities, have begun to look for new interpretations which could be incorporated within the essential core of their own tradition. In practical terms this means that Western and to some extent also Islamic calligraphers no longer see the actual readability of a text as the only way to communicate but, rather like Far Eastern calligraphers, let the shape of letters and the overall composition enable the onlooker to reach a deeper and more direct understanding of the meaning of a text.

Bibliography

Chinese calligraphy

Atil, E. *The Brush of the Masters, drawn from Iran and India.* Washington: FreeGallery of Art, 1978.

Brown, Y-Y. *Japanese Book Illustration,* London: British Library, 1900.

Earnshaw, C. J. *Sho, Japanese Calligraphy: an in-depth Introduction to the Art of writing Characters.* Tokyo: Charles E. Tuttle Co., 1989.

Ellsworth, H. *Later Chinese Painting and Calligraphy, 1800-1950.* New York, 1987.

Fu Shen, C. Y. (et al), *Traces of the Brush — Studies in Chinese Calligraphy*. New Haven: Yale University Art Gallery, 1977.

Fu Shen, C. Y., Lowry, G. D. and Yonemura, A. *From Concept to Context: Approaches to Asian and Islamic Calligraphy*. Washington: Smithsonian Institute, 1986.

Gaur, A. *A History of Calligraphy*. London: British Library, 1994.

Kim, Y-Y. *Hanguk Sohwa Immyong Saso: Biographical Dictionary of Korean Artists and Calligraphers*. Seoul, 1959.

Kotzenberg, H. *Bild und Aufschrift in der Malerei Chinas: unter besonderer Beruecksichtigung der Literatenmaler der Ming Zeit (1368-1644) T'ang Yin, Wen Cheng-Min und Shen Chou*. Wiesbaden, 1981.

Lauf, D. I. *Tibetan Sacred Art: the Heritage of Tantra*. London: Shambhala Publication Inc., 1976.

Ledderose, L. *Mi Fu and the classical Tradition of Chinese Calligraphy*. Princeton: Princeton University Press, 1979.

Legeza, L. *Tao Magic, the Secret Language of Diagrams and Calligraphy*. London: Thames and Hudson, 1975.

Mote, F. W. and Chu, H-L. (ed) *Calligraphy and the East Asian Book*. Princeton: Shambhala Publication Inc., 1988.

Nakata, Y. *Chinese Calligraphy*. New York: Weatherhill, 1983.

Stanford, J. H. *Ikkyu Sojun: A Zen Monk of fifteenth century Japan*. Harvard: University Press, 1972.

Tsien, T-H. *Writing on Bamboo and Silk: the Beginning of Chinese Books and Inscriptions*. Chicago: University of Chicago Press, 1962.

Willetts, W. *Chinese Calligraphy - its History and aesthetic Motivation, Record of an Exhibition held at the University of Malaya in 1977*. Oxford: Oxford University Press, 1981.

Yao, M-C. *The Influence of Chinese and Japanese Calligraphy on Mark Tobey (1890-1979)*. San Francisco, 1983.

Islamic calligraphy

Abbott, N. *The Rise of the North Arabic Script and its Kur'anic Development*. Chicago: University of Chicago, 1939.

Ahmad, S. B. *Introduction to Qur'anic Scripts*. London: Curzon, 1984.

Babinger, F. *Die gross herrlichenTughra: Beitraege zur Geschichte des Osmanischen Urkundenwesens*. Leipzig, 1975.

Dodd, E.G. *The Image of the World: a Study of Quranic Verses in Islamic Architecture*. Beirut, 1981.

Edgu, F. *Turkish Calligraphy*. (English trans.). Istanbul: Ada, 1980.

Gaur, A. *A History of Calligraphy*. London: British Library, 1994.

Khatib, A. and Sijelmassi, M. *The Splendour of Islamic Calligraphy*. London: Thames and Hudson, 1976.

Lings, M. and Safadi, Y. H. *The Qur'an*. Catalogue of an Exhibition of Qur'an Manuscripts at the British Library, 3 April-15 August 1976. London: 1976.

Minorsky,Y, V. *Calligraphers and Painters; A Treatise by Qadi Ahmad son of Mir-Munshi (ca. A. H. 1015/A.D. 1606)*. Translated from the Persian with an introduction by B. N. Zakhoder. Washington: Smithonian Institute, 1959.

Nath, R. *Calligraphic Art in Mughal Architecture*. Calcutta: Iran Society, 1979.

Rice, D. S. *The unique Ibn al-Bawwab Manuscript of the Chester Beatty Library*. Dublin: Chester Beatty Library, 1955.

Safadi, Y. H. *Islamic Calligraphy*. London: Thames and Hudson, 1978.

Schimmel, A. *Calligraphy and Islamic Culture*. 2nd edn., London: I. B. Tauris and Co., 1990.

Schimmel, A. *Islamic Calligraphy: Iconography of Religions*. Leiden: Brill, 1970.

Welch, A. *Calligraphy in the Arts of the Muslim World. Catalogue of an Exhibition shown in Asia House Gallery in the winter of 1979*. Austin: University of Texas Press, 1979.

Western calligraphy

Aris, R. *Explicatio Formarum Litterarum: The Unfolding of letters from the first century to the fifteenth.* Minneapolis: The Calligraphy Connection, 1990.

Bischoff, B. *Latin Paleography.* Cambridge: University Press, 1990.

Boyle, L. E. *Medieval Latin Palaeography, a Bibliographical Introduction.* Toronto: Univeristy of Toronto, 1984.

Brown, M. P. *A Guide to Western historical Scripts from Antiquity to 1600.* London: British Library, 1990.

Child, H. (ed.), *The Calligrapher's Handbook.* new edn., Pentalic, Faber and Faber, 1985.

Child, H. (et al). *More than fine Writing: The Life and Calligraphy of Irene Wellington.* New York: Overlook Press, 1986.

Child, H. (ed.), *Calligraphy Today: Twentieth-century Tradition and Practice.* 3rd edn., London: Blackwell, 1988.

Cobbden Sanderson, T. J. *The ideal Book; or the Book Beautiful, a Tract on Calligraphy.* Berkeley: University of California, 1982.

Drogin, M. *Medieval Calligraphy: its History and Technique.* London: Montclair, 1980.

Fairbank, A. *The Story of Handwriting: Origin and Development.* London: Faber and Faber, 1970.

Fairbank, A. and Wople, B. *Renaissance Handwriting: an Anthology of Italic Scripts.* London: Faber and Faber, 1960.

Filby, P. W. *Calligraphy and Handwriting in America 1710-1961 assembled and shown by the Peabody Institute Library, Baltimore, Maryland, November 1961-January 1962.* New York: 1963.

Gaur, A. *A History of Calligraphy.* London: British Library, 1994.

Gray, N. *A History of Lettering: creative Experiment and Letter Identity.* Oxford, Phaidon, 1986.

Jackson, D. *Copperplate Calligraphy.* London: Macmillan, 1979.

Johnston, E. *Formal Penmanship and other Papers.* ed. Heather Williams. London: Lund Humphries, 1971.

Johnston, E. *Lessons in Formal Writing.* eds. Heather Child and Justin Howes. London: Lund Humphries 1986.

Johnston, E. *Writing and Illumination and Lettering.* J. Hogg 1906, re-issued Pitman 1948, re-issued A and C Black, Tapling, 1983.

Knight, S. *Historical Scripts: a Handbook for Calligraphers.* London: Blackwell, 1984.

Lindsay, J. *William Morris: his Life and Work.* London: 1975.

Parkes, M. B. *English Cursive Bookhands 1250-1500.* Oxford: Clarendon Press, 1969.

Shelley, D. A. *The Fraktur — Writings or Illuminated Manuscripts of the Pennsylvanian Germans.* Allentown: Pennsylvanian German Folklore Society, 1961.

Stansky, P. *Redesigning the World: William Morris the 1880s and the Arts and Crafts Movement.* Princeton, 1985.

Tarr, J. C. *Calligraphy and the Chancery Script.* San Leandro, California, 1973.

Whalley, J. I. *The Pen's Excellence. Calligraphy of Western Europe and America.* Tunbridge Wells: Midas Books, 1980.

11. What is a book?

The purpose of a book is to store intellectual information for multiplication and further transmission. To this end the author can make use of codified symbols (scripts) but also pictures, photographs, drawings, musical and other notations or mathematical formulae. A book can either be written by hand (manuscript from the Latin *manu* — hand and *scripti* — writing), printed (by block print or moveable type) or lithographed; it can also be a computer printout or a disk. An inscription, however often copied, is not a book — neither is a private document. A book is, furthermore, meant for circulation; it must therefore be portable and have a reasonable amount of physical stability. Circulation in turn presupposes organisations for production, distribution and sale, as well as arrangements to ensure preservation in private or public libraries. Books are valuable private and/or public property, property which has to be safeguarded by appropriate laws.

Shape and material

Overall agreement exists as far as the purpose of the book is concerned. But when it comes to its physical appearance and shape, we are confronted by widely different facts and concepts. Broadly speaking, the shape of the book is greatly influenced by the material used for its production. The reason why a particular material is chosen at a particular time, in a particular place, depends in turn largely on geographical availability and the stage of technological development. Some materials, such as wood, leaves, bones, tortoiseshells or tree bark seem to suggest themselves, being freely available in most parts of the world and needing only a minimum of treatment to turn them into books. In this way bamboo seemed the obvious choice for China (being replaced by wood once the administration moved to areas where bamboo was no longer freely available), palm-leaves for India and southeast Asia, clay bricks for Mesopotamia and papyrus for Egypt, as long as the plant grew plentifully in the Nile Valley. Some materials became possible only after a capability for handling and transforming (or recycling) raw materials had been reached. Into this category fall metals, cotton, linen, silk, parchment, vellum and finally paper. Tradition can have a modifying influence when choosing materials suitable for book production. Parchment was practically never used further east than Iran since Hindu and Buddhists alike would have deemed it unthinkable to use so 'unclean' a material for their sacred texts. Right through recorded history human ingenuity has applied itself to the problem of providing suitable writing materials and in the process arrived at a variety of widely different yet equally successful solutions.

Cultural traditions not only influenced the choice of material but often also the type of book chosen by a particular group. A further consideration, which brought its own problems, especially when trying to speculate about the early stages in the development of certain scripts, is the question of durability. Much may have been written on simple leaves which perish quickly in adverse climate conditions. Indian palm-leaf manuscripts, for example, are easily prey to insects and the damp monsoon weather. In consequence, most manuscripts found in India itself seldom predate the 15th century; the few surviving early examples come mostly from the northwest of what is now Pakistan or from central Asia. Even papyrus, a fairly durable material, does not withstand European weather conditions; the majority of early Greek examples still extant have been found in Egypt, where the dry climate protected them from destruction.

Nowadays most Western people and people influenced by Western concepts will automatically associate the term 'book' with the codex — a collection of folded pieces of paper, all cut to the same size, covered with print on both sides and held together, between covers, by glue and string. Yet the codex gained dominance only after 400 AD. Effectively, paper was not used in Europe before the 14th century and European printing did not start before the middle of the 15th.

The form of the book the codex replaced, after having existed with it side by side for some 400 years, was the scroll (or roll, the term being interchangeable in common usage), which had dominated the cultural life first of Egypt and later of Greece and Rome. The format that provided the model for the codex was the waxed tablet (Bowman, 1983) used in the ancient and classical Mediterranean world and also in the Near East (wax-tablets dating form the 8th century BC have been found in the Assyrian city of Nimrud). The material which made the codex possible was parchment; papyrus splits easily when folded and is better suited for being inscribed on one side only. Parchment had been known in Rome since the 1st century BC. According to a story told by Pliny the Elder, King Eumenes II of Pergamum (hence the term) in Asia Minor (197-158 BC) invented it in response to an embargo of papyrus, instigated by a jealous Pharaoh who was a rival book collector. Political as well as religious considerations play a considerable part, not only in relation to scripts and writing systems, but also as far as the choice of writing material and the shape of the book are concerned. This is hardly surprising since the book, being easily moveable and easy to consult, can serve the infrastructure more effectively than any, however splendid, inscription.

Scrolls, made from sheets of papyrus, originated in Egypt. Papyrus is an exceedingly pleasing and, in the right climatic condition, reasonably durable material. The earliest extant example so far discovered comes from a grave in Saqqara and dates from the Early Dynasty period (c. 2925-2775 BC), which indicates that by then knowledge of making papyrus was well established. There are also some stone inscriptions of the same date that depict scribes with scrolls. Since the days of antiquity much has been written about the use and the production of papyrus. Basically, carefully cut pieces from the inner stem of the plant are laid cross-wise (one layer on top of the other) on a special table, pressed and beaten together and then dried in the sun. Some type of adhesive was probably used (starch, a special type of glue or just Nile water) but none of the classical Arab writers is very clear on this point. Several sheets stuck together constituted a scroll, which could be of varying length, the average being some 20 sheets. Exceptionally long scrolls, like the Great Harris Papyrus (c. 1766 BC), now in the British Museum, are an exception. The text could be written continuously across the whole scroll from top bottom — exceeding awkward for consultation. Later, especially in Greek and Roman times, a method was preferred by which blocks of writing were arranged in columns some 7 to 8 cm wide, which followed each other — the first attempt of what we would later call a page. This method was adopted, more or less unchanged, once parchment took the place of papyrus. When not in use, a scroll was kept with an *umbilicus*, a rod inserted in the middle to give it more stability. Leather or pottery containers were used for what would later be called book covers and an indication of the subject was written either on the outside of the scroll or on a piece of papyrus affixed to it. The papyrus scrolls in the great library of Alexandria (founded c. 184 BC) were carefully indexed according to the *incipio*, the first word or sentence of the text — a forerunner of what later became a book title. Papyrus was never a cheap material and at times some scrolls were not only inscribed on both sides but the original text was washed off to make room for a new one — a scroll used in this way is referred to as a palimpsest (from Greek *palin* — again; and *psestos* — scraped, rubbed).

Leather scrolls, documented in Egypt from the 24th century BC, which later played an important role in Jewish ritual (to this day the Torah used in the synagogue must be made of leather), were more durable than those fashioned from papyrus; they were also heavier and altogether more cumbersome. It was only after parchment, more flexible and offering the possibility of being inscribed on both sides, came into general use in the 2nd century BC that a further step was made towards the codex format.

If parchment provided the ideal material, the 'book' which gave the codex its decisive shape was the waxed writing tablet. A pile of wooden tablets held together by clasps, with a leather cord passed through pierced holes, already looked quite similar to a modern codex. Indeed the Latin term *codex* was first used to describe a plurality of writing tablets. Other elements that favoured the change of format were the ability to increase the size of the book to accommodate even the most lengthy texts (especially after folded parchment sheets stitched together replaced wood); the possibility of using space more economically (writing could now be done on both sides); and, last but not least, the easy accessibility of passages anywhere in the text. All this may, however, not have been enough to bring about so revolutionary and far-reaching a change, especially since it necessitated the elimination of long established and highly regarded conventions. Only a combination of cultural change, together with technological innovation, could overcome the natural conservatism of professional scribes and that of the book-using section of society. Writing a codex demanded new skills: it meant calculating space ahead, keeping sheets in their right order (pagination), problems not inherent in the production of a scroll. The main intellectual and, as it turned out eventually, also political force behind the change was in all likelihood the advent of Christianity, a text and book oriented, proselytising religion which between 100 and 400 AD replaced the old, state related, Roman cults and rituals.

The emerging status of the codex, suitable for more than note-taking, is first mentioned in Latin texts. Martian (40-104 AD), in a number of somewhat controversial passages (*Epigrams* XIV. i. 1) refers to literary publications in (parchment) codex form, adding that because of its format the codex was especially suited for travellers and bibliophiles. The next, more decisive evidence can be found in the writings of Roman lawyers who, when drawing up wills and bequests, had to make a clear distinction between a book and a private document. Paulus, who became Praetorian Prefect in 223 AD, finally defined the book as a self-contained unit, independent of material and form (*Sententiae* iii. 6. 87). He also mentioned, for the first time, the term *codex*, thus providing the new book format with an official status, something that had up to then been the prerogative of the papyrus scroll.

During the three millennia when the book had predominately been a scroll, first in Egypt and later also in the Mediterranean countries, another format dominated Mesopotamia and the ancient Near East: the clay tablet (see Plate 68). Together with Egyptian papyrus sheets, clay tablets were the first reliable writing material produced by artificial means. Specially prepared clay, suitably inscribed, was either dried in the sun or, depending on the importance of the text, baked in a kiln. Despite their unprepossessing appearance, clay tablets constituted books of remarkable durability. Even the great temple and palace fires, which periodically swept through attached libraries, only served to hardened them. In addition, like the codex, clay tablets could easily be carried around, taken on journeys and held in one hand while writing or reading.

Physically their format differed. The earliest examples, dating from around 3000 BC, were small, square, thumb-sized tablets. By 2800 BC larger tablets made an appearance, which warranted a different way of holding a tablet during writing; this, in turn, greatly influenced the direction of the script.

When at the beginning of the Christian area the power structure inside Mesopotamia collapsed and cuneiform was replaced by simpler writing systems, traditional book production came to an abrupt end. Unlike in Western countries, and as we shall see later in the Far East, there was no indigenous transition to another form of the book. The Mesopotamian clay tablet books, together with the cuneiform script and the languages they had both served, became obsolete and in time forgotten. The once splendid cities with their vast palace and temple libraries vanished under mounds of rubble; eventually even their location was forgotten. It was not until the 19th century that the clay tablet book and the cuneiform script were, so to speak, 're-discovered'.

At the time when the book was predominately a papyrus scroll in Egypt and the Mediterranean and a clay tablet in Mesopotamia, in China it was a collection of thin bamboo strips. In place of bamboo, wooden slips (of the same shape) were also used and there exists a theory that bamboo was replaced by wood once the administration moved into areas where bamboo was no longer readily available. Both bamboo and wood slips had notches which enabled them to be laced together (see Plate 69) to accommodate even the most lengthy texts.

With the arrival of paper the shape of the book changed. According to tradition, paper was invented by Cai Lun, a eunuch at the court of the Han Emperor Wu Di, in the year 105 AD. It is, however, more likely that Cai Lun was in reality the supervisor of an on-going project, charged with collecting information about experiments in paper-making, based on the knowledge of making paper out of the still very expensive silk rags. Whatever the exact date of the invention (and fragments pre-dating the 2nd century AD have recently been discovered), paper was considerably cheaper, since it substituted tree bark, fish-nets and old rags made of raw fibres for silk. Once paper had

Plate 68. Clay tablets were one of the earliest forms of the book. After having been inscribed they would be dried in the sun or baked in a kiln. They were carefully kept and indexed in vast palace and temple libraries and, despite their unassuming appearance, proved remarkably resilient. Two tablets found in Tell Mardikh (Ebla) showing a tabulation of sheep (left) and of articles of clothing (right). The impression of circles and half-circles represent numbers. c. 2,400-2,000 BC.

come into common use, the Chinese book took on the form of a scroll, inscribed on one side only and kept rolled up when not in use. The most famous Chinese book, dated, complete and already printed, is a Chinese translation of the *Diamond Sutra* from the year 868 AD; it is now in the British Library.

Together with Buddhism the scroll format was transmitted to Korea and Japan. There are basically two different scroll formats: hand scrolls or horizontal scrolls and hanging scrolls; the latter could be hung on the wall of a scholar's study. Similar hanging scrolls (*tangkas*), painted or embroidered with Buddhist themes, were also popular in the Himalayan countries: Tibet, Nepal, Sikkim, Bhutan and Ladakh. Painted scrolls illustrating the Hindu epics can still be found in India and until recently also in East Java.

Within Islam the book has always stood at the centre of the religious, intellectual and political life of the community. Western manuscripts were only one avenue for artistic innovation; in the Muslim world the book was, from the 8th century onward, the primary aesthetic source. As such it forged a unique relationship between verbal and visual expressions which made it one of the most distinguishing features of Islamic art. Royal patronage and the *madarasas* (schools) attached to mosques promoted the book as the main vehicle of learning. The Koran presents the sum total of divine revelation given in Arabic to the Prophet. The words of the Koran are deemed to have been culled

Plate 69. Early Chinese books consisted of bamboo or wood slips which could be bound together to accommodate even the most lengthy texts. This, a military register of munitions supplies for a government office at a far western military base, consists of 77 wooden slips altogether.

from the *Uma al-Kitab* (the Mother of Books), which is written with the celestial pen, recording all that has and will happen in the course of time.

In south Asia the earliest references to writing can be found in the Pali Buddhist Canon of the 5th century BC, where various writing materials are mentioned: leaves, wood, metal and bamboo slips. We are told nothing about the nature of these leaves but they could hardly have been those of the talipot palm which is indigenous to southern India. It is interesting to note that despite the fact that much is known about the social history and the material culture of ancient India, there exists an almost total silence about books as physical objects. The lengthy inventories about what Buddhist monks could and could not own never mention books — yet books seem to have existed in one form or another, as the recently discovered example of a Buddhist Canon written on birch bark demonstrates. At the time of Alexander's invasion (326 BC) narrow slips of bark were used, sometimes rolled up, which has provoked occasional speculation about connections with Greek papyrus scrolls. Some (much) later bark leaf books, consisting of folded sheets between leather covers, could create a codex-like appearance. But again, it would be inaccurate to see this as proof of foreign influence. The possibilities of suitable materials are, after all, limited and the discovery of their usefulness was most certainly not made just once in just one place.

The Indian book *par excellence* was, however, well into the 19th century, the oblong palm-leaf manuscript. Three species of palm trees provided material suitable for writing: the talipot palm, the palmyra palm and, especially in southeast Asia, the lontar

Plate 70. Palm-leaves were until quite recently the most important material for making books in India, Sri Lanka and parts of southeast Asia. In Thailand this material was called bailan *and the script was no longer always incised with a stylus but often also painted in gold or lacquer on a black or red background. All three examples are written in the Khmer script.*

palm. To prepare them for writing (with pen and ink in the north and with a metal stylus in the south) each leaf has to be separated from the centre, cut to size, then soaked and boiled (in milk and/or water), dried, usually several times, until it is finally smoothed down with a cowry shell or a stone. Individual folios were secured between wooden boards by a cord running through one or two holes and the cords was then tied around the whole book (see Plate 70). Though wood is the most commonly used book cover, in the case of especially important manuscripts or those commissioned by rich clients, gold, ivory or silver was sometimes used, especially in Sri Lanka and southeast Asia. The shape of the palm-leaf greatly influence the appearance of the book in India, and also in southeast Asia. Even when lacquer, cloth, metal, copper (for charters acting as title deeds), ivory or eventually, after the 13th century, paper were used, the characteristic oblong shape was frequently retained. Despite the fact that there was no longer any need for a cord securing the pages, empty spaces were still left in the text in the appropriate places. Since they no longer served any practical purpose, they eventually became convenient centres for ornamentation (see Plate 71).

Another book format is the folding book (see Plate 72) which appears in geographically widely different locations: in southeast Asia, Japan and also in pre-conquest Mesoamerica. Only few Mesoamerican examples have survived which, for

Plate 71. A palm leaf-shaped paper manuscript of the Jain Kalpasutra, *from Gujarat, dated 1502/1445. The large spots mark the places where previously the cord was passed through the palm leaf folios to secure them to the wooden covers.*

some reason, are wrongly referred to as *codices*. They were folded concertina-wise, with the last page meeting the first and, when not stored, could be hung on the walls of houses.

Bookbinding

The idea of putting protective covers around a book occurred at quite an early stage of development. Since parchment has a tendency to buckle when subjected to changes in temperature, stiff covers were necessary to protect the codex. Such covers were usually made of wooden boards and fastened with a clasp — similar to the methods used for waxed writing tablets. In due course the wooden boards were covered with leather; especially valuable books would have covers encrusted with engraved gold or silver, enamel, ivory or precious stones (see Plate 73).

The basic form of the codex consisted of sheets of parchment or vellum, all cut to the same size and (usually rectangular) shape, which were folded to form what is called a 'gathering'. A sheet folded once made a folio of two leaves, four sheets making eight folios or sixteen leaves produced a *quaternio*, a term from which comes the word 'quire'. The folded packages were subsequently stitched together and placed between thin wooden covers. In fact, the codex was in many ways responsible for the introduction of bookbinding, both as a practical necessity and eventually also as an art form. The earliest elaborately decorated bindings were those made for books used at the altar. Book covers provided an opportunity to decorate the outside of the book in the same way as illustrations decorated individual pages. Apart from various binding techniques which developed in the course of time, some basic elements had to be considered, such as the direction of writing. Christian books, using scripts running left to right (the Greek or Roman alphabet) stitched the sheet on the left side, Arabic and Jewish book on the right.

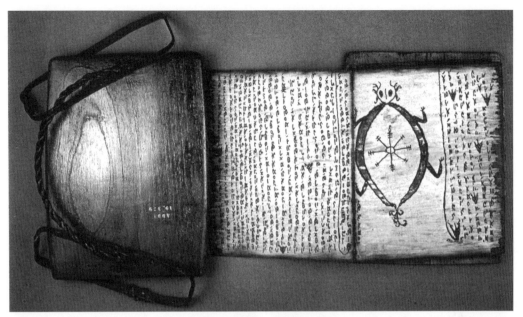

Plate 72. A pustaha *(from the Sanskrit word for book,* pustaka) *as used by the medicine men of Sumatra. The inner bark of a tree is fashioned into long strips and then folded accordion-wise; the writing is done with black or white ink. Usually such books have protective wooden covers, sometimes decorated with carvings in low relief; two strings of plaited bamboo provided additional security. Since medicine men were essential to the welfare of the whole community, a* pustaha *could protect the carrier when walking though hostile territory.*

Modern books are still bound in very much the same fashion. Paper sheets are thinner; they can also be larger and it is possible to fold them more often. Since both sides of a sheet of paper are identical — unlike parchment which distinguishes between recto and verso — a page replaced the folio as the smallest accountable unit. The four basic elements necessary for the production of a codex are the folded sheet, the gathering, the stitching and the protective covers.

Some of the earliest Egyptian Coptic book bindings consisted of papyrus leaves pressed together, with the cord going directly from section to section, rather like the modern machine sewn book. Later, leather was used. The oldest known leather bindings were those used for Coptic manuscripts in the 7th and 8th centuries; they precede by more than 500 years all but a handful of Western examples. From Christian Egypt the craft of bookbinding extended to other parts of the Near and Middle East; in the wake of Islam it spread to Syria, Arabia and across North Africa to Spain. Ethiopic books were bound between boards and in addition often kept in leather bags called *mahedar*. The bags had attached straps so that the book could be carried slung over the shoulder or hung on a peg in the house.

The earliest form of the Japanese book modelled itself on the Chinese hand scroll, a format that was to dominate the Far East for nearly a millennium. Scroll books are

Plate 73.1a and 73.1b. A traditional Coptic book binding: packets of leaves between wooden covers.

 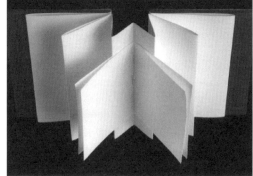

Plate 73.2a and 73.2b. Two examples of a concertino books binding, one of triangular shape.

 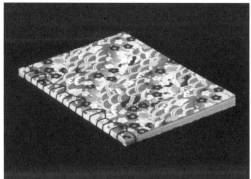

Plate 73.3a and 73.3b. Examples of Japanese book binding.

All bindings in Plate 73 have been made by the contemporary book binder Hilary Henning.

easily stored but awkward to read (unroll). During the Heian period (794-1185 AD) some additional books forms, also based on Chinese models, developed. The simplest one was the folding books with covers on both sides. A popular format, the so-called butterfly book, developed at the same time. It consisted of sheets of paper each folded into half with the text facing inward. These were stacked and then pasted together along the spine-fold, so that the back of each sheet was attached to the back of the neighbouring sheet. This style lasted until the 17th century and derived its name from the fact that the open pages of the book stood out like the wings of a butterfly.

Since pasted bindings were sensitive to insect damage, a new type of thread-sewn binding developed in the 12th century. It no longer relied on Chinese examples but was uniquely Japanese. Known as the multi-section book, it resembled Western signature bindings. A number of pages were stacked and folded into half to form a section, then several sections were stitched together through the centre fold. This type of book was mostly used for handwritten anthologies, novels and diaries. After the 14th century it was replaced by pouch binding, a Chinese type of sewn binding that eventually supplanted all other styles and is now considered the most typical format of the Japanese book. It is made of sheets, inscribed or printed on one side only, folded in half with the text on the outside, and stacked together. Covers are added on both sides and the book is stitched along the spine (the edge opposite the fold) so that each double-leafed page forms an envelope which is open on the top and also at the bottom of the page.

In Japan printing was for many centuries a Buddhist monopoly and, until the 17th century, religious subjects constituted the bulk of all printed material. Paper was expensive and only monasteries, centres of wealth and learning, could afford to produce it. During the Edo Period (1603-1868 AD) the unification of the country and the growth of cities brought about an increased demand for books. The Meiji Restoration of 1868 introduced Western technology and with it Western-style books where the text was printed with metal type on machine-made paper. Nowadays, traditional types of books and traditional book binding are in the hand of a limited elite of dedicated binders, scholars, artists and bibliophiles who cater for a small but select audience.

Illustration and illumination

The purpose of illustration can be twofold. It can support the meaning of the text, highlight important ideas and passages but it can also re-tell the text in visual terms for the benefit of those with little or no knowledge of reading. The latter has been a consideration in the case in many Christian, Buddhist, Hindu and Tibetan books, as well as certain types of southeast Asian manuscripts which consist primarily of pictures. Sometimes the illustration can be dominant with the text serving only as an explanation. Children's books and the popular strip-cartoons fall into this category. In some cases illustrations tell a story quite different from the written text. Pertinent examples for the latter come from Sri Lanka where texts are never illustrated because Theravada Buddhism does not encourage monks to take delight in visual beauty. But the wooden covers, which are the work of lay craftsmen who are not bound by such restriction,

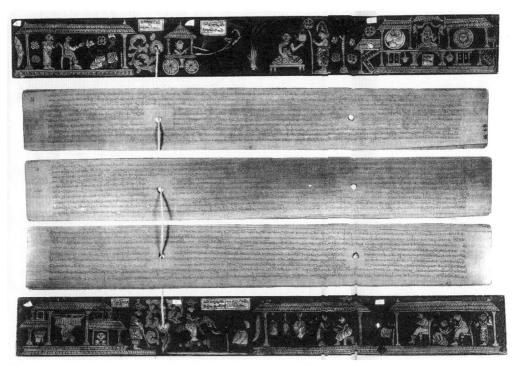

Plate 74. A palm leaf manuscript from Kandy. Theravada Buddhism, as practised in Sri Lanka, is closer to the original austere teaching of the Buddha. It does not encourage visual representation, which could distracts monks from the importance of the text. Only the wooden covers, made by lay craftsmen, bear illustrations. They usually represent tales from the Jatakas *(the previous lives of the Buddha) but the stories often bear no relation to the actual text of the manuscript.*

often portray colourful illustrations from the *Jataka* (tales about the previous lives of the Buddha) and in many cases bear no relation to the actual text (see Plate 74).

The close connection between picture and script — the pictorial and the scriptorial — which already exists in calligraphy, is also the main purpose of calligrams. The term was first introduced by the French poet Guillaume Apollonaire in 1918 to describe his own work, where the text is arranged in the shape of its contents. But text-pictures as such have a much longer tradition. They can be traced back to the Greek poet Simias who in the 4th century BC wrote poetry in the shape of an egg, a double axe or the wings of a bird. Calligrams were quite early on introduced to Christian Europe and in the 6th century AD the Bishop of Poitiers wrote his poems *De Sancta Cruce* in the shape of a cross. The tradition has remained popular right up to the present, when the Concrete Poetry Movement of the 1960s took it up with renewed vigour. Calligrams were used for amulets in the Far East and also in certain areas of Islamic calligraphy. Thus the *basmalah* (the formula which opens each *sura* of the Koran) can be written in the shape of a mosque, a bird or a lamp (to remained the faithful that God is the light of heaven and earth), to give just a few examples.

In ancient Egypt the idea of illustration was already inherent in the script itself which freely intermixed the pictorial with the scriptorial. This symbiosis between writing and illustration, text and picture, word and symbol, is also a characteristic element of Mayan and Aztec manuscripts. The earliest extant Egyptian papyrus roll, the Ramesseum papyrus dating from the 20th century BC (now in the British Museum), shows some 30 figures drawn along the bottom of the scroll. Later examples, especially the 'Book of the Dead' (a sort of guide book buried with the deceased to enable him/her to find the way in the other world) uses a method of simple text illustrations with some elaborate compositions reserved for key issues. After the Greeks settled in Alexandria in the 4th century BC, they learned from the Egyptians the organisation of large *scriptoria* and, having adopted the Egyptian method of illustration, passed it on to the Greek and Roman world.

Much has already been written about the methods and the way illustrations, illumination and other forms of ornamentation used in the medieval Christian codex were produced, at first in the *scriptoria* of monastic establishments and, after the Church began to lose its monopoly of book production and education, increasingly in secular workshops (Jackson, 1968). Religions hostile to pictorial representations like Islam, Judaism and iconoclastic forms of Christianity, as well as Mahayana Buddhism, have always done their best to preserve the purity of the text. But their struggle has seldom been totally successful. In one way or another the picture, in the form of ornamentation or illustration, forced its way past the barriers. There are, for example, the notes to the Jewish Masoretic texts, painstakingly composed in micrographic writing which represent humans, animals or plants (see Plate 75), or the previously mentioned wooden covers of Sri Lankan Buddhist manuscripts. Only Islam has succeeded, much more effectively, to keep the offending picture away from its most sacred text. However, once Islam extended its influence to countries with different traditions, pictures appeared in non-religious literature: the illustrated Persian and Indian manuscripts are some of the most splendid examples. But even there a certain sense of unease does at times manifest itself. Illustrated Persian manuscripts were often kept in the women's quarters. In some cases faces had either been erased or a fine line drawn through the neck of a person, symbolically indicating disapproval and negation of the offending picture.

Illumination is not the same as illustration, though in common usage the two terms are often intermixed. The illuminator (from *illuminare* — to light up, to throw light upon) works not only with colours but also with precious metals, applying thin leaves of beaten gold to initials or the background of a miniature. Illumination is one of the most striking features of medieval writing; here colours are meant less to decorate than to enhance the significance of the text. In a way, illumination restores some of the spirit of a text which the alphabetic script could neither underline nor express. The ultimate aim of medieval reading was to learn the text by heart. The reader was invited to see a page as a symbolic diagram of a series of words, remembering it as such in total. The illuminated page became a form of memory aid, designed to help the onlooker, who was not always fully (if at all) literate, to understand and remember the text and its message.

Illumination was not restricted to Christian manuscripts. It was used to great effect in Jewish manuscripts, many of them having been prepared in the same workshops as

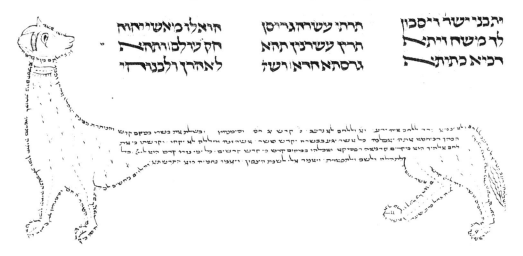

Plate 75. Together with Islam, Theravada Buddhism and certain iconoclastic forms of Christianity, Judaism is strictly opposed to the representation of living forms in the sphere of religious literature. Only the notes to the Masorah (the original text of the Hebrew Old Testament ascertained by Jewish scholars in the 10th century) can show in the margin of the text figures, often fantastic, of animals, people and plants.

Christian manuscripts. Islam, of course, kept itself strictly separate and the dazzling pages of some Korans retain to this day their own cultural identity.

The danger of books

Books spread information. Under certain circumstances this in itself beneficial quality can however also become a dangerous instrument for subversion. If writing had been looked upon with mistrust by societies where oral learning ensured ownership and a position of power, the book — more permanent and at the same time more mobile — was in an even stronger position to spread heresy and undermine the established political order.

In China, where the ability to write — and write well — has always been an essential precondition for entering the ranks of the ruling elite through the civil service examinations, any piece of writing was considered imbued with power. It was in fact considered unlucky to destroy a piece of paper that contained writing, a concept used by Daoist priests to fashion talismans (see Plate 76). In 231 BC the first Qin Emperor Shi Huang Di ordered that '. . . all books in the historical archives, except the records of the Qin, be burnt, that all persons in the empire except those who hold a function under the control of the official scholars, daring to store classical literature and the discussions of various philosophers, should go to the administrative governor, so that these books may be indiscriminately burnt . . .' In this way all texts not in harmony with the emperor's ideological position were destroyed and their authors killed. To eliminate knowledge of the achievements of one's predecessors was, however, in no way limited to China or to any particular period. All through history Christian as well as Muslim rulers have

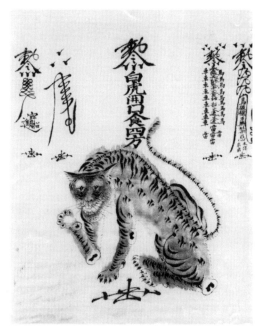

Plate 76. Chinese Daoists drew diagrams which they considered to be imbued with supernatural power. Such talismans could be pasted on walls, burnt to send messages to the spirit world or made into pills to be used as medicine. A Chinese secret society banner made of silk with the picture of a tiger and a talismanic drawing.

periodically destroyed the libraries of their predecessors to erase knowledge and claims contrary to their own.

By the time the Spaniards first appeared in Mexico indigenous book production could look back on a long history of at least a millennium. Manuscripts prepared of deer skin or *amatl* paper give accounts of maps (ownership and stories of migrations), dynastic histories and the all important calendrical accounts and dates. When the Franciscans arrived in 1524 they tried to introduce the Bible as the legitimate basis for conversion. But the Aztecs failed to be impressed. They pointed out that they had their own books and that those books told a different and much longer story of genesis and human culture, providing them with a sound basis for a different political agenda. The missionaries saw their work greatly threatened by this store of indigenous knowledge and soon commenced with the burning of hundreds of native books (see Plate 77), ransacking libraries and often burning their owners as well (Brotherston, 1995). This attitude was in no way a new development restricted to the conquered territories of Mesoamerica. In Spain itself they had, when sending Jews to the pyre, often burnt them together with their Talmud. In other Christian countries the same fate was handed out from time to time to all those who wrote, or even merely possessed, what the Church considered heretical literature.

The 20th century, often mistakenly considered more civilised, saw similar pogroms initiated by Communists as well as Nazis. After the end of the Second World War a similar destruction of Nazi-tainted literature was carried out. In China the Cultural Revolution showed a deep mistrust not only of literacy but of education as such by not just burning books and authors but by closing universities and printing presses and sending all intellectuals (or those who were perceived or merely denounced as intellectuals), if they were not killed outright, to work in the rice fields — a disastrous policy repeated by the Khmer Rouge in Cambodia. After the incorporation of Tibet into China much Buddhist literature and traditional knowledge was destroyed and an effort was made to teach the children Chinese writing instead of Tibetan.

Not so long ago the British government made a desperate, and at times somewhat hilarious effort, to prevent the publication of a book entitled *Spy Catcher*, advertised as 'the candid autobiography of a senior intelligence officer' (1987), despite the fact that, since the book had already been printed in America, copies could easily be obtained through friends returning from the USA. As it turned out, the fear of the book had greatly exaggerated its danger and thus unwittingly contributed to its commercial success.

Modern technology and the talking book

Modern technology has added a further, and in some cases, totally different dimension to the book. The British scientist John B. Dancer had by 1839 already invented microphotography which could reduce printed material to a size no longer readable to the naked eye. Microforms did not however begin to make an impact before the late 1930s, when high-quality film and commercial-grade equipment first became available. If the codex had reduced the size of the book, microfiche did so to an, until then, unimaginable degree. In the optimistic 1960s, at the time when computers began to make their first realistic impact, there was much talk about the possibility of converting whole library collections to the new medium and to store them in a fraction of the space so far required. But the 'paperless office' and the demise of the book — which McLuhan had so confidently forecast for the more or less immediate future — has (at least until now) never really happened. This does not mean that no progress has been made in the new direction. Electronic publishing, the electronic book held on disks that can be updated at will (creating new problems for the principle of copyright), have now a secure place in certain areas of publishing. The book is no longer a definite, incorruptible entity but a flexible tool. Microforms are also an invaluable aid to conservation — precious manuscripts need no longer be endangered by non-essential use. But the conversion of large collections like those held in the British Library or the Library of Congress will (at least at present) prove enormously expensive, both in labour as well as in real money terms. In addition, microforms need periodical replacement, being far less stable than the papyrus scroll, the parchment/paper codex or even Indian palm-leave books. The future has taken a long time in coming and, certainly up to now, not fulfilled all its original promises.

Whereas microfilm, microfiche and computer disk storage still follow established traditions, changing in effect only the format of the book, a totally new element has been introduced with the creation of 'talking books'. Libraries have held sound recordings in their collections since the invention of the Edison cylinder in 1877. Technological improvements have added disks, magnetic sound and videotape, as well as compact disk formats. But the 'talking book', which allows us to listen to the recitations of novels, poetry, historical and other educational and informative material falls into a quite different category. It does, in fact, for the first time introduce elements which could make books obsolete. In many ways, it is a return to oral traditions. A text is no longer written and read but spoken and listened too. We are only at the beginning of this new development and it is impossible to predict how far it will intrude into our lives and how far the future of the book itself will depend on it.

Plate 77. After the military conquest of Mexico the Spaniards started a brutal regime of economic exploitation and ideological persuasion through the offices of the Church and the Viceroyalty. Post-conquest codices, mixing local forms of writing with the script of the conquerors and traditional pictorial representations, like the Historia Tlaxcal *written by Diego Munzo Camargo, provide an ample account of what took place. Especially after 1524, with the arrival of the 'Twelve Apostles' (Franciscan friars), many indigenous books and much literature and ritual paraphernalia were indiscriminately burnt and destroyed.*

Bibliography

Arnold, T W. and Grohmann, A. *The Islamic Book: a Contribution to its Art and History from VII-XVIII century.* London/Florence, 1929.

Arvin, L. *Scribes, Scripts and Books: The Book Art from Antiquity to Renaissance.* London: British Library, 1991.

Birt, Th. *Die Buchrolle in der Kunst: archaeologische und antiquarische Untersuchungern zum antiken Buchwesen.* Leipzig, 1907.

Blackhouse, J. M. *The Illuminated Manuscript.* Oxford: Phaidon, 1979.

Bland, D. *A History of Book Illustration: The Illuminated Manuscript and the Printed Book.* London: Faber and Faber, 1969.

Bowman, A. K. *The Roman Writing Tablets from Vindolanda.* London: British Museum, 1983.

Brown, L. N. *Block Printing and Book Illustration in Japan.* New York: E. P. Dutton, 1924.

Brotherston, G. *Painted Books from Mexico.* London: British Museum, 1995.

Brownring, L. L. *Mediaeval Book Production: Assessing the Evidence.* London: Red Gull Press, 1990.

Brownring, L. L. *Making the Medieval Book: Technique and Production.* London: Red Gull Press, 1995.

Chibbett, D. *The History of Japanese Printing and Book Illustration.* Tokyo: Kodansha International, 1977.

Cloonan, M. V. *Early Bindings in Paper.* London: Mansell, 1991.

Cockerell, D. *Bookbinding and the Care of Books. a Text Book for Bookbinders and Libraries,* 5th edn.. London: Pitman, 1978.

Dawes, L. G. *Japanese Illustrated Books.* London: H.M.S.O., 1972.

De Hamel, C., *The History of Illuminated Manuscripts.* London, Phaidon, 1986.

Diringer, D., *The Illuminated Book its History and Production,* 2nd. edn.. London: Faber, 1967.

Gaur, A. *Oriental Writing Materials.* London: British Library, 1975.

Gray, B. (ed.), *The Arts of the Book in Central Asia, 14th - 16th Century.* London: Serindia, 1979.

Harthan, J., *Bookbinding.* London: HMSO, 1961.

Harthan, J. P., *The History of the Illustrated book: The Western Tradition.* London: Thames and Hudson, 1981.

Hobson, G. D., *English Bookbinding before 1500.* Cambridge: University Press, 1929.

Hollander, A., *Bookcraft.* New York: Van Nostrand Reinhold, 1974.

Hughes, S., *Washi: The World of Japanese Paper*. Tokyo: Kodansha International, 1978.

Hunter, D., *A Papermaking Pilgrimage to Japan, Korea, and China*. New York: Pynson Printers, 1936

Hunter, D., *Papermaking: The History and Technique of an Ancient Craft*, 2nd edn.. New York: Dover Publications, 1978.

Hussein, M. A., *Origins of the Book: Egypt's Contribution to the Development of the Book from Papyrus to Codex*. Greenwich: New York Graphic Society Ltd., 1972.

Ikegami , K, *Japanese Book-Binding: Instructions from a Master Craftsman*, translated from the Japanese by D. Kinzer, 6 edn.. New York: Waterhill, 1995.

Isaac, P. C., *Development of Written Languages and early Writing Material*. Leeds: University Library, 1989.

Johnson, A., *Bookbinding*. London: Thames and Hudson, 1992.

Johnson R., *The Roll of Parchment in Graeco-Roman Antiquity*. University of California, 1968.

Lanham, R. A., *The Electronic World: Democracy, Technology and the Arts*. Chicago: University of Chicago,1993.

Laver, M., *Computer and Social Change*. Cambridge: University Press, 1980.

Lewis, A. W., *Basic Bookbinding*. New York: Dover Publications,1957.

Lewis, N. (ed.), *Papyrology*. Cambridge: University Press, 1985.

Mitchell, C. A., *Inks, their Composition and Manufacture including Methods of Examination and a full List of British Patents*. London: Charles Griffin & Co., 1904.

Parkinson, R. & Quirke, S., *Papyrus*. London: British Museum, 1995.

Pattie, T. S. & Turner, E. G., *The Written Word on Papyrus*. London: British Library, 1974.

Pinner, H. L., *The World of Books in Classical Antiquity*. Leiden: A.W. Sijthoff, 1948.

Putnma, G. H., *Books and their Makers during the Middle Ages: a Study of the Conditions of the Production and Distribution of Literature from the Fall of the Roman Empire to the Close of the 17th century*, 2 vols.. London: 1996/7.

Reed, A., *Ancient Skins, Parchment and Leather*. London: Seminar Press, 1972.

Reed, A., *The Nature and Making of Parchment*. London: Elemete, 1976.

Regmemorter, B. van, *Some Oriental Bindings in the Chester Beatty Library*. Dublin: Chester Beatty Library, 1961,

Roberts, C. H. & Skeat, T. C., *The Birth of the Codex*. London: Oxford University Press, 1983.

Roberts, M. T. & Etherington, D., *Bookbinding and the Conservation of Books; A Dictionary of Descriptive Terminology*. 1982.

Sassoon, R. *Computers and Typography*. Oxford: Intellect, 1992.

Tidcombe, M.,*The Dover Bindery*. London: British Library, 1991.

Tidcombe, M., *The Bookbindings of Lucien Pissarro and a Bibliographical List of Eragny Books*. London: The British Library, 1984.

Tsien, T., *Written on Bamboo and Silk: The Beginnings of Chinese Books and Inscriptions*. Chicago: University of Chicago,1962.

Turner, E. G., *Greek Papyri: An Introduction*. Oxford: The Claredon Press, 1968.

Turner, E. G., *Greek Manuscripts of the Ancient World*. Oxford: The Claredon Press, 1971.

Verveliet, H. D. L. (ed.), *The Book through 5000 Years*. London: Phaidon, 1972.

Whalley, J. I., *Writing Implements and Accessories. From the Roman Stylus to the Typewriter*. Vancouver: 1975.

12. Printing, the writing masters and the Internet

Printing is the uncorrupted multiplication of graphically stored information by mechanical means, the two key words being 'uncorrupted' and 'mechanical means'. Scribes did copy manuscripts but, apart from the fact that this was a time-consuming effort, they could, and did, make mistakes (see Plate 78). Mechanical duplication ensures that a text remains exactly the same — in other words, reliable. This not only standardises the information, it also introduces elements of legality and, most of all, of intellectual ownership. An author owns the text he has published; additional copying needs his explicit permission. Printing is part of the market economy in a way the manuscript was never meant to be. It is true that today rare manuscripts are sold in auction houses at often highly unrealistic prices. But these are not sold as intellectual property in order to protect the rights of the person who originally composed the text, or those of the scribes and illuminators who laboured on its production — their value is in many ways totally artificial, based solely on the fact that each manuscript is unique as a physical object.

We are usually told that there are two possibilities of printing: block printing and printing with moveable type. But the concept of printing, the idea of duplicating information correctly, incorruptibly, and as such legally binding, goes back much further. In a way, printing started when seals were first cut in the ancient Near East the Mediterranean countries, and in the mysterious cities of the Indus Valley. They ranged from simple stamp seals for marking property to highly sophisticated roll seals which combined written information with pictures — text with illustration. In the market economy seals play an important role by documenting and safeguarding property. Seals could also give authority to the message conveyed in a text. In China personal seals not only furnished proof of the authorship of a painting or a piece of calligraphy, they were also at times used by owners, providing us with important information about provenance. In a similar though more elaborate way, the Turkish Thugras (stylised representations of a Sultan's name) provided the ultimate authorisation of a particular document and their use was guarded by strict laws.

If seals were the earliest examples of block printing, we also have at least one very early example of moveable printing in that still mysterious object referred to as the Phaistos disc (see Plate. 79), dating from about 1700 BC. Here seals seem to have been used exactly like moveable type to print what to all intents and purposes looks like a text. The fact that the characters bear no resemblance to any other contemporary script and that the disk itself remains the only object of its kind ever discovered has led to a number of speculations, one being the possibility that it is a fake. But why go to the trouble of cutting 45 different seals/type for the sake of faking just one object? The jury is still out on this particular subject.

Block printing as we now know it originated in China. But much of our knowledge concerning its early stages is based on circumstantial evidence. It seems, however, fairly certain that by the end of the 2nd century AD all the elements necessary for printing were in place: paper, ink and a technique for making impressions (by rubbing or ink squeeze) from inscriptions carved in stone. By the 6th century AD this technique had further improved so that it was now possible to make copies of high calligraphic quality and, most important, perfect authenticity, not only from stone but also from wood, metal or baked clay. This was already remarkably close to actual block printing. Since repeated copying was likely to damage the original, the next step was to prepare, on wood blocks, a faithful copy of the original, at first in negative and later in positive characters cut in relief. The result was black script on white paper — a print.

Though block printing has in the Far East for long remained the preferred option, experiments with moveable types (see Plate 80), made from clay and glue hardened by backing, were already made between 1041 and 1048. In 1313 AD a magistrate by the name of Wang Zhen had some 60,000 characters carved on wooden moveable blocks so as to be able to print a treatise on the history of technology. From China printing reached Korea in the 13th century. In 1403 AD — almost half a century before Europe discovered typography — the Korean king Htai Tjong commissioned 100,000 pieces of type made from bronze During the 15th century printing with metal type was practised with great skill in Korea. In Japan moveable type was introduced almost simultaneously in the latter part of the 16th century from Korea and from Portugal. Although typography was short-lived in Japan, lasting no more than half a century,

Plate 78. Reconstruction of the monastic scriptorium *in Shrewsbury, showing a scribe at work. The sack of Rome in 410 AD brought about the destruction of nearly all public and private libraries and with it an almost total loss of the existing literary output. Book production passed into the hands of the newly emerging Christian church, whose existence in turn depended on the authority of (written) biblical texts. The need for authentic copies was already recognised by the founders of monastic orders. Thus the rules of St Benedict (c. 480-543 AD) made it obligatory for monks to set aside certain hours of the day for study and writing. Gifted monks began to work as scribes, illuminators and bookbinders. Their importance to the community was fully realised; indeed an Irish law prescribed the same punishment for the murder of a scribe as that meted out for a bishop or king.*

Plate 79. The disc, dating from c. 1700 BC, was found in Crete in 1908. Altogether 241 signs, arranged in groups (words?) and divided by vertical lines, have been impressed with punches similar to printing. Forty-five different signs have been used for the text, which runs in a spiral from the centre outward. These signs bear no resemblance to any known contemporary script and nothing similar to the disc has so far been found in any other place.

some fine examples were produced during this period. In the 17th century typography more or less disappeared in the Far East — for practical as well as aesthetic reasons — until it was eventually re-introduced from Europe.

Whereas printing developed more gradually in China, from where it was introduced together with Buddhism to Korea and Japan, in Europe it seems have been vitalised by just one event: the 42-line Gutenberg Bible printed with moveable type in 1455. Though Gutenberg himself appears to have reaped little financial reward from his venture, he is generally referred to as the inventor of Western printing as such. But was it really an invention, considering that the term invention customarily refers to a totally new concept? As in China, all the elements essential for printing were already at hand by the middle of the 15th century: the oil press, the art of cutting punches as practised by goldsmiths (Gutenberg himself having worked in this profession) and, most of all, the ready availability of paper (see Plate 81).

Without paper the so-called printing explosion, which signalled the start of the modern period based on an increased and more readily available volume of information, would probably not have been possible — some of the earliest Bibles printed on parchment used the skins of up to 300 sheep.

If writing had long served as an effective part of the infrastructure, printing fulfilled this role even more efficiently. It was quick, less labour intensive, in the long run cheaper and it could aim at a much larger audience. In Europe it was from the beginning a commercial enterprise directed at the mass market; this by necessity, created questions of ownership and standardisation. But for any new configuration to succeed, there must first be a primary need.

In the Far East the development of printing had been closely connected with the expansion of administrative needs and the sudden and rapid diffusion of Buddhism in the middle of the first Christian millennium, first in China itself then also in Korea and Japan (see Plate 82). The spread of Buddhism and the concept of a Confucian-based administration throughout the Far East, together with the Chinese language and the Chinese script, represented a form of cultural colonisation not directly based on commercial rewards. The activists in this enterprise were people who had at their

Plate 80. *By the 11th century Chinese printers were able to work with movable type. But the nature of the Chinese script made this a complex and in the end far less satisfactory option than block-printing. There was first of all the expense (and the time-consuming labour) of manufacturing thousands and thousands of different characters for each font, arranging them for printing, storing them, cleaning them and eventually re-sorting them for re-use.*

disposal two essential elements: time and free labour. In addition, unlike copying by hand — a somewhat solitary endeavour — printing is based on team effort: trees have to be felled, wood cut, the text must be written, first on paper, then transferred to the wood block and the block has then to be fashioned according to need. Even the preparation of paper alone is time-consuming and needs the close cooperation of a group of people employed in successive tasks — all this before printing can even begin. The places where such a pool of (unpaid) labour was readily available were the large Buddhist monasteries.

We need here not repeat the well-researched history of European printing or the role played by Gutenberg and his associates (Sternberg, 1979). What interests us is the interaction between printing and writing and its effect on literacy, not just as an individual achievement but as a decisive factor in a changing infrastructure. Most of all, why did printing suddenly replace writing which for so long had served as a reliable medium for the storage and distribution of information?

The reasons were both religious and economic, or better, the power shift in the interaction between both elements. By the 15th century the Church had lost its monopoly of scholarship and learning; it no longer controlled the way information was stored, manipulated, made available and used. The gradual secularisation of society had led to the foundation of independent schools and universities. Information was no longer just stored and transmitted (mostly in subtly censored form) but it was now also increasingly more often questioned. The manipulation of the infrastructure was no longer in the hands of the Church alone or that of a Church-sanctioned hierarchy which could be trusted to serve the same purpose. In a way, printing in Europe not only prepared the way for the industrial revolution but for revolution as such.

¶ Mors resecat/mors omne necat quod carne creatur
Magnificos premit & modicos/cunctis dominatur.

¶ Nobiliu tenet imperiu nulli retinetur
Tam ducibus & principib9 cõmune habetur.

Plate 81. This is the earliest known representation of a Western printing shop as shown in La grande danse macabre, *Lyons, 1499 AD. On the left Death is leading off a compositor and two pressmen. The compositor holds in one hand a composing stick in which he is just about to arrange types taken from the compartments on the trestle table in front of him. Beside him is a two-page forme which he is setting up. The forme would be inked by the man with the ink-balls in the background. On the right side of the page is a cubicle built into the main room where the finished books are stored and sold over the counter.*

¶ Nunc tibi iue/tibi seø/tibi voø/tibi flos inuenisis.Hic nisi pus/nisi seø/nisi terre præso visie.

¶ Le mort ¶ Le mort

¶ Venez danser vng tourdion
Imprimeure sus legierement
Venez tost/pour conclusion
Mourir vous fault certainement
Faictes vng sault habillement
Dresses/z capfee vous fault laisser
Reculer ny fault nullement
A sourtage on congnoist sournier.

¶ Les imprimeurs

¶ Helas on auoins nous recours
Puis que la mort nous espie
Imprime auons toue lee cours
De la saincte theologie
Loiz decret/z poeterie/
Par nre art plusieurs sont grans clers
Reseruee en est clergie
Les vonsous des gens sont diuers

¶ Sue auant vous ires apres
Baistre libraire marches auant
Vous me regardez de bien pres
Laisses vos liures maintenant
Danser vous fault/a quel galant
Pettes icy vostre pense
Comment vous reculez marchant
Cõmencement nest pas fuse

¶ Le libraire

¶ Ce fault il maulgré moy danser
Je croy que oup/mort me presse
Et me contraint de me auancer
Pesse pas bute destresse
Des liures il fault que ie laisse
Et ma boutique desormais
Dont ie pers toute tresse
Cel est blece qui ney peult mais.

6

With the spread of literacy came a growing demand for books. Printing not only endangered the old order, it also began to usher in what eventually became a consumer society which, by definition, feeds on ever-increasing and often artificially created demands. In the rich towns wealthy merchant began to turn their hands to book collecting and the monastic *scriptoria* were no longer able satisfy all needs. Professional scribes, who for some time had worked side by side with their monastic colleagues, began to set up independent workshops and formed themselves into guilds to protect their interests (Jackson, 1968). Copying books became a well-organised and lucrative enterprise but it was still hampered by the inherent slowness of the process and, predictably, hard pressed scribes were apt to become less reliable.

In the beginning printers tried hard to imitate scribes as closely as possible (see Plate 83). Gutenberg himself had spent a good deal of time studying manuscripts before designing his fount. There was, at first, a mixture of mechanical and manual elements: space might be left after the text had been printed so that initials, ornamentation and illustrations could be added by hand or with the aid of a printing

*Plate 82. In fear of a rebellion raised by one of her ministers, the Japanese Empress Shotoku ordered the printing of one million Buddhist charms (*dharani*), which were distributed in specially designed little pagodas throughout Japan. This was a massive operation which considerably strained the resources of the country, and took six years (764-770 AD) altogether to complete.*

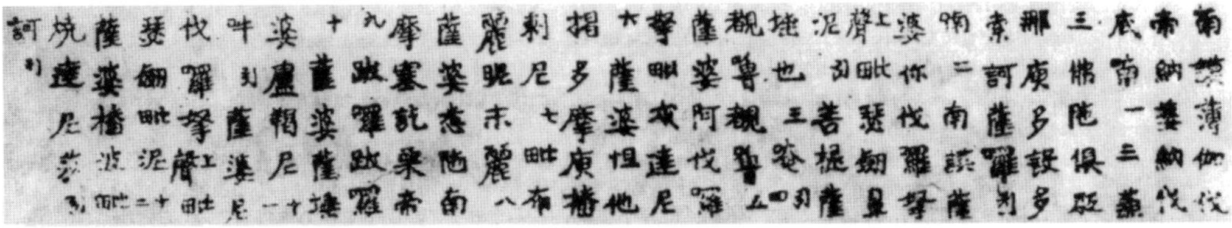

Plate 83 *A page from Gutenberg's 42-line Bible printed at Mainz between 1453 and 1455. Initially the printers clearly felt themselves in competition with scribes, who had so long dominated the market. Their aim was to make the printed book look as similar to a manuscript as possible. Initials were sometimes added at a later stage with the assistance of wood or metal blocks or space was left for the illuminators and illustrators to complete a page by hand.*

block. But before long printers became conscious of the inherent autonomy of their craft and it soon looked as if the calligrapher, and even more so the copyist, who for so long had been indispensable in the running of religious and secular affairs, was to become obsolete.

Mass production, and the increase in literacy, rapidly enlarged the size of the reading audience. This created new opportunities and some enterprising calligraphers/scribes were quick to exploit the situation. Not only did more people want to be instructed in writing so as to improve their chances in an increasingly more consumer-orientated, commercial, environment but by using the new possibilities of mass production, scribes willing to act as instructors could win themselves a share in the steadily growing market. In 1522 the Roman calligrapher and printer Ludovico degli Arrighi (fl. 1510-1527) published a small booklet entitled *Operina da imparare di scrivere littera cancellaresca* which gave simple instructions, illustrated by wood-cut examples, about how to learn the author's favourite Cancellaresca style in 'a few days'. His publication is widely held responsible for the creation of a new profession: that of the writing master.

Two years later, the Venetian chancery scribe Giovanni Antonio Tagliente (fl. 1491-1531), after having spent many years as a teacher, published his *Presente libro*; and in 1540 Giovanni Palatino's *Libro nuovo d'imparare a scrivere*, the most widely disseminated copy-book of the 16th century, appeared in Rome. Other professional calligraphers, who had seen their livelihood threatened by the new invention, were quick to follow suit and over the next 50 years a host of similar manuals appeared in print: in Germany those of Johann Neudoerffer (1538), Caspar Neff (1549) and Jonathan Sautter (1555); Clément Perret (1569) and Jan van den Velde (1605) in the Netherlands, Juan de Yciar (1548) and Francisco Lucas (1577) in Spain; Gerard Mercator (1540) in Holland; and Geoffroy Tory (1525), Pierre Hamon (1561), Aert van Meldert (1585) and Guillaume Le Gangneur (1599) in France.

Printing, the writing masters and the Internet

Though commercial printers, publishers and book distributors seemed to control the newly-emerging market, the writing master began to act as an arbiter of taste and fashion. In the second half of the 16th century Cancellaresca, the Italian chancery hand, became the script most favoured in court circles and among humanistic scholars. Introduced to England in 1570 by the Huguenot scribe Jean de Beauchesne (c.1538-1610) and John Baildon with *A Book containing Divers Sortes of Hands,* the new style soon found acceptance. Not only did Queen Elizabeth I, amply instructed by Roger Ascham, and her contemporaries make use of this style, it also served for schoolbooks and daily correspondence on a wider scale. In addition, educated Europeans continued to write Black Letter Secretary and at times (together with Shakespeare) made light of their new 'sweet Roman hand'. Indeed in the German-speaking countries cursive versions of the Gothic style survived as the script of correspondence and government business until the early parts of the 20th century. The principal French style of this period was a national Black Letter cursive called *Lettres Francoises* (or *financieres*) for everyday and business affairs and the more aristocratic Italian Bastarda, a compromise script which mixed common Gothic cursive with the more fashionable Italic, going back to a manual (*Opera nella quale si insegna a scrvere*) published by Vespasian Amphiareo (d.1563) in 1554. Bastarda (still rather an ornate script) was introduced to Britain under the name 'new mixed cursive' through Edward Cocker's (1631-1676) copy-books (1661/1668/1672). Cocker, who engraved his own work, was the most prolific and best-known English writing master of his time, much admired for his calligraphy and his exuberant flourishes. By the beginning of the 18th century a more simple and businesslike script had developed from it, originally propagated by John Ayres (fl.1608-1705) and his contemporaries, to serve commercial demands.

As the 17th century drew to its close and during most of the following centuries, the purpose of writing moved from calligraphy towards utilitarianism. At the same time an enormous number of copy-books flooded the market. Italian writing masters declined in favour of northern scribes. The fact that more people wanted and were able to write brought about a decline in standards. With this the writing master's position too declined; he was no longer a calligrapher or even a craftsman but a mere teacher. As the market grew more and more competitive, some tried to attract pupils by ever more fanciful letter shapes, baroque decorations and elaborate flourishes. But by the 18th century the accelerating demands of commerce, trade and colonial administration, especially in England, began to create a need for a clear and fluent hand that was easy to read and easy to write — unlike the rather difficult 'Secretary hands' which had in the past been used for public and private documents. The main aim was no longer the development of an aesthetically pleasing, or even eye-catching style, but legibility. The growing importance of the commercial sector had in some way been foreshadowed in Arrighi's second publication *Il modo de temperare le penne* (1523), which had set out separate models for styles suitable for the use of merchants, notaries, scribes designing apostolic briefs and so on. Arrighi's publication also included two pages of type specimens, an illustration of the new role the writing master was now adding to his brief: that of the type designer (see Plate 84).

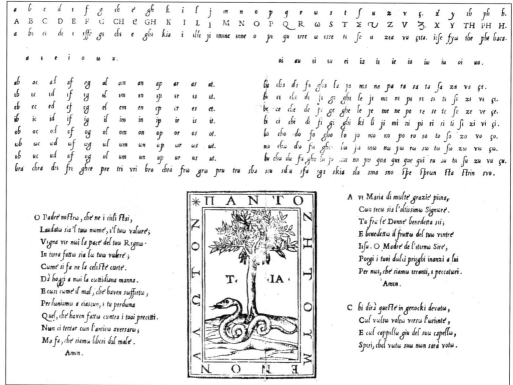

Plate 84. The publication of Ludovico degli Arrighi's Operina da imparare di scrivere littera cancellaresca *in 1551 encouraged some calligraphers to turn themselves into writing masters. This is a type-sheet produced by Janiculo of the second Italic type of Arrighi, which was engraved after his designs by the goldsmith and medalist Lautritio di Meo Rotelli of Perugia in Italy in c. 1529 AD. Rotelli had been a reputed seal maker and was as such well suited for the work of cutting metal punches.*

Writing masters acting as printers and type designers were to wield considerable influence, not only on the way books were printed but also on the way people wrote (or thought they ought to write). Originally masters such as Arrighi, Tagliente, Palatino and Cresci had used wooden blocks to illustrate their books with calligraphic examples of their own script. However in the early 1570s Guilantonio Heroclani created a new controversy by using copperplate engravings for his *Essemplare utile di tuttu le sorti di lettere cancellaresche correntissime, et altre usate*. Though Hercolani himself employed this method with a certain amount of restraint, his decision had far reaching consequences. The main tool for engraving, a short piece of sharpened steel called burin, is held almost stationary while the engraver moves the copperplate with his left hand. This method could imitate the fine hairlines and elaborate flourishes so cherished by writing masters, anxious to impress prospective pupils, much better than the wood block. Before long, handwriting began to imitate printed models. During the following century this new method was widely used and became the inspiration for the so-called copperplate writing of the 18th century. In due course it also became the preferred script of the ever-increasing army of clerks labouring in government offices and commercial houses.

Commercial considerations at times outweigh artistic integrity. Moreover, the calligraphy propagated by some writing masters in their copy-books was very often not their own true handwriting. Writing masters like Urban Wyss, George Bickham (see Plate 85) and Edward Cocker, who could double as master engravers, were the exception rather than the rule. Indeed, quarrels between writing masters and engravers became increasingly more common and many copy-books are full of complaints about the way the author's style had been corrupted by the engraver. Unlike in China, where the master's calligraphy was directly transferred to the wood block, in the West it was often simply copied by the engraver. This introduced problems of interpretation and ability between the writing master and his printed copy-book.

After the new Education Act of 1840 in England, which introduced literacy to a much larger cross section of society, copy-books, now teaching mainly the same plain and rather dull script, became a cherished tool for self-help and self-improvement, not only in Europe but also, and even more so, in America. In the 17th century copy-books had already been introduced from England but they were soon replaced by indigenous American examples. Together with 'colleges' which taught writing and related arts, their main aim was 'self-improvement' — teaching 'young people' how to acquire a good handwriting so as to improve their chances in life.

In the last four decades desk-top publishing has revolutionised book production. The infrastructure resting on the availability of essential information can now be manipulated by practically everybody who is computer literate and owns the appropriate appliances. More sophisticated machines allow users to design their own letter forms and to create typefaces based on personal handwriting. But this new freedom has inherent problems. Western calligraphy and good typography have to a large extent always been based on an awareness and the successful manipulation of letter forms. Since too little importance has long been accorded to the study of letter forms in primary and secondary education, an appropriate knowledge, let alone the ability and necessary training, is not likely to be found among the bulk of computer users. Moreover, to produce, write and design letters is not a natural ability, nor something that can simply be acquired. In other words, while everybody can be taught how to write, not everybody can become a calligrapher — or, for that matter, even obtain full proficiency in writing. While everybody can learn how to use a computer, one has to be taught, and have the ability, to become a type designer. Without good type designing, computer print outs are a possibility but they cannot hope to rival good printing.

Many of today's leading calligraphers have indeed stepped into the place of the writing masters and successfully turned their hand to type designing or to creating a style of handwriting which assists children in the learning process. Names like William Morris, Sidney Carlyle Cockerell, Edward Johnston, Stanley Morison, Eric Gill, Hermann Zapf, Rosemary Sassoon and others come to mind.

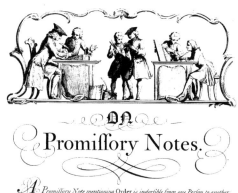

Plate 85. The expansion of commerce in the 18th century needed the support of an ever-increasing army of clerks who commanded a good and legible hand. Writing masters like George Bickham found much profit in providing the necessary publications (The Universal Penman, 1743) and tuition. The top of the page illustrates the way work was carried out in an office: on the left side sits a clerk taking down dictation; in the middle, two of his colleagues are engaged in re-shaping their quill pens; and on the right another clerk copies from a book which is held open for him.

But the most worrying aspect of this new, unchecked and universal ability to access and manipulate the infrastructure based on the storage and dissemination of data is the fact that data is no longer safe. It can be corrupted, interfered with and misused by anybody with the appropriate knowledge owning any of the freely available appliances. It does not even require a great deal of talent or unique ability. Teenage boys have been known to hack into national defence systems, disgruntled employees in danger of losing their jobs are able to interfere with the infrastructure of their organisations, corrupting information, changing data, even implanting information which eventually can destroy essential information altogether. The Internet, the much advertised 'highway of knowledge', is not just a highway to knowledge but a possibility for corruption and crime. Paedophiles can (and do) set up networks to inform each other about the availability of vulnerable children, terrorists can use it to teach even those with little intelligence and skill how to make destructive devices. Manuscripts and printed books could be controlled and if necessary censored. Today the question is not so much whether censorship is justifiable but whether it is possible at all. Apparently not. Since the Internet has no central provider there is no central point that can be held responsible. This is a long way from prehistoric cave paintings, monastic *scriptoria*, scribal workshops, even from the traditional position of authors, printers and publishers. In fact, even the most irresponsible tabloid editor carries some ultimate responsibility for the information he produces and can, if necessary, be called to account. Nobody apparently carries any ultimate responsibility for the information transmitted through the Internet. This is a totally new situation and not everything a new situation has to offer is beneficial. The answer — if there is an answer — has not yet been found.

Bibliography

Benson, J. H., *The first Writing Book: an English Translation & Facsimile Text of Arrighi's La Operina, the First Manual of the Chancery Hand*. Oxford: 1955.

Blake, N. F., *Caxton and his World*. London: Andre Deutsch, 1969.

Blumenthal, J., *Art of the Printed Book 1455-1955: Masterpieces of Typography through five Centuries from the Collections of ther Pierpoint Morgan Library*. London: The Bodley Head, 1974.

Blunt, W., *Sweet Roman Hand*. London: Jana Barrrie, 1952.

Carter, H.G., *A View of early Typography up to 1600*. Oxford: Clarendon Press, 1968..

Carter, T. F., *The Invention of Printing in China and its Spread Westwards*, Revised edn.. New York: Ronald Press, 1955.

Carter, S., *Twentieth-century Type Designers*. London: Lund Humphries, 1995.

Cassel, D. and Jackson, M. *Introduction to Computers and Information Processing*. Reston: Virginia, 1981.

Chibett, D. *The History of Japanese Printing and Book Illustration*. Tokyo: Kodasha International, 1977.

Davies, J. of Hereford, *The Writing Schoolmaster or the Anatomy of Faire Writing*. 1663.

Dean. H. *Analytical Guide to the Art of Penmanship*. Salem MA, 1805.

Dreyfus, J. *Into Print: Selected Essays on Typography, Printing History and Book Production*. London: British Library, 1994.

Dreyfus, J. *Morris and the Printed Book: A Reconsideration of his Views on Type and Book Design in the Light of later Computer-aided Techniques*, London: William Morris Society, 1989.

Dunton, A. R. *Duntonian System of Penmanship*. New Orleans, 1843.

Einsenstein, E. L. *The Printing Revolution in early Modern Europe*. Cambridge: University Press, 1983.

Einsenstein, E. L. *The Printing Press as an Agent of Change*. 2 vols., Cambridge: University Press, 1970.

Fisher. G. *The Instructor, or American Young Man's Best Companion, containing Instructions for Reading, Writing and Arithmetic and many Other Things besides the Art of Making several Sorts of Wine*. [1748].

Foster, V. H. L. *Vere Foster's Copy-Books. Bold writing, or Civil Service Series*. London: Blackie and Son, 1870.

Fragg, R. *Everyday Handwriting*. London: Hodder and Stoughton, 1962.

Grey, N. *History of Lettering. Creative Experiment and Lettering Identity*. Oxford: Phaidon, 1986.

Harling, R. *The Letterforms and Type designs of Eric Gill*. Westham: Silversted, 1976.

Heal, A. *English Writing Masters and their Copybook. A Biographical dictionary 1570-1800*. Introduction on the development of Handwriting by Stanley Morris, Cambridge: University Press, 1931.

Holborn, A. *The Writing Masters Amusement. A new Alphabet in Knot-work: Adorned with a Variety of Scripture-Pieces, Written in all the Hands of Great Britain, and embellished with Borders, the Whole performed by the Pen*. 1767.

Jarman, C. *The Development of Handwriting Skills*. Oxford: Basil Blackwell, 1979.

Krimpen, J. van. *On Designing and Devising Type*. New York: Sylvan Press, 1957.

Larisch, R. von. *Unterricht in ornamentaler Schrift*. Achte Veraenderte Auflage, Vienna, 1911.

Marchand. *Nouveaux principes d'ecriture itallienne avec des examples suivant l'ordre de Madame de Maintenon pour les demoiselles de la Maison Royal de St. Louis etablie a St. Cyr. Par le maitre a ecrire de Madame la Duchesse de Bourgogne*. Paris, 1721.

Mather, W. *Young Man's Companion*. London, 1681.

McLuhan, H. M. *The Gutenberg Galaxy, the Making of Typographic Man*. London: Routledge and Kegan Paul, 1962.

Nash, R. *American Penmanship 1800-1850: a History of Writing and a Bibliography of Copy Books from Jenkins to Spencer*. Worcester: Colonial Society of Massachusetts, 1959.

Osley, A. S. *Luminario: an Introduction to Italian Writing Books of the Sixteenth and Seventeenth Century*. Miland: Nieuwkopp, 1972.

Rand, B. H. *A New and Complete System of Mercantile Penmanship*. Philadelphia, 1814.

Rubinstein, R. *Digital Typography — an Introduction to Type and Composition for Computer System Design*. Reading, MA, 1988.

Sassoon, R. *A Practical Guide to Lettering*. London: Thames and Hudson, 1985.

Sassoon, R. *Computers and Typography*. Oxford: Intellect, 1992.

Sparling, H. H. *The Kelmscott Press and William Morris, Master Craftsman*. London: Macmillan, 1924.

Spencer, P. R. *Spencerian Key to Practical Penmanship*. 1866.

Spencer, P. R. *Spencer and Rice's System of Ladies Epistolary and Ornament Penmanship, carefully prepared for the Use of Public and Private Schools and Seminars*. New York, 1848.

Standard, P. *Arrighi's Running Hand: a Study of Chancery Cursive*. New York, 1979.

Sternberg, S. H. *Five Hundred Years of Printing*. 3rd edn., London: Penguin Books, 1979.

Todd, W. B. *The Gutenberg Bible, new Evidence of the original Printing*. University Library, University of North Carolina, 1982.

Twitchett, D. *Printing and Publishing in Medieval China*. London: Wynkyn de Worde Society, 1983.

Updicke, D. B. *Printing Types: their History, Form and Use: a Study in Survival*. Cambridge, MA: Harvard University Press, 1922.

Widman, N. (ed.), *Der gegenwaertige Stand der Gutenbergforschung*. Stuttgart. 1977.

Whalley, J. I. *English Handwriting* London: H.M.S.O., 1969.

Worthy, W. *The Renaissance Handwriting Books*. London: Chatto and Windus, 1954.

Zapf, H. *ABC-XY Zapf. Fifty Years of Alphabet Design*. ed. J. Dreyfus and K. Erickson, London, 1989.

13. What is literacy?

In asking this question we first of all have to decide whether we want to restrict ourselves to the English word 'literacy' or whether we want to examine the concept of literacy as such. In English, because of the close, and in consequence often implied, connection with the term 'literature', literacy has all too often been identified with the ability to read and write, to produce and understand written texts. But in other languages different terms are used which have different implications. For example, Barthel (1972) in his *Konnte Adam schreiben: Weltgeschichte der Schrift* (in itself a curiously naive title) states 'im einundzwanzigstem Jahrhundert wird es auf Erden kaum noch Analphabeten geben' (in the 21st century hardly anybody on our planet will be illiterate). Only the word chosen for 'illiterate' is *Analphabet*, which literally translated means 'somebody unable to master the alphabet'. Apart from the fact that his confidence was, as we now see, greatly misplaced, literacy becomes by this particular definition not just equated with the ability to read and write but to do so in just one system, the alphabet.

Gelb, by calling his work *A Study of Writing, the Foundations of Grammatology*, stays more closely within the traditions of his own culture. Medieval Europe inherited its language of scholarship from classical Rome. What was known as Latin was simply a particular system of letters and orthography. But medieval writers did not use the term Latin; they called this system 'letters' (*litterae*) or 'grammar' (*grammatica*). To them Latin was not a foreign language, it was simply the correct way to speak and write. (Clanchy, 1992). Though it was in no way difficult to write in any of the vernacular languages, to do so would have been considered illiterate, ungrammatical, un-Roman and, with it, un-Christian. Such 'illiterate' texts were at times provided for new converts but they became obsolete once the newcomer understood 'grammar' and the new religion.

But is literacy indeed restricted to the alphabet, to post-Roman cultural conventions or even to written texts? We should here perhaps ask ourselves once more the question raised at the beginning of this study: what exactly is writing or, perhaps even more pertinent, what exactly is the purpose of writing? We have stated that the purpose of writing, indeed its only purpose, is the storage of information, information essential to the well-being of a particular community. The kind of writing — graphs, notches, pictures, objects, pictograms, mixed scripts, phonetic scripts, etc. — is in the final instance irrelevant as long as the system successfully supports the needs of the community in question. Any system which fulfils this purpose is proper writing, however it may appear to somebody not part of this particular community or period. As such writing forms an essential function within the infrastructure of a community and by being part of the infrastructure it becomes subject to political manipulation.

What then is literacy? Who can be called literate? Quite simply, all those who understand, can make use of, perhaps even contribute to the (written) infrastructure of the society they live in. In other words, the paintings and kerbs in the Netholitic caves of France and Spain supported the existing infrastructure of their society. Those who could understand their purpose and meaning were, just as those who produced them, literate within the sphere of their own community. We, looking at them, are not. We can at best make guesses which in the final instance will always remain more or less arbitrary.

The suggestion has been made that those pictures could not have been writing since they represented real-life objects, not the words which stood for those objects (Finegan, 1999). Apart from the fact that this would leave all non-pictorial forms of information storage unexplained, and even if we accepted the preposition that writing must have a connection with words — how exactly do we know that the pictures did not represent words or sounds? Why should we even think so? We have in fact absolutely no way of knowing and very little chance of ever finding out. We shall just have to accept our ignorance and consequent lack of 'literacy'. But we are in no way justified in making retrospective assumptions, from the point of our own cultural experience and conventions, of a civilisation long since gone and totally different from our own.

Literacy is basically an interactive process. Cultural literacy, a term now often used in connection with ethnic division and conflicts between minority and majority groups, is simply another description of the pool of shared experience within which literacy has always functioned. Just as there are few true inventions, there are few truly new situations. Definitions, being more dependent on a particular historical, social and cultural climate, may change but the facts and problems connected with them remain basically constant, as does the ability (or, more often than not, inability) to solve those problems.

Benefits and pitfalls of literacy

Literacy is by definition a political act (see Plate 86). It is connected with empowerment, imposing stratification, control. Since, unlike language, it is not a natural by-product of being human, it has to be consciously imparted — taught. This places those able to teach (those in possession of the essential information) automatically into a more dominant position by enabling them to manipulate the information and to decide on how much of it should be passed on to whom. Literacy is nowadays usually seen as a means for the advancement of the individual or a particular group. To be literate is an achievement; to be illiterate, or not sufficiently literate, signifies failure. But literacy is also a precariously double-sided tool and just as there existed (and in times of conflict still exists) a fear of books, there can be unease about the wider spread of literacy in societies which depend more on an inherent hierarchical structure than on individual ability and merit. We do not have to go back to ancient Egypt, Vedic India or even Vietnam to illustrate this statement: we can find pertinent examples much nearer home. When in 1807 the Bill for Universal Elementary Education was put before the British parliament, the president of the Royal Society felt called upon to write: ' . . . giving education to the labouring classes of the poor . . . would in effect be found to be prejudicial to their morale and happiness; it would teach them to despise their lot in life, instead of making them good servants in agriculture,

Plate 86. In China calligraphy, owing to its inherent prestige, has always played a significant role in the cult of personality and was in this capacity frequently used for political purposes. Thus the calligraphy of famous emperors had traditionally been engraved in stone. Although calligraphy itself was for some time looked upon with some unease as an elitist form of expression by Chinese Communists, the tradition itself was too deeply ingrained to be extinguished by the new creed. During the time of his ascendancy, the handwriting of Chairman Mao Zedong was widely displayed on posters, as newspaper headlines or, as here, a whole book of his poems was produced in his own handwriting.

and other laborious employment to which their rank in society had destined them; instead of teaching them subordination, it would render them factious and refractory, as was evident in the manufacturing countries; it would enable them to read seditious pamphlets, vicious books, and publications against Christianity; it would render them insolent . . .'

Not for the first time did the question of literacy or, better, the effects and possibilities implied in literacy, put the dominant group into an ambivalent situation. If printing had encouraged the spread of literacy, the industrial revolution made a certain basic amount of it necessary. Just as the unification of China under the Qin had created a need for more administration, and with it more written documents, so the changing pattern of economic life following the industrial revolution, and consequent overseas expansion (territorial, political and commercial), required a large army of numerate clerks capable of writing a legible business hand. As in imperial Rome, written instructions had to be issued to overseas territories, support overseas business interests. The question has always been how to handle such a situation, create improvements without destabilising the established order. England in a way handled the situation with remarkable aplomb by promoting a two-tier education system: expensive public schools to educate what would hopefully become the governing elite and poorly-funded state schools, growing out of the 18th century Sunday and Charity

Schools. The latter aimed less at encouraging upward mobility than on imparting just enough literary knowledge to teach the children of the poor how read the Bible and learn from it how to be industrious, while still accepting their place in a carefully graded society. This worked perfectly well. The Communist revolution did not, as Marx had thought, begin in an industrialised county like Britain but in agrarian societies like Russia and eventually China. In this way the limited and carefully graded introduction of literacy was for the time being a success.

Unfortunately, in Britain the aftermath of this system is still with us. A fair number of state schools (for better or worse still under the jurisdiction of local councils and in consequence often used as political footballs) are, despite the often superhuman efforts made by their teaching staffs, not overtly successful. This is not because of a large number of minority or immigrant groups — the convenient scapegoat here as well as in the USA. In fact, the school results of many Asian and black children are often above those of their Western cohorts, partly because they come from homes where achievement and ambition — and literacy — are greatly valued, something that cannot always be said of their native compatriots. I well remember a meeting of parents, head teachers and governors where one father stood up and said, in all seriousness, he did not see why he should work hard to help his son with his homework just so that the teacher could get the praise. The idea that he might want to work with his son so that his son would get praise had not even occurred to him. Instead of blaming teachers, it is the overall (predominately white) home culture that needs changing. But then only a hundred years ago the results of those underachieving children would have been considered perfectly acceptable. Unfortunately for them and, by implication for all of us, the pattern of life, the culture of the work place and the possibilities for gaining an acceptable livelihood, have drastically changed in the last decades. We no longer need a large quota of obedient servants, soldiers barely able complete a form, industrious agrarian or factory workers, women satisfied with becoming copy typists or at best secretaries. Such work can now be done, more quickly and more efficiently, by machines and computers. The information explosion, so long forecast, has finally arrived; the future we were promised is here. But it seems we have been slow in making adequate provision for it and one often wonders whether, even now, we are quite sure how to do so.

It would, however, be wrong to say that all 19th century education and that of the following decades was based on cynical manipulation. As the 19th century progressed a genuine enthusiasm for spreading literacy crept in. The growing prosperity and the political power of Western countries, where the majority of people could in one way or another read and write, became a further incentive. Educators, and also a good many missionaries, began to look upon literacy as the key to better health, a better character, greater sensibility, a better life. Universal franchise, when it eventually arrived, was an added inducement for the spread of literacy; as in classical Athens, citizens in a democratically run society ought at least to be functionally literate. The French Revolution did away with the blind acceptance of a divinely-sanctioned social stratification. If, at least in theory, all are equal, upward mobility, the way to the top becomes possible through personal achievement.

As far as overseas territories were concerned, the belief that the ability to read and write would automatically provide a panacea for all social evils held, unfortunately, an additional and, as it was to turn out, in many cases dangerously fragile promise. Since literacy seems to have made the West prosperous and dominant, then literacy would enable people in ex-colonial third world countries to achieve not only political freedom, self-determination and democracy but, above all, personal economic prosperity — the latter being in the mind of many a more or less automatic by-product. But just as writing is proper writing only when it fulfils the needs of a particular community, so literacy becomes beneficial only if it forms part of the overall socio-economic pattern. Apart from being sent semi-literate into our post-modern world dominated by an increasingly more sophisticated information technology, nothing is quite as frustrating, as having reached a reasonably high level of literacy to find that your own society does not as yet have a place for you.

The often well-meant enthusiasm for literacy encouraged many students from disadvantaged homes to consider an education certificate a guarantee of employment and material prosperity. In many cases, here as well as in overseas countries, this has often not only put the credibility of education into question, but also brought about an alienation from the original community. Having gained a certificate in town, it is difficult to come back to the village empty-handed. However, a number of enterprising young men (less is expected from young women who can conveniently, if in many cases unhappily, retreat into traditional family life) in Africa or India have partially solved the problem by taking on the role of literacy mediators — acting as scribes for their communities. Writing letters, filling forms, reading notices, advising grown-up men, perhaps even the head of the village *panchayat* on his rights in a legal case, not only provide an income but also a reasonable amount of self-respect. In the end it is not the education certificate but what an individual is able to do with it that counts. This is however at best an intermediate, certainly not a final, even less a fully satisfactory, solution.

Functional literacy

What then of 'functional' literacy'? Politically it is often seen as a means of keeping whole groups in society within certain restricted boundaries. This is without doubt at times the case but, in the final instance, we are all only functionally literate. In fact, in today's highly specialised world it is totally impossible to be anything else. The time of 'Renaissance man' has long since gone. However we look at it, the shared pool of experience that was needed to communicate through objects or pictures and which the little girl in Kipling's *Just So* story very nearly got wrong, is again becoming an essential element in our highly differentiated society.

Functional literacy need not be a hindrance, providing it is large enough to cover not only our needs but also provide us with the possibilities to step outside the narrow confines of our original social group. To teach children only what would not divide them from their birth community (not something they have chosen in the first place) would condemn them to stay within their original confines without any hope of further advancement. Literacy is truly a relative term. It should not limit us to the expectations of our own group, whatever that group might be. In fact, the idea (at one time much propagated) that children should not be taught anything that might separate them from their original background is one of breathtaking arrogance. It negates anything connected with ambition, merit and social mobility. By this theory, no revolutions would ever have been possible.

When talking about literacy we should not forget that ultimately it is the individual who motivates society. Literacy does not solely depend on the ability to read and write. Literacy can be used as a tool but even without this tool truly exceptional individuals have never been restrained by the expectations of their immediate community. For better or worse, neither Chingiz Khan nor Theodora allowed themselves to be limited by the expectations of their own social group. The first was an illiterate tribal chief, the second started life as a circus woman and became, against all odds and all contemporary laws, Empress of Byzantine.

Oral literacy

Literacy does not depend on writing, even less on the use of a particular form of script which is supposed to enhance, by its very nature, critical thinking. There exists in fact no clear dichotomy between oral and written language, between oral and written traditions. Both have long been closely linked.

Writing itself hardly ever started with 'literature' and 'texts' but with a need for counting goods, proving dynastic legitimacy or providing a reckoning for the more abstract concept of time. Moreover, literary texts can and have existed without writing. And not just literary texts but text relating to grammar, phonology, law, religion, philosophy and science.

In India, literacy — a highly refined and sophisticated form of literacy — pre-dates the use of writing by at least a millennium. It is true that as far as the orally composed and orally transmitted Vedic texts were concerned there existed a definite element of ownership. Knowledge of them, and the permission to use them, was highly exclusive and since such knowledge brought very definite benefits to the 'owners', it could serve as a political tool the elite used, not just for the benefit of the community but certainly also for that of its individual members. In fact, not only knowledge and its use but also permission to listen to those texts was subject to definite restrictions. According to Manu's code of laws, dated approximately to the 5th century BC but probably looking back on earlier (oral) traditions, precise forms of punishment were laid down for low caste persons who had, even unwittingly, listened to the recital of Vedic hymns. But this, of course, in no way detracts from the fact that the hymns were very definite literary texts which, moreover, because of the care their 'owners' took, were meticulously preserved until they eventually found their way — still with a good deal of reluctance — into writing. But oral texts and oral traditions are not restricted to literature; they can include subjects such as grammar, phonology, archival history, semi-historical tales, even treatises on laws.

Another example of a sophisticated society based largely on oral traditions was that of the Iron Age Celts (Brown, 1998). From 600 BC onwards the Celts spread through most parts of Europe and Asia Minor until eventually Rome and her successors forced them back into Brittany, Ireland and the northern parts of Britain. The binding element of their society was, however, less rooted in political power than in a common culture based on oral traditions. This tradition was safeguarded by the *Aes Dana*, a highly trained elite of shamans, bards, jurist and Druids. To become a professional bard, and with it a trusted guardian of orally transmitted knowledge, required a long training in specially designed establishments. In fact, it took a good deal longer and probably more effort than was required to become a scribe in ancient Egypt. Classical literature tells us that the Druids were in no way ignorant of Greek and Roman writing but that (like their Indian counterparts) they put more trust in oral tradition to safeguard the knowledge essential to their society. But when it comes to the often quoted relationship between oral tradition and ownership, we should not forget that writing and the knowledge of writing too implies ownership. It has to be taught and those able to teach can decide to whom to teach it.

Codified text like the Bible and the Talmud started in the form of oral literature and were only written down at a later date. '. . . tracing the precise historical development of [this process] . . . is a complicated and somewhat hypothetical enterprise. We do not possess records which clearly described the process involved. Nevertheless a good deal of information can be derived by inference. Since the beginning of the 20th century, biblical scholars have detected signs of oral lore in the earliest strands of [biblical traditions] . . . The notion of an ancient Israelite "epic tradition" which originally existed in oral-poetic form was further developed . . . [This] epic tradition was passed down via oral recitations until the 10th/9th centuries BC when it was adapted to written form . . .' Similarly, 'moving on to laws and prophecies, the Pentateuch largely portrays Moses as transmitting laws orally to the Israelites, although there are occasional directives to commit particular clauses to writing. . .' When it comes to 'the role of oral interpretation of received traditions . . . this issue touches primarily on the interpolations of laws, since the laws, which were viewed as divinely ordained, needed to be rendered fully operative and mutually compatible to each other. Even a cursory reading of the Pentateuch laws, or what the Jewish tradition refers to as the "written Torah", highlights the necessity for . . . oral traditions and oral interpretations . . .' (D.A. Glatt-Gilad, 1999).

The great Indian epic the *Mahahbharat*, the ancient story of two rival dynasties (which incidentally contains the much-lauded though often totally misunderstood *Bhagavadgita*) is nothing but a collection of (at first orally transmitted) tales, as are the *Arabian Nights*. The verses of the Koran were at first orally transmitted by the Prophet to his follows. It was only when, in the wars following the Prophet's death, many of the Huffaz, who were by tradition entrusted with memorising the verses, were killed that the Caliph Abu Bakr (r. 632-634 AD) ordered his secretary to collect all verses in one written work which to this day is still the proper text of the Koran. Interesting in this context is the position of the Huffaz. The Arabs themselves had always been a highly literary people, an element no doubt encouraged by the fact that their language can use up to 30 different words for one term. It had been the task of those men to memorise the tales and stories and teach them to young disciples who would continue the tradition.

The tradition of the professional storyteller is known in almost all cultures. He is entrusted with remembering events essential to the community: its genealogy, the origin of his people, and, once elements of 'written' information storage appear, interpreting the song boards and other memory aids for the benefit of the community. Far from text and literature (as well as literacy) beginning with writing, or as some extreme representatives of this theory would have, being made possible by writing, oral traditions have always stood before written traditions. The step from oral tradition to writing was often made via some form of memory aid designed to safeguard the correctness of the rituals and texts without endangering their exclusiveness, since it was only the trained priest who could understand (read) them correctly.

Oral tradition did not end with the evolution of writing or the widespread use of a definite writing system. Ancient Rome was a highly literate society; in fact, the level of literacy that existed in the 1st century AD was never matched in Europe until the 19th. Reading was widespread amongst educated people but writing itself was considered an inferior activity, left mostly to slaves who wrote to dictation. Speeches made in the Senate were written down with the assistance of the Tironian *notae* on wax-tablets which were well-suited to support such a semi-oral culture. Texts taken down by scribes in the course of discussions could later be copied out in full on more permanent material. In the monastic *scriptoria* dictation too played an important role, either in the form self-dictation — the monks reciting aloud the text they knew by heart — or one monk dictating to the whole *scriptorium*.

During the last decades an increasingly more self-satisfied form of value judgement has been introduced when comparing orality with writing. Ong (1982), for example, maintains that 'non-literate folk' reason, communicate and remember information differently from 'literate folk'. Really? Winterowd (1989) and others claim that 'reading and writing made Western technology, science, philosophy and technology possible'. But much of what we call 'Western' technology has really come to us from the East (the non-alphabet writing countries): paper-making (essential for the success of the printing revolution), the concept of writing itself, an understanding of the concept of zero, much medical knowledge, the use of the wheel, as well as that of money, irrigation, phonology, printing — even many of our classical Greek traditions that lie at the root of the Renaissance have reached us via Arabic or Hebrew translation. Not to mention Christianity, which is in reality nothing but a Jewish heresy.

A recent study of African Yoruba plays (Fielding, 1996) points out that they are unscripted, improvised and collectively produced by an interaction of performers with each other and also with the audience. There is, in this form of entertainment, no cultural divide between 'oral' and 'literate' culture. The study links orality with the pre-colonial past, which exists right into the present and which is seen as something different from the 'indigenous' African culture. These improvised plays, we are told, belong therefore to the non-elite, such as agrarian workers, motor mechanics and so on. This of course is to a large extent a retrospective, non-indigenous value judgement. In ancient India the Vedic priests composing their hymns and the ancient grammarians evaluating their speculation which so decisively influenced the study of linguistics in 19th century Western countries were without doubt part of an indigenous non-writing but certainly not non-literate group. Being elitist and indigenous does not automatically have to be exclusive. Changing into our more immediate past, plays such as those composed by Moliere and performed for the most elitist group in the country (the Royal court) were often only written down during the performance by members of the audience, who then produced printed versions of rather doubtful fidelity.

Written culture is nearly always based on a preceding oral culture, something to which we should perhaps give more consideration in our modern (Western) education systems. In traditional Sanskrit schools, Indian children first learn to recite the texts by heart before being instructed in their meaning; similar customs prevail in Muslim *madarasas*.

Western concepts of literacy have always been more egocentric. Well into the 19th century the ability to write one's name (sign, and thus authorise a document, even if there was in fact no proof at all that one had understood it) was considered the first step towards being literate (see Plate 87). Is the insistence in today's nursery schools to make children write their names, however inadequately and however far removed they are from any knowledge of writing, a reminder of such past concepts? Education would perhaps be more successful if more weight were initially given to the recitation and remembering of oral texts, by encouraging oral creativity.

In the area of modern politics the written text is often subordinated to the spoken message. Speeches by leading politicians will be listened to by a wide and often quite diverse audience. The aim of a political speech is to create consent by the skilful use of language (Swanson and Nimmo, 1990; Fairclough, 1995). Here the power rests with the politician's ability to convince his audience through his speech. He may have the text written down before he confronts his audience but if he is a good speaker and a skilled politician he will be sensitive to the reaction of his audience and make ad hoc changes as he goes along.

Like the lawyer, the politician has to rely on the 'art of persuasion'. The purpose of his rhetoric is to win over the opposition. Government institutions need rhetoric in order to unify the audience, legitimise their pronouncements, orient their listeners and finally convince them so as to be able to implement policies. Speeches serve to unify society and create a sense of belonging among the group of listeners; they foster identification between the audience and those in power. As Aristotle pointed out, rhetoric solves problems by offering choices and encouraging discussion. However, once the speech has been made, the text will be written down and eventually published and broadcast. Here the speaker loses at times much of his original power to the writer who can (more or less arbitrarily) select parts of the speech and in the process often considerably changes the original meaning.

In fact, there has never been a clear break between oral and written culture in the sense that the one spells the extinction of the other: both have always existed side by side. Just as printing did not mean the end of writing, it is unlikely that information technology will totally eradicate the use of paper and of what we still call books. In any case, what about radio plays, radio news reporting, educational radio programmes — the talking book? Are we to think of them as falling outside literacy?

Plate 87. Signatures are the ultimate expression of authority. They can legitimize a contract, an edict, a legal decision, the order for an execution. They have therefore always been jealously guarded and their unauthorised use was considered a serious offence. They were also, up to the beginning of the 20th century, taken as proof of (an at least elementary) form of literacy, implying that the person signing the document knew what he/she was doing (i.e. had been able to read the document).

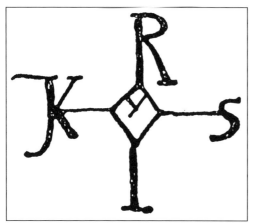

Plate 87a. Charlemagne (742-814) did much for the reform of education and the standardisation of book production. In the process he was instrumental in the creation of Carolingian, one of the finest styles of Western calligraphy. He did, however, never manage, despite much effort on his part, to become himself fully literate. His signature was in fact more an iconic cipher of authority than a representation of his actual name.

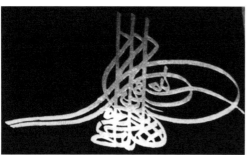

Plate 87b. The Tughra, an elegant and elaborate device based on the names and titles of the reigning Ottoman Sultans, served as signature to legitimise official degrees. The complexity of a Tughra was meant to protect it from forgery; any unauthorised use carried the death sentence. This example has been photographed over the entrance of a mosque inside the Topkapi Palace in Istanbul.

Plate 87c. Contemporary signature of a senior British civil servant. It does not actually reveal the name and it is practically as intricate, and certainly as difficult to forge, as a Turkish Tughra.

Information overload?

When information technology first began to play a serious part in our everyday lives, reservations were at times expressed about the way this new tool might be used to control, perhaps even limit, our access to information. It seemed that, more than ever, the storage and accessibility of information was in danger of becoming an instrument of political control. Such considerations are in fact neither unfounded nor totally restricted to the realm of science fiction. But it now seems that there is another, perhaps even more dangerous element to be taken into consideration — that of constantly overloading people with masses of information they do not need, do not fully (if at all) understand and which is, in consequence, not so much manipulative as simply misleading.

Information, as a mass product, is not only losing its credibility but also its usefulness. Far from increasing levels of knowledge, such as those based on properly acquired literacy, the constant overload of unsolicited information endangers many people's ability to absorb and make use of what seems so freely available.

To learn through oral transmission demanded time, a face to face effort, a willingness on the part of the instructor as well as on the part of the learner. Even if oral traditions limited the amount of information and did not encourage enough original thinking, they did at least provide a secure basis of contemporary knowledge. They enabled the learner to access, at least in part, the pool of shared experience. This introduced what we may now call functional literacy but it was nevertheless literacy that enabled people to function within their own sphere and community. To learn how to read and write is time-consuming too and demands considerable effort. To produce and commission a manuscript needed a well above average amount of resources — intellectually, as well as economically — and it also took time. Even to buy a printed book is based on a definite desire to possess this book, read it and the willingness to pay what the buyer considers an appropriate and affordable price. All this is the result of a number of definite decisions; definite efforts have to be made, which will make it more likely that the reader/buyer wants to obtain the information contained in the manuscript/book.

To switch on the TV may be a definite decision. But in many households the TV is switched on practically all day and what is supposedly information is hardly more than a background to everyday living. Against this everyday background parts of the information may from time to time be absorbed. But will they be understood? Understood not only in their own context but also in a way that renders them useful? Does this daily bombardment of information benefit education? In theory, perhaps, but in practice the exact opposite seems to be true. One has, for example, only to think of the detailed and explicit sex education already given to children at primary school level. One would think them more knowledgeable than their parents who 'learned it at the playground' (now frowned upon) and therefore better equipped to manage their lives in a way beneficial to themselves. But exactly the opposite seems to be true. A most important part of the message, namely how not to get pregnant, does not seem to sink in. More and more underage girls become pregnant (married or unmarried — it hardly matters) and many condemn themselves, seemingly voluntarily, to a shadowy existence in drab council flats, living on meagre state handouts, without stimulation and not much hope of personal achievement. All this despite the fact that their education has made them 'literate'.

Just like the insidious cameras which now monitor our every move in the work place, in shopping malls and on the street (supposedly for our own safety), so information is blasted at us from the TV screen, advertising boards and radio broadcasts all the time. But does this make us more or less literate? Does this encourage literacy fit to prepare the next generation for the 21st century? Somehow, sooner or later, and the sooner the better, we will have to address this question.

Bibliography

Adams, M. J. *Beginning to Read. Thinking and Learning about Print.* Cambridge, MA: MIT Press, 1990.

Aldrick, R. *An Introduction to the History of Education.* London: Hodder and Stoughton, 1982.

Assmann, A. and J. and Hardmeier, C. (ed.), *Schrift und Gedaechtnis. Beitraege zur Archaeologie der literarischen Kommunikation.* Munich, 1983.

Barr, A. and Feigenbaum, E. A. *A Handbook of Artificial Intelligence.* vol. 1. Los Altos: Heuris Tech Press, 1981.

Barthel, G. *Konnte Adam schreiben: Weltgeschichte der Schrift.* Koeln: Du Mont Schauberg, 1972.

Berlin, I. (ed.). *The Age of Enlightenment.* New York: Mentor, 1956.

Berry, J. W. *Human Ecology and Cognitive Style: Comparative Studies in Cultural and Psychological Adaptation.* New York: Sage/Halsted, 1976.

Brown, S. (ed.) *The Pressure of the Text. Orality, Texts and the Telling of Tales.* Birmingham: University of Birmingham, 1995.

Chall, J. S. *Learning to Read: the Great Debate.* New York: McGraw-Hill, 1967 (updated 1989).

Clanchy, M. T. *From Memory to Written Record: England, 1066-1307.* Oxford: University Press, 1979.

Cook-Cumperz, J. (ed.), *The social Construction of Literacy.* Cambridge: Cambridge University Press, 1986.

Cooper, R. *Language Planning and Social Change.* Cambridge: University Press, 1988.

Daniel, P. J. *The first Civilizations: the Archaeology of their Origin.* London: Thames and Hudson, 1968.

Dilke, O. A. W. *Reading the Past: Mathematics and Measurements.* London: British Museum, 1987.

Dowing, J. and Leong, C. K. *Psychology of Reading.* New York: Macmillan, 1982.

Fielding, P. *Writing and Orality.* Oxford: Clarendon Press, 1996.

Foley, J. M. *The Theory of Oral Compositions.* Bloomington, Indiana University Press, 1988.

Fry, D. *Homo Loquens: Man as a talking Animal.* Cambridge: University Press, 1977.

Goody, J. *Literacy in Traditional Societies.* New York: Cambridge University Press, 1968.

Goody, J. *The Interface between the Written and the Oral.* Cambridge, University Press, 1987.

Goody, J. *The Domestication of the Savage Mind.* Cambridge: Cambridge University Press, 1977.

Glaser, M. and Pausch, M. *Between Orality and Writing.* Amsterdam: Rodopi, 1994.

Gregg, L. W. (ed). *Cognition in Learning and Memory.* New York: John Wiley, 1972.

Havelock, E. A. *Origins of Western Literacy.* Toronto, Ontario: Institute for Studies in Education, 1976.

Henderson, L. *Orthography and Visual Word Recognition in Reading.* London: Academic Press 1982.

Ifrah, G. *Universalgeschichte der Zahlen.* Frankfurt: Campus, 1989.

Irvine, S. H. and Berry, J, W. (ed). *Human Abilities in Cultural Context.* New York: Cambridge University Press, 1988.

Johnson-Laird, P. N. *Mental Models: towards a Cognitive Science of Language, Inference, and Consciousness.* Cambridge: Harvard University Press, 1983.

Joseph, G. G. *The Crest of the Peacock: Non-European Roots of Mathematics.* New York: Tauris Publications, 1991.

Kessing, R. M. *Cultural Anthropology: a Contemporary Perspective.* 2nd edn., New York: Holt Rinehart and Winston, 1981.

Leakey, R. *The Making of Mankind.* New York: Dutton, 1981.

Martlew, M. (ed.) *The Psychology of Written Language: Development and Educational Perspective.* New York: John Wiley and Sons, 1983.

Miller, G. A. *Language and Communication.* New York: McGraw-Hill, 1951.

Olson, D. R. Torrance, N. and Hildyard, A. (ed). *Literacy, Language and Learning: the Nature and Consequences of Reading and Writing.* New York: Cambridge University Press, 1985.

What is literacy?

Ong, W. J. *Orality and Literacy: the Technologization of the Word*. New York: Metheun, 1982.

Ong, W. J. *Interfaces of the World, Studies in the Evolution and Consciousness of Culture*. London: Cornell University Press, 1977.

Osgood, C. A., May, W.H. and Miron, M. S. *Cross-cultural Universals of Affective Meaning*. Urbana: University of Illinois, 1975.

Paradis, M., Hagiwara, H. and Hildebrandt, N. *Neurolinguistic Aspects of the Japanese Writing System*. New York: Academic Press, 1985.

Pattison, R. *On Literacy*. Oxford: University Press, 1982.

Pike, K. L. *Phonemics: A Technique for Reducing Language to Writing*. Ann Arbor: University of Michigan, 1947.

Pontecorvo, C. and Blanche-Benveniste, C. *Proceedings of the Workshop on Orality versus Literacy*. Siena 24-26 September 1992. Strasbourg: European Science Foundation, 1993.

Purves, A. C. and Jennings, E. M. (ed.), *Literate Systems and individual Lives: Perspective on Literacy and Schooling*. Albany: SUNY Press, 1993.

Reynolds, L. D. and Wilson, N. G. *Scribes and Sources: A Guide to the Transmission of Greek and Latin Literature*. Oxford: University Press, 1974.

Scribner, S. and Cole, M. *The Psychology of Literacy*. Cambridge: Harvard University Press, 1981.

Smith, F. *Understanding Reading*. London: Holt, Rinehart and Winston, 1982.

Sternbarg, R. and Wagner, R. (ed). *Practical Intelligence: Nature and Origins of Competence in the Every Day World*. New York: University Press, 1986.

Taton, R. *Ancient and Medieval Science from Prehistory to AD. 1450*. trans. A. J. Pomerans. London, 1963.

Taylor, I. and Olson, D. R. (ed.), *Scripts and Literacy: Reading and Learning to Read Alphabets, Syllabaries and Characters*. Dortrecht: Kluwer Academic Publishers, 1995.

Taylor, I. and Taylor, M. *The Psychology of Reading*. New York: Academic Press.

Terrace, H. S. *Nim, the Chimpanzee who had Sign Language*. New York: Knopf, 1979.

Thompson, J. W. *The Literacy of the Laity in the Middle Ages*. New York: 1963.

Thurstone, L. L. *Primary Mental Abilities*. Chicago: University of Chicago Press, 1938.

Unger, J. M. *The Fifth Generation Fallacy: Why Japan is Betting its Future on Artificial Intelligence*. New York: Oxford University Press, 1987.

Vansina, J. *Oral Traditions as History*. London: James Curey, 1985.

Wagner, D. A. (ed). *The Future of Literacy in a Changing World*. Oxford: Pergamon Press, 1987.

Wang, W. S-Y. *The Emergence of Language: Development and Evolution*. San Francisco: W. H. Freeman, 1991.

Winterowd, E. R. *The Culture and Politics of Literacy*. Oxford: University Press, 1989.

Worthy, W. *The Renaissance Hand-written Books*. London: Chatto and Windus, 1954.

UNESCO. *The current Literacy Situation in the World*. Paris, 1985.

Some final thoughts

1. This study is more interested in posing questions than finding answers, to show how much we do not know about scripts, writing systems and their origin. It offers no final solutions — a concept so dear to the majority of 19th, as well as many 20th century scholars, who turned their thoughts towards this subject.

2. By looking at writing (all forms of writing) as an important element of the political infrastructure, we can see that the need for such an infrastructure goes much further back in historical as well as prehistoric times than has generally been assumed. This, especially in the case of sign languages, brings new possibilities to the question of where exactly lies the line, not between pre-writing and proper writing, but between the cognitive recognition of pictures and codification. However simple (even unlikely) some may look to us, they were probably for their own societies extremely complex achievements.

3. Writing and mathematics, considered separate entities today, go back to similar basic needs. Any further attempts at a history of writing should therefore also concern themselves not just with what we call writing but also with the history of numbers and the creation of mathematical concepts. The still largely prevailing Euro-centric approach to writing is even more apparent when it comes to mathematics. The American scholar Morris Kline in his *Mathematics, a Cultural Approach* (1962) sees the Greeks as the true originators of all worthwhile knowledge and dismisses the contributions made by the Egyptians and Babylonians as 'almost insignificant'. We have still a long way to go from freeing ourselves from prevailing (and often grossly self-satisfied) preconceptions when looking at past civilisations.

4. As for the future, this will have to take care of itself. We can neither predict not control coming developments and needs. All that seems certain is that we are in the middle of a tremendous upheaval which sees the change from an industrial society, where wealth rested on the availability and use of raw materials, to one dependent on scientific knowledge and the use of intellectual property. It is no longer the Sultan of Brunei but Bill Gates who is the richest man in the world. In this new society an infrastructure based on the efficient and inventive communication of information will be of prime importance. But this new literacy will neither be tribal nor will it depend on national boundaries or even on linguistic considerations. It will, for the first time, have to satisfy and explain truly global needs. But whatever else the future may bring, there will be — as always — winners and losers. We are at present simply not in a position to ascertain who will fall into which category and, with it, we are powerless to prevent, or even accurately predict, any (but unavoidable) new forms of inequality.

Index